MOMENTUM

ON RECENT
SOUTH AFRICAN
WRITING

Edited by
M J Daymond
J U Jacobs
Margaret Lenta

MOMENTUM

ON RECENT
SOUTH AFRICAN
WRITING

Contents

Contents continued overleaf

Contents

CRITICAL
ESSAYS

Contents

SOUTH AFRICAN VOICES
FROM ABROAD

Introduction

Lionel Trilling once said that modern literature, more than the literature of other ages, could be divided into two parts: its produced artefacts (fictions, poetry, plays) and the manifestos which governed or emerged from their production. This is no less true of South African literature than of the literature of America and England to which Trilling was referring. Its produced artefacts and its manifestos have reflected, analysed and theorised about South Africa and South Africans for more than a hundred years.

To fix a date when English-speaking writers living in this country took South African life as their subject is to risk the censure of the literary historian, but as we write this introduction at the end of 1983, it is impossible not to think of Olive Schreiner and *The Story of an African Farm*, published in 1883.

The manifestos too have certainly not been lacking. Manifestos by creative writers themselves, as well as publications which elicited from individual writers their personal literary credos, have also been important in South Africa — as in *Voorslag*, *The Classic* and *Drum*. Mphahlele's *The African Image* is a voice of this kind. His statement about himself as writer made for this present book shows, like that of Mafika Gwala, how frequently black writers are drawn to cultural assessment through the self-portrait — a form of reportage which spans the divide between artefact and manifesto. Perhaps the most important influence of today which has led writers, especially black writers, to think about their practice and the theoretical basis which underlies it, is *Staffrider*. Partly because of the growing tradition of the literary manifesto, and partly because of the need — to which writers testify in the first and last sections of this book — to understand the ways in which literature can intervene to change South African society, there have been a number of conferences on South African writing.

These have been held both in the country and abroad, providing an opportunity for writers to reveal and compare their literary beliefs. One of the most recent and influential of these conferences was that in 1982 in Gaborone, entitled *Culture and Resistance*, where all the arts, including literature, came under consideration.

Although the formal study of South African writers was a late introduction in our school and university syllabuses (the 1969 English Academy conference in Grahamstown saw relatively few white academics supporting its inclusion), both the artefact and the manifesto have been subjects for extensive literary debate in recent years in South Africa. A complete catalogue of these debates must be impossible here but these names at least call for acknowledgement: Lionel Abrahams, Guy Butler, Michael Chapman, Cherry Clayton, Jack Cope, Tim Couzens, Dorothy Driver, Nadine Gordimer, Stephen Gray, Don Maclennan, Roy Macnab, Jean Marquard, Es'kia Mphahlele, Lewis Nkosi, Cosmo Pieterse and Richard Rive. They have been prominent contributors to both critics' and writers' awareness of what they themselves are doing and must do. We in turn know that thanks to these critics we enjoy the luxury of joining an already established discussion.

It is because of the co-presence of artefact and manifesto in our literature that we conceived of *Momentum* in its present form. It consists of three sections. The first, Voices from South Africa, and the last, South African Voices from Abroad, contain statements by the artists themselves about their work. We approached writers whose work is well known in English in South Africa. The middle section, Essays on South African Writing, contains critical commentaries on recent fiction, poetry and drama. What we wanted to create was a forum where writers, resident or non-resident in the Republic, could write about their practice, their motivation and their theory, and an accompanying area where critics would discuss South African writing today. We took as our 'today' the period beginning with the events of 1976. In the letter sent to writers asking them to contribute, we explained our purposes thus:

> As matters become more than ever difficult for all writers in this crazy society of ours, and as writers themselves are debating publicly their role ... it will be very valuable, especially to scholars, to have a firsthand account from writers of how they experience and conceive of their activity.

To explain the thematic focus of the book, we said that

> we would like the [critical] articles to be linked by some attention
> to the way writers are seen as responding (or not) to crises in
> South African affairs. Soweto '76 is an obvious landmark, but we
> aren't suggesting to anyone, writers or critics, that response to
> national events is a criterion of some kind. We would just like to
> raise the question of how, directly or indirectly or not at all,
> the events are reflected in current writing.

The critical articles come from members or ex-members of the
Department of English at the University of Natal, Durban. (Sheila
Roberts is now at Michigan State University and Ian Steadman at the
University of the Witwatersrand.) This is partly because their working
interests are known to us as editors and partly because we felt that the
varied critical productions of a connected group are of interest in their
own right. The book's critical range has been determined by the spontaneous interests of the contributors, though we did make specific
suggestions in one or two cases. It was of course clear to us from the
start that we could not hope to cover contemporary South African
literature in its entirety, and that the selection of works for discussion
would not satisfy everyone. We decided to include all three essays that
were offered on J M Coetzee's novels, despite the omissions that such
weighting necessitated. The recent degree of interest aroused abroad, as
well as the sustained attention his novels have received here in South
Africa, has, we think, vindicated this decision. An article on *Staffrider*
by Es'kia Mphahlele could not, to our regret, be completed in time for
inclusion. Our book could only have been the better for the presence of
so eminent a writer discussing a phenomenon as important as *Staffrider*.

As for the responses from writers, we liked Karel Schoeman's
suggestion that our book should contain the response in Afrikaans of
at least one South African writer and have therefore included his
Afrikaans article with a translation into English. We have not attempted
to impose any uniformity of form or style on the writers' contributions.
Douglas Livingstone and C J Driver chose to write in verse; the interviews with Athol Fugard and Nadine Gordimer also differ in form
from the statements written by the other writers.

It is difficult to draw a single conclusion from the statements in this
book. The extraordinary tensions of South African life, its conflicting
and dividing loyalties, the fact that South African literature of today is
composed of writings from at least two groups, resident and non-

resident South Africans, as well as the fact that the circumstances of black and white writers in this country differ in many ways, some of them described within our book — all these factors prevent the emergence of any agreed or even widely experienced sense of what it is to be a South African writer.

Divisions between groups of writers, though they are more obvious, are not more profound than divisions within writers themselves. Ahmed Essop writes of "the twin temptations" which inevitably face South African writers, either "'to take up arms against a sea of troubles' or to retreat into misanthropy and solipsism". Sheila Fugard, writing of her Irish and Afrikaans ancestry and her own perception of the diversity of cultures in South Africa, speaks of her "sense of rootlessness". At eight years old, she says, she was already "a divided person". Stephen Gray's sense of the strange position of present-day South Africans is different in emphasis, but related; he sees us as "suspended between African historical moments that should have coincided: we are postcolonial beings, but still we are pre-independent". Although she is writing primarily about life away from South Africa, a similar tension is registered by Rose Moss who claims that a particular kind of irony, that of "seeing simultaneously from two or more points of view", is an inescapable feature of her vision. Another kind of irony is evident in the position of resident South African writers. Richard Rive describes the predicament of writers who feel morally obliged to struggle against oppression by continuing to live in South Africa while writing about its problems, and are nonetheless subjected to continual condemnation by exiled and foreign writers as collaborators with the oppressor. Perhaps the most concise expression of the South African plight is given in the Gramsci sentence which Peter Wilhelm quotes as used by one of his reviewers: "The old is dying and the new cannot be born: in this interregnum there arises a great diversity of morbid symptoms". Nadine Gordimer chose the same quotation as an epigraph for her most recent novel, *July's People*.

Wilhelm's comment, "Every age is an interregnum, but it requires a dissociation from effective life to perceive it as such", places the function of the writer in any age. In responding to the contemporary situation, it is necessary to remember that our literature is affected by all of our history. As Athol Fugard says, we are still "watching the consequences" of a war which occurred eighty years ago. And he himself is still responding to Sharpeville, let alone to Soweto, therefore he is right to warn that it would be "incredibly presumptuous" to claim to understand what happened in 1976 and what the consequences will be. But to remember that this is so is not to minimise the importance of the events of our own day or of the questions we put to writers and critics. South Africans will be living out the consequences of Soweto '76 for a good eighty years to come and the least we can now do is to recognise and discuss the forms of literary response there have been to the events of those months. Elsa Joubert writes of "the need to bear witness" of which she herself first became strongly aware in 1960, when her journalist-husband actually saw the Sharpeville shootings, and of the years which she spent informing herself about the lives of black people, urban and rural, so that her testimony, when she was able to offer it, might be both true and profound. Zakes Mda, Mbulelo Mzamane and Daniel Kunene are among the many writers living abroad who have acknowledged that events in South Africa are still the primary influence on their writing.

Certain phenomena, particularly certain laws, must be recognised as inhibiting, or determining in an adverse sense, South African literary production within the country and as preventing or restricting the circulation here of books published elsewhere. The Internal Security Act, which is concerned with the utterances of people deemed politically undesirable, and the Publications Act, which is concerned with propriety of language, as well as with wider moral issues, are the most obvious of these laws. Not only can the officials who administer them decide, sometimes on the advice of officially-appointed experts, what South Africans can be allowed to read, but the knowledge that a book may be banned is ever-present to writers themselves, as well as being a potentially strong check on publishers, who must suffer the financial loss which banning involves. Great credit is due to those South African publishers who have been willing, time and again, to run this risk.

The fear of banning, as Sheila Roberts has admitted, and as we ourselves have been compelled to accept, may shape literary works themselves. Alex la Guma most generously agreed to contribute to this book if we could give him a guarantee that his contribution would be published; as he is banned and may not be quoted in South Africa, we were powerless to supply this assurance. Colin Gardner's essay on Dennis Brutus also could not appear. In it Gardner argues that Brutus exists as a black hole in the South African firmament; the censorship laws have ensured that this darkness shall continue.

It remains for us to thank, most sincerely, all our contributors, most of all for their writings, but also for their kind forbearance during the period between our call for contributions and the actual appearance of this book. The reasons for delay were largely economic, and we are therefore sure of the sympathy of all writers and critics: we hope that the reasons for our book's compilation and eventual publication will seem equally cogent to all its readers.

MARGARET DAYMOND
JOHAN JACOBS
MARGARET LENTA

December 1983

VOICES
FROM SOUTH AFRICA

Lionel Abrahams

Quoting a forgotten source, Barney Simon long ago gave me a dictum I found resonant: "A man must have a place and a face".

It is not merely incidental that at the age of fifty-four I can lay claim to only one and a quarter published volumes of my own writing. Other work lies scattered in magazines, anthologies and files and promises to yield two further books shortly; I have edited perhaps a dozen volumes of other people's work and sundry magazines — but I have never been anything near a steadily working prolific author. A similar slightness appears in each of the other areas of my literary work: I am a critic without scholarship or theory, a reviewer without consistency or industry, an editor without professionalism, a publisher without organization or capital, and a teacher of 'creative writing' without a philosophy of method or depth of culture.

My achievements, relying on flashes, feelings, prophetic tinglings, are patchy, but some things I have done as editor, publisher, and teacher leave me with a solid sense of satisfaction, even of privilege. Temperament and opportunity have equipped me to play what has been, I believe, an unusual role in the early recognition and support of talent in others, helping them in one way or another to persist or to become better known. Perhaps every one of them would have come to light without my intervention (Bosman's posthumously published work would have come out somewhat later, but — who knows? — possibly to better advantage at the hands of more professional editors), but as it happened I was allowed some obstetrical functions, ranging from encouragement and critical advice (for such as Barney Simon, Ruth Miller, David Farrell and Jeni Couzyn) through editing and guiding (for Modikwe Dikobe and Ahmed Essop), to the full range of aid from recognition to actual publication (as in the cases of Oswald Mtshali, Wally Serote and Eva Royston).

A less fruitful but more topical expression of my commitment to my "place" was my participation in the dramatic non-racial phase of the Johannesburg PEN Centre. I participated perhaps with misguidedly altruistic motives, wanting to give something to potential writers across the colour line — as well as receive from our interaction some of the richness inherent in this South African world. As an executive committee member I enjoyed a privileged view of the experiment. Those three years of association with political people did nothing to persuade me of the error of my individualistic-liberal ways. Instead they produced a graphic demonstration of the confusions, destructiveness and self-destructiveness inherent in that form of power drive which is the radical approach to things. Whatever possibilities it holds out for the rectification of society, it yields, at any rate, nothing desirable for the pursuit of literature beyond the farcical and tragic stories it generates. My deepest quarrel is with the doctrine that literary values like subtlety, complexity, disinterested verisimilitude, individual imaginativeness and general human appeal are bourgeois and Western prerequisites and hence not African. Were I not acquainted with the best achievements of such as Mofolo, Mphahlele, Nakasa, Nkosi, Dikobe, Mtshali, Serote and Sepamla, my spell in PEN, an extended exposure to the kind of protest writing that radical criticism defends, might have afflicted me with a brand new category of racial prejudice.

Some of my opinions on these and other issues have found their way into articles and letters, both published and unpublished. Whether I have given more space to my disputes with those on the left or my anger over cruelties and stupidities from the other side (like that preposterous form of censorship known as gagging) I do not know. Opinions, and reactions to 'the situation' have also flowed to some small extent into my 'situationist jingles' and some other poems.

So much for my "place". The concerns with "place" and "face" are not simply separable, and though my poetry and fiction are overwhelmingly matters of "face", that is to say, personal and private in their preoccupations, I have taken great pleasure from several testimonies to the effect that my stories have been found to be evocatively South African. I take that to be a measure of some kind of truthfulness. My 'novel' *The Celibacy of Felix Greenspan* is a small, odd, anomalous book, not *one* fictional structure out of the imagination, but an edited bundle of stories that were spontaneously precipitated out of a rather arbitrary selection of memories, and happened to cohere into a vague unity on the themes of childhood and growing up, religion, love and

4

sex. Three critics have complained of a certain self-centred (or should I say "face"-centred?) lack of social awareness in *Celibacy*. So be it. This is the main body of my prime creative work. I am justified as a writer if, and only if, my poetry and my fiction have enough in them of truthfulness, passion, humanity and expressive skill to reach out and move people who have never known me.

Guy Butler

"The problem is to find a super-racial reference point from which to plan and map," I wrote in 1950 in *Vista*, a student magazine of the University of the Witwatersrand, where I was teaching at the time. I went on to say:

> The emergence of cultural cohesion in Western Europe out of the ruins of the Roman Empire may illustrate my point. Western Europe during the fifth century presents certain parallels with Africa in the twentieth: sophisticated, skilful, consciously superior Romans mixed with raw energetic barbarians speaking other tongues and utterly different in culture. Out of this unpromising mixture came Dante and Notre Dame, Shakespeare and St John of the Cross. Without minimising economic and other factors, it seems to me that, as always, cohesion and order came from man's consciousness, that is, from above, not from below, not from mere economic dynamics. Western Europe derives from the synthesis of certain ideas, Grecian, Roman and Hebraic . . . . It was achieved, consciously, by men such as St Augustine . . . . Looking at the chaos — economic, cultural, religious, racial — that followed on the collapse of Rome, he did not throw up his hands in despair, nor submit to 'the historical process' (Marxist) nor 'the destiny of his race' (Fascist), but, pivoting history and himself on the cross and its tremendous claims for man, declared for a common citizenship, for duties and privileges which are far more important than Roman or Germanic or Celtic culture. . . . Out of it, gradually, there came a new society, a new synthesis, carrying along with it much of the ruined civilisation which had given it birth.

With that precedent before me, what choices did I have? I could have simplified my life by emigrating to an entirely Western country. I could continue to live on a white island in Africa as a European exile; or I could try to be more and more present where I was, as I was:

> I have European origins, but am committed to Africa, here, to this most original, unholy, unjust chaos. I am part of this, as well as being part of the European mess. I cannot clarify either or begin to control or synthesise them until at least part of me is above and outside both. Before I write I must get above or outside, or I shall make confusion worse confounded. How shall I get above or out? God alone knows.

In 1950 the Council of Cultural Societies asked me to speak on South African Literature:

> First, the CCS assumes that South Africa has, and is going to go on trying to have, a culture of its own. This, I think, is an unwarranted assumption. The few things which most South Africans have in common are taken from outside, from Europe and America, which is tantamount to saying that the forces making for cohesion . . . are neither characteristic nor indigenous. Most cultural forces in South Africa tend to divide rather than unite. In this country we have not one culture, but at least three, each mutually resentful and suspicious: Afrikaans, English and African . . . . Surely before our writers can be said to contribute to South African culture, the peoples living in South Africa must recognise and accept each other in some very real and deep sense.

Conscious recognition and acceptance was hampered if not hamstrung by the political and social strictures of apartheid legislation. (Now, at last, after a disastrous, wasted thirty years, there are signs of change, which in moments of innocent optimism I believe to be more than cosmetic; and which in spells of self-indulgent pessimism I fear are too little and too late.)

But however procrustean the political dispensation, I had experienced enough of fellow South Africans of all shades of opinion and pigmentation to know that below and above the laws there were common loves and loyalties. The articulation of these has been one of my deepest preoccupations. Three lessons I learnt quite quickly: it is very difficult for a person of one language group to get inside the skin of someone from another. Most attempts struck me as unconvincing and

7

presumptuous. (I've never found a Frenchman convinced by a portrait of Frenchmen drawn by an Englishman, or vice versa.) The second lesson was not to hate or write off one's own kind: this has been very difficult at times. The third was to trust my intuitions and those of other poets and not to write according to the prescriptions of politicians or other specialists in abstractions. I suppose this means I am a Romantic. The decision "to be more and more present where I was" led me in directions which many of my colleagues thought idiosyncratic. As a Professor of English in South Africa it seemed proper for me to ask questions about the odd little group of about a million English-speakers whose children I was instructing, whose forebears started arriving in Southern Africa about one-and-a-half centuries ago. What effect had Africa had on their language and literature? This meant reading what they wrote, mainly diaries and letters (many still unpublished) rather than what others wrote about them. 'Settlers' do, and do not, conform to what all the various schools of historians say about them: useful ammunition either way, they are mostly interesting people, incorrigibly human. At the same time I made a steady effort to catch up with Afrikaans and black poetry. With the former I made considerable progress because I knew the language: and reading Krige, Opperman, N P van Wyk Louw and others in the 1950s provided me with many epiphanies. How, for instance, could Afrikaner Nationalist poetry-lovers rejoice in N P van Wyk Louw's *Raka*, possibly our best short epic to date, with its African hero and setting? With regard to black writing, having no African language, I had to be content with translations. I read much history and folklore. I wrote angry protest poems; and for three years attended mass fairly regularly in the Church of Christ the King, Sophiatown.

Many of my friends were Left or Left-inclined. I could heartily sympathise with much socialist economics and concern for equality of opportunity, but I found it impossible to accept dialectical materialism. This nineteenth-century European gospel struck me as being less suited to Africa than Christianity, if only because of its rejection of ancient pieties and sanctities. African thinking, it seemed, was still blessedly family- and kin-centred, organic and sacral. Further, the Left's dubious technology-based atheism, espoused by many as an absolute religion, seemed to me ultimately more inhuman than the ruthless rough and tumble of capitalism. Nor, lily-livered old-fashioned liberal that I was, could I accept a social gospel which advocated the preaching of class and/or racial confrontation as the only course open to a decent man.

I clung stubbornly to the notion that there were new thoughts, new shapes, new forms about to be born in Africa, strange, perhaps terrifying, Dionysian, fresh. Some of these might appear in English, which might become in time an African language. For myself, I no longer expected an unconscious synthesis (although that might happen), nor the eliciting or imposition of a pattern (although inherited patterns or myths might help one to think or be receptive); it was a matter of listening, of waiting patiently. (As a citizen one might sometimes act very impatiently indeed.)

I must insist that for me words like primitive, savage and barbaric were not necessarily pejorative, nor were words like civilised, European or Western necessarily words of praise. On study leave in Europe in 1954, I wrote *Home Thoughts*: perhaps the isolated, waiting, listening poet could act as a catalyst.

I was, of course, not alone. Isolated as I felt myself to be in the 1950s, there were others, younger and less hung-up than myself, who rejected the 'Answer-guys' of both the Left and the Right:

> 'History
> surprise us!' is one petition.

> 'Society
> save us!' is one petition. (*Residuum*)

For Sydney Clouts, petitions to such vast abstractions were retrogressive, reptilian, "speeding the lizard". Like Blake and others before him, he urged the need to escape "dead thought swarming with tyrannical flies," (*The Situation*) and to get back to miraculous particulars such as grains of sand:

> Thingbedded mutterings delay.

> Listen, listen among the particles.

> A vigil of the land as it appears.

> Open. Open.

> Enter the quick grain: everything is first. (*Residuum*)

Listen, listen. And what one hears, at last, loud, and not always very clear, is a multitude of African voices (some white): anger, anguish, hope, nostalgia; many responses predicted by the 'Answer-guys', but by no means all. Africa was not created merely to affirm or corroborate European political or social theories:

> Too succulent for quinces comes
> this fresh quo vadis,
>   Africa
>
>   the bud
>   the blossom
>   the scent
>   of intimate lightning. (*Intimate Lightning*)

Only rarely have I achieved the condition of "being fully present where I was". This is partly owing to the restrictions on movement and social contact, and the inhibiting conflicts and barriers of our complex society. But the main reason may be a sceptical streak in my nature as a result of which the excitements, dangers and gratifications of overwhelming convictions, religious or political, have been withheld from me. I am capable of only limited, unheroic responses to party, church or state. Such beliefs as I hold have been granted to me. I do not retain them by reason or by act of will: the strength to hold them comes from what I take the source of those beliefs to be: the love of God for all men, and their limited ability to respond to it, and in responding to find each other.

In 1950 it had seemed to me that the European synthesis had been achieved consciously by men like St Augustine. Thirty years later I still believe in the creative role of conscious thought. Perhaps, now, I would add that there might be some connection between that great African's powers of synthesis and his sanctity; and sanctity is not entirely a matter of conscious choice.

J M Coetzee

A NOTE ON WRITING

In an essay dating from the late 1960s, Roland Barthes discusses the verb 'to write' in terms of the grammatical oppositions past versus non-past, transitivity versus non-transitivity, and active versus passive.[1] What Barthes (following Benveniste) has to say about time and person are not relevant to my purpose here; but I will summarize what he has to say about voice.

Though modern Indo-European languages retain morphologically distinct forms for only the active—passive opposition, the phantom presence of a *middle voice* (a voice still morphologically present in Ancient Greek and Sanskrit) can be felt in some senses of modern verbs if one is alert to the possibility of the threefold opposition active—middle—passive. 'To write' is one of these verbs. To write (active) is to carry out the action without reference to the self, perhaps, though not necessarily, on behalf of someone else. To write (middle) is to carry out the action (or better, to do-writing) with reference to the self. Or — to follow Barthes in his metaphorical leap from grammar to meaning — "today to write is to make oneself the centre of the action of *la parole*; it is to effect writing in being affected oneself; it is to leave the writer (*le scripteur*) inside the writing, not as a psychological subject . . . but as the agent of the action." The field of writing, Barthes goes on to suggest, has today become nothing but writing itself, not as art for art's sake but as the only space there is for the one who writes.

Whether Barthes's essay is best thought of as a piece of speculative linguistics or as academic propaganda for a post-modernist practice of

1 Barthes, Roland "To Write: An Intransitive Verb?" in *The Languages of Criticism and the Sciences of Man* edited by Richard Macksey and Eugenio Donato (Baltimore: Johns Hopkins 1970) 134—156.

writing I do not know. Perhaps it is of no more value than as a demonstration of how deeply a literary conception can be embedded (metaphorically) in linguistic categories (are there any deeper linguistic categories than those of tense, person, voice?) I would not be spending time on it here if it did not, tangentially, speak a word of caution about constructions that we often run across in literary criticism in South Africa, particularly at the level of reviewing:

> to use language
> to write a book
> to create characters
> to express thought
> to communicate a message.

One of the things these core phrases have in common is grammatical structure. The verbs are all transitive, their voice (in form and, as I read them, in intention) active. They reflect a common conception of the subject — a subject prior to, independent of, and untouched by the verb — and of the relation, or lack of relation, between subject and object. Within the conception of writing reflected here, a paradigm sentence would be

> I | am writing | a note,

with the bars standing for bars between subject and verb, verb and object, subject and object.

I am not suggesting anything about value here. It may be truer in some cases, in some conception of value, to say "A wrote X" and in others to say "B | wrote | Y", but such a distinction would say nothing about the value of X or Y. Nevertheless, it is an interesting exercise to reflect on the two sentences

> I am writing a note (active)
> I am writing a note (middle),

asking oneself which of them describes the act one is performing. (But: *to perform an act* or *to perform | an act*?)
One might also want to think of

> A is-written-by X (passive)

as a linguistic metaphor for a particular kind of writing, writing in stereotyped forms and genres and characterological systems and narrative orderings, where the machine runs the operator. The three voices active, middle, passive may then be thought of as a cautionary chorus always to be lent an ear when one is doing-writing.

Patrick Cullinan

I sometimes wonder if it is not absurd for a man of fifty to be so pre-occupied, obsessed rather, with words. I wonder if poetry is not some kind of minor ailment and whether I am not some kind of malingerer on the outskirts of healthy society.

This infatuation took hold very early in my life and I know there is little I can do about it now. Words, tunes, ideas, pictures, memories knock about inside my head and sooner or later I start a poem. Most of these artefacts have to be abandoned or thrown away: for without precision, the right cadence, a resonance, the words do not work. They are not poems.

But, successful or not, when the poem is made I wonder again what the activity has produced. Is it not obscene or trivial to have written a poem about my personal obsessions when I live and work in a society so monstrously unjust as ours? This question would have no cogency if put in Western Europe or the United States; but we don't live there and the question here is a very real one. Embarrassingly, I have no argument against political poetry anyway. English has a magnificent tradition of polemical verse. Dante, the poet I admire most, was fanatically partisan about his 'political' allegiance. More to the point and to complete the argument, fellow poets in South Africa have written most movingly and intelligently against injustice and the apartheid state.

But beyond this, beyond words almost, I feel most passionately about the condition of this country. I believe that writers should demonstrate visibly their loathing of racism, of imprisonment without trial, of the whole *apparat* of apartheid. The only question is how this is to be done: outright polemic so often falls into rhetoric and protest poetry can so easily degenerate into facile slogans that have no edge and thus become self-defeating. But the makers of words must continue to struggle, to be accurate and consonant and true with their words.

14

Only this kind of dedication will have effect and will survive. There has always been injustice and there is no reason to think it will end. What matters is that the makers do their job.

I have, then, never been able to write a successful, overtly political poem, though, God knows, I have tried. I once showed such an effort to Lionel Abrahams, that fine critic who well understands the need for such writing and has himself so ably succeeded in doing it. Lionel just hung his head. True friend, his silence was all the reproof I needed.

It may be that there is some kind of filter in a writer's consciousness that sieves out what he cannot do, that says this is not precise: it is rhetoric; this has no inner resonance: it is platitude. It is possible that for me verse is not the right vehicle for this passion; the feeling is too raw, too immediate for this form. Nevertheless I believe that the verse I have published could only have been written by someone with a South African commitment, with my beliefs and background. Indeed if my verse has any strength it gets it from those elements.

It is hard to remember which faction Dante belonged to in four-teenth-century Florence. What remains is the passion. If we survive as writers, six hundred years from now, our factions will seem as vague as those of the Guelfs and Ghibellines. Let us hope the passion will endure.

Wessel Ebersohn

My country is a battlefield, a place of conflict where the rewards differ depending on the group to which you belong. For those now dominant the reward is survival, and especially survival of that position of dominance. For those subordinate and without influence, power is the spur.

In such a situation neither side looks kindly on those who do not conform to the group's requirements. The black man who tries too hard to understand white motives finds himself in much the same position as the white who identifies himself too closely with his black compatriots. Neither side can afford the luxury of nonconformism. The only thinking that may be permitted is those thoughts to which the group subscribes. Among black South Africans no one dare doubt the happy and beneficial outcome of the revolution. To do so places him in league with his people's enemies. Among whites no one dare question the adamantine control necessary to ensure our perpetual dominance.

It is this control that is the chosen vehicle for white survival and it is this control that bears as its fruits devices like the Prisons Act, the Defence Act and the Publications Act: measures structured to weigh and sift the information and influences reaching the public. Conventional liberal wisdom has it that such laws are *breaches of the public's right to know, oppressive draconian measures, assaults on the freedom of the press, the eroding of human rights* . . . . What seems to have been lost amongst the clichés of enlightened thinking is that these laws are nothing more nor less than the tools of a people's survival. Whether they are the best tools for the job is open to debate, but whether I like them or not I am faced with the reality of what they are.

It is in this culture, where those in authority exercise control over what is read and perhaps try to influence the writer in what he should write, that our literature seeks to grow. It would seem to be barren, infertile soil. I believe that the opposite is true. Times of conflict, wars, revolutions, the death of a love, illness and decay, all may be tragedies to the normal and sane among us, but to the literary artist they are mother's milk.

It is reasonable to suppose that out of a placid, uncomplicated life the literature produced would be equally unremarkable. Happily I am not cursed with such a situation. If at the end of this period in our history it is adjudged that no great literature was produced then you can accept with reasonable certainty that no one alive at the time was capable of producing it. The raw material certainly existed.

So the writer is faced with a wealth of circumstances that define most aspects of human behaviour more clearly than anyone could wish, drama and conflict surpassing the least reasonable desires, happiness and sadness in close contrast, dominance and submission, pleasure and pain . . . . Balanced against this is the possibility that his work might never be published in his own country. And if he is not fortunate enough to see it published abroad it might never be published at all. This could be seen as a reactionary factor, inhibiting the production of great literature. I doubt though that such a view would be valid. The writer who could stop writing because he might never be published is not a true writer and is not likely ever to have produced anything of worth.

Examining my position in the society into which I was born and the rights I claim for my trade, I find that I am in a battlefield, gripped by sympathy for one side and held by blood ties to the other, hoping by my work to add a little sanity to the proceedings, but aware that such hopes are probably futile. And did I really expect civil rights in the centre of a battle? The possible censorship of my writing must surely be a small matter when a society's survival is at stake. And when the present loser in the battle in time becomes the victor, as he surely must: under this future Marxist government, these happy purveyors of liberation; at that time am I going to enjoy greater freedom than I do now? It is possible, but it seems a little unlikely. The African liberal of whatever colour is not blessed with a lot of company. And, like it or not, liberalism is the common disease that afflicts all writers of real ability.

It is a matter of surprise to me that the authorities allow as much as they do in terms of challenging and controversial literature. Two of my own books that have been passed for local distribution after first being banned seemed at the time to be far beyond the limits I could expect the authorities to allow. Given the degree of our national desperation, I am surprised at the tolerance shown to writers. It is true that books are banned. It is also true that many books that reflect

17

the most hideous aspects of the system under which we live go unbanned.

Lately I have been hearing about a new sort of writer, the committed artist, and I have understood that this commitment is not to the pursuit and production of prose, poetry or whatever. I understand such a position. When surrounded by so much that is unjust the desire to help to change it is natural. But if such a commitment grows larger than the commitment to writing the writer so afflicted is to be pitied.

For myself, I write my stories because they are mine. I feel that they are intimately my property. If they exert an influence I am pleased, but in truth they are no more than a reflection of my own perception, such as it is. If I must be censored I think I understand why. But write I must, censored or not, with or without a publisher. And as I work I am a little surprised to be alive and still working in the centre of a battlefield. It is a privileged position.

Ahmed Essop

For a writer to elucidate his perception of self or of reality as it occurs in his work is very difficult, for the genesis of any piece of writing rests on too many factors in the environment and in the human psyche. Therefore, whatever is said in this brief essay is tentative and general.

The South African social order imposes itself on most writers, especially on those who have a deep reverence for all manifestations of life and consider themselves passionate humanists. Like so many other writers I have been profoundly disturbed by the structural violence of our society. It is buttressed by many convergent forces, among them historical causes and precedents, human frailties, psychological determinants, and, on the religious plane, the Judaeo-Christian ethic of the chosen guardians of final truth. There is also the larger context: the Western world's continual display of its arrogant ego in its relations with the peoples of Africa and the East and its historical record of plunder, oppression and cultural annihilation.

Impositions are seldom innocuous. Our social order can present a serious threat to the writer. As I see it, the threat is not so much to what one wants to write about, but to the creative consciousness and the creative imagination. Under the pressure of a crushing social reality, there is the danger that the creative imagination can become constricted. Instead of the writer being many-voiced, he may become single-voiced. The voice of the comedian, the satirist, the wit, the historian, the allegorist, the lover and sensualist, the lyricist, the psychologist, the philosopher and visionary may not be heard. The writer may reduce himself to the level of the secretary, the journalist, the zealot, the demagogue; and as passionate commitment to social and political change becomes the principal end of writing, abandon the formal aspects that control creative literary performance. To be many-voiced, it will be admitted, is not easy; the demands on our intellect, emotions and imagination are formidable. But I believe that the creative imagination reveals perceptions and truths that are not otherwise discoverable; meanings and values that exist in all forms of reality and experience, in that which is individual and related, and in that which displays recurring universal patterns. This is so because the creative imagination is a unifying principle of consciousness; it perceives the identity between subject and object, the psyche of man and the material universe; it is ever-changing and evolving. In my own writing I have tried to be as many-voiced as possible. I am interested in life's multiple and complex dimensions and have addressed myself to the variety of its manifestations as seen in the light of the creative consciousness. I do not believe that a single-minded devotion to one aspect of life can offer a comprehensive statement. And surely it is because of the complexity of life and its multiple dimensions that those who seek to reduce us to one-dimensional beings will ultimately fail. The human spirit will always manifest itself in all its variety and richness and break out of all imposed moulds.

In saying that the social order can be a threat I do not wish to imply censure of writers for suppressing their creative potentialities and renouncing the claims of 'universal truths', or for disregarding 'literary technique' and 'aesthetic canons'. That would be not only an insensitive response to their work, but also an example of a totalitarian view of the writings of others. 'Universal truths', 'literary technique' and 'aesthetic canons' do not guarantee any piece of writing literary validity. There is no reason why a single-minded devotion to one aspect of reality cannot lead a writer to produce work of literary value. Literature is not a science and has no fixed axioms which constitute a definition.

Of course the social order can equally be a threat to the writer who has not been oppressed. He may be tempted to enter the territory of liberal sympathies by exploiting the racial situation in his work, or he may retreat into the wasteland of avant-garde writing where experiment and form become preoccupations. But there is nothing to impede him from producing valid literature as long as the creative imagination is the source of it.

Events in South Africa (the long and bitter struggle for liberation, the '76 and '80 pupil and student revolts) are terrible burdens on every writer. One cannot ignore them in one's work if one hopes to leave a record of the times to future generations. Indeed, it is often an epic struggle to maintain one's equilibrium in the worsening social malady and not give up writing altogether. The twin temptations, "to take up arms against a sea of troubles" or to retreat into misanthropy and solipsism are ever present. Human destiny has been shaped so often by people who are insensitive to life-values. Political figures like Gandhi are so rare in this world.

In my own lifetime, besides the daily agony of living in South Africa, there have been the Second World War and conflicts in Vietnam, Cambodia, Africa, South America, Afghanistan and recently Lebanon. Though I have been, like many other people, profoundly affected by the immensity of the human tragedy, I have tried to keep my poise in the act of writing. I believe that literature has an important contribution to make to human understanding, peace and happiness. The impact of creative writing is not only immediate; it reaches beyond the emotional and intellectual sensibilities into the deeper reaches of the human psyche. It is perhaps there that the possibilities of authentic moral renewal lie. In this age, the morally unevolved consciousness, with its claustral notions of racialism, nationalism, patriotism, together with religious fantasy and dogma, still throws its penumbra over the world. But a time shall come when it shall evanesce. Then the work of writers may come to be seen not only as a testimony of the times and a revelation of the human condition with its potentials and possibilities, but as an important contribution to the metamorphosis of society into a rational, humane and compassionate one.

Athol Fugard

Please tell us something about the techniques you have used when writing your plays.

Fugard: The first thing I'd like to point out is that in the body of work that has my name, whatever its final value may be, I have used two radically different techniques — sets of tools, for that matter — in the making of a play. I like to use the word 'making' of a play to avoid any conceit about being an artist — that sounds very proud and affected. My profession is play-wrighting — a maker of plays, like the wheelwright and all the others.

The two radically opposed methods I have used are, first, the orthodox concept of a writer, which is somebody who disappears into his ivory tower with a stack of blank paper and emerges sometime later. It might take me a year to write a play; I'm very slow. The other technique I've used is to go into a rehearsal room — having given myself no time privately as a writer beforehand — with a loose mandate (an image, or sometimes more than that) and through work with actors, using techniques like improvisation, I've evolved a text, an experience which we put on the stage. There is a specific personal history involved in my decision to change from writing a play to making a play by working with actors. After my play *Boesman and Lena* which I think dates back to '68, '69, I began to develop a writer's block. Somehow I felt myself frustrated by the orthodox method of just sitting in my room and writing a play. I was running out of juice: every attempt, and I made several, to write plays after *Boesman and Lena*, miscarried because those techniques had gone stale on me. Then came the opportunity Professor Sneddon gave me to present *Boesman and Lena* in Durban. She gave me *carte blanche* to do anything I liked on the stage — she didn't ask for an orthodox production: she said, "Stage it any way you like." Yvonne Bryceland and I came up with what for us at that point was revolutionary; we relied just on ourselves and a pile of rubbish and the word. Out of that experience came the sense that there were other methods of making a play. The important influence on me at about the same time was the Polish theatre man, Grotowski, and I felt that he shared with me one very important idea, that the actor need not necessarily be just an interpretive instrument; he also has creative potential. By and large, although a measure of creativity is recognised in an actor's interpretation of, say, King Lear, he is not considered as the creator of the substance of his stage role. Grotowski worked with his ensemble in Poland (incidentally, I have never seen them, because at the period of which I'm talking I was without a passport and unable to leave the country). This was the time when Grotowski was showing most of his work in the West. But I read his book, *Towards a Poor Theatre*, and I found it enormously provocative. I was given the opportunity to go into a rehearsal room with three actors, Yvonne Bryceland, Val Donald and Wilson Dunster, and I had a loose mandate. I still don't properly understand the relationship between the two ideas that I coupled: the one was my fascination with Clytemnestra, Agamemnon and her killing of him in revenge for what he did before the Trojan War, and the equally tragic incident from our own history involving John Harris and the station bomb in Johannesburg. We had to make our tools as we went along — I had no experience of working in this way — and it turned out to be a very controversial experience. Just about every critic in the country described it as a load of rubbish, but we did have a faithful following of people who found the experience meaningful. That experience left me with a set of tools for making a play with actors which I continued to use, working with John Kani and Winston Ntshona. There was one difference: in the case of *Orestes*, I rightly described myself as just a scribe, but when it came to working with Kani and Ntshona, although I didn't want to write the play, the experience and the techniques that I had acquired as a playwright were all-important in shaping and in some cases even rewriting the material that emerged as we worked together in the rehearsal room. It's a form of instant play-making: *Sizwe Bansi* took us two weeks; *The Island* took us ten days, from the moment we first walked into the rehearsal room and I presented my idea, to the point when we gave our first performance.

I'm critical of those two works; I think they suffer from that haste. I think there is a limit to the density, the subtlety, even the complexity of the text which emerges under those conditions. Actors aren't playwrights: they can deal with an experience, and the best of them, if you use certain techniques correctly, can arrive at some articulation of it, or an articulate response to a situation you've created, hoping to release something in them. But it's important to distinguish between the actor's articulate response and the very different, savage, ruthless, painful discipline that is involved in professional play-wrighting.

In exactly the same way as the orthodox disciplines had ended up frustrating me, this alternative method of play-making ended up frustrating me as well. I did become progressively more conscious of the extent to which, although the experience was a powerful one, and may be more powerful because of its simplicity, it was a limited one. There was a very specific ceiling. I don't think there is really a ceiling, in the same sense, to what can happen when a writer sits down with a blank paper. There is no way of defining the ceiling involved in a play like *King Lear*, a play like *Long Day's Journey into Night*, or Ibsen's *Hedda Gabler*; they just go on soaring. I was frustrated, and that is still the case now.

My essential definition of myself is: a writer. I directed plays because the writer in me needed them; I've acted in them because it helped me to learn a little more, but my essential sense of myself is that I'm a writer and I've now returned finally to the old orthodoxies.

Could you talk about other influences besides Grotowski which have been important to you in the writing of your plays?

Fugard: I start writing every play — and in the current notebook I'm keeping I make the same observation — as if I'd never written any other one. The writing of one play doesn't help me write the next, and the reason for that is that every experience involved in a play, every essential experience, poses different demands, makes different requirements, needs a different style. In *Boesman and Lena*, I had to make a new set of tools that would allow me to capture and put down on paper very specific requirements in terms of dialogue. The high-flown, possibly at times over-inflated style of *Dimetos* is very different from that memorable line which opens *Boesman and Lena*, "Jou moer!" I'm always proud that an English play starts that way. That desolate landscape with two people, nothing else, a sense of interminable time, of disorientation, of the pointlessness of existence — I realise now, and it's something critics realised long before, that Samuel Beckett was an influence. I certainly had read him, and it was at that particular moment that his influence began to operate, but I wasn't conscious of it. Many influences operate as I write but I can only come back a year later and tell what they are. In *Hello and Goodbye* I think I definitely relied on influences from American plays. Certainly, in a more recent play, *A Lesson from Aloes*, I was influenced by my experience of Eugene O'Neill; it's a dramatically orthodox play in its structure, and I learnt from him. But there was a very specific requirement in the case of *A Lesson from Aloes* that had me going back to study and learn from someone else, whom I admire most profoundly — Chekhov. This need to go back to Chekhov arose from the fact that, more than in the case of other plays I've written, the creational concept operated under a bland surface of words, particularly in that very strange first act, where, with the exception of one or two little explosions, the real movement is taking place subterraneously.

To what extent do you base your plays on actual people and events?

Fugard: That has varied enormously; a very specific example is the genesis of *Sizwe Bansi is Dead* which lies in a photograph I saw in a little back-street photographer's studio. It was a photograph of a smiling man in an obviously newly-bought suit, and a pipe in one hand and a cigarette in the other. He was just so bloody joyous, so celebratory in his testimony to something which cannot be broken in the spirit of people. I remembered it for years and when John and Winston said to me, "Let's make a play; we want to be professional actors," we tried a few ideas out and all of them ground to a halt. And then I told them about the photograph: the play is specifically based on it. Actual experiences of John's came into the play, and actual experiences of Winston's. To give an example of a play not made with actors, but made entirely by myself, the genesis of *Boesman and Lena* lies quite simply in five seconds when I was in a car, paused at a traffic light at night, and in the headlights I saw a man and a woman, coloured, both heavily burdened. What the chemistry is, or the alchemy, I don't know: I just knew that I had an appointment with those two. It took me a long time: I don't keep my appointments immediately; there's a period of gestation when the incident sinks down and much later it surfaces, and the time has come to do battle. Plays can be based on experiences as small as that. *A Lesson from Aloes* relies massively on actual incidents. It deals with a man who is politically involved; as a result of a series of incidents, he's mistakenly thought of by the other comrades as being a police informer. That man was actually in my life: I never subscribed to the suspicion, but it and all the appalling consequences of sending a man to Coventry actually happened to that man. The play contains actual characters, actual incidents.

1976 was a crucial date for South Africa, likely to affect the work of all writers. Do you feel it has affected you?

Fugard: Obviously I start with a total agreement that 1976 was a crucial date; there can be no question about that. But we're talking about a shattering event in South African history which is only six years behind us and I think it would be incredibly presumptuous on anyone's side to try to understand the consequences of that in either personal terms or in a broader social context. What happened in Soweto is still so close to us and is still operating so that an objective perspective on it — let me repeat myself, either personally or in a broader social context — seems impossible at this stage. It's still happening; those Soweto riots are still happening in the individual psyche and in the social psyche of this country. When does an event run out of consequences? We are still watching the consequences of the events of the years 1899 to 1902—3, now, eighty years later; and I think in eighty years' time we will still be watching the consequences of 1976 in Soweto. And that's really what I'm trying to say — that it's presumptuous to claim to know what that event has done or is doing. 1976 is only six years behind us and the consequences of those days in Soweto are in a sense only beginning to operate now. Also, lurking behind that question is a much bigger question: What is a writer's or an artist's relationship to a major political event like that? Now I can be very specific in dealing with that. In 1976, when it all started to happen in Soweto, Ross Devenish and I were making a film seemingly totally unrelated to the politics of South Africa, about an episode in the life of the Afrikaans poet — a naturalist, a drug addict — Eugene Marais. At the time, as I read the newspaper reports about what was happening in Soweto, as I saw the posters on the streets, when we went out to a day's shooting on the Marais film, about the number of deaths there had been in the latest riots, I subjected myself to a fairly ruthless cross-examination about the relevance of making a film about Marais. I wondered about going back to the year 1926, in a time when the political situation in Soweto and in South Africa generally was so charged, so terrible, and I've satisfied myself on that score. I never lost any faith, any sense of the significance of making that film, but it raises the question now, now that Soweto has in fact happened, whether I will be able to make a film like that again — a film which on the face of it dealt with

26

nothing of the immediate politics of that situation. And my unequivocal answer is that if I hadn't made the Marais film in 1976 and the opportunity came now to make it, I would still make it.

How do you choose the subject matter of your plays?

Fugard: I chose to tell the story of *Boesman and Lena* and *Sizwe Bansi* for exactly the same reasons as I chose to tell the story of Johnny and Esther Smit in *Hello and Goodbye*: they were stories that fascinated me and I wanted to tell them. In the case of *Hello and Goodbye*, I seem to have told a story which does not resonate politically. The *Boesman and Lena* story does resonate politically, as to a certain extent does my latest play, *'MASTER HAROLD' and the boys*. But I would be violating a very important relationship with myself if I were to say: the situation in South Africa is so terrible that I'll only tell the stories that on the face of them resonate politically. I just couldn't do that. My whole motivation, my choice of the stories I tell, belongs in a very secret area of my life which I reveal to no one. And I've also got a public act, which is the play when it gets onto a stage. Before I get round to a relationship with South African society around me, the good and the bad in it, there's a relationship with myself. That's my secret. I can't turn that necessary area of secrecy in me into a public relationship with South Africa.

Do you attempt to influence people in your plays?

Fugard: Just how potent politically my form of story-telling is, is something I still find myself debating. What I have settled for, and I think that this is as far as I can go with any conviction, is that I do believe art is a civilising influence, and God knows, I think that South Africa is a country that can do with all the civilising influences that come its way. And I believe that my plays have made a contribution there; they have heightened the awareness of both white and black South Africans of certain social issues. I hope they are amusing too. It does seem to work out that way, judging by audience reaction to them. In America recently, for example, that was part of the audience's reaction to the intellectual conceit of the seventeen-year-old white kid in *'MASTER HAROLD' and the boys*; he thinks he knows all the bloody answers, which he doesn't. He says at a certain point to Sam, a black man who's trying to persuade him that ballroom dancing is very significant, "Don't confuse art and entertainment". Sam gets a chance later to talk about his ballroom dancing and what emerges is that ballroom dancing for Sam is an enormous political vision, because it's a world without collisions. You realise that this black man sees in ballroom dancing a vision of what the world should be like, where people know the steps and as he puts it, "dance like true champions, not like a bunch of beginners".

I've arrived at a stage where I really find myself almost incoherent when trying to explain the hows, whys or whens of my operation as a playwright. And yet at the same time, I have a very secure sense of my own voice. My sense of myself is that I'm essentially a story-teller: I have on any number of occasions found myself saying and writing in my notebooks that the only safe place I've ever known is at the centre of a story as its teller.

Sheila Fugard

A CASTAWAY IN AFRICA

The opening paragraph of my novel, *The Castaways*, reads: "I have always known shipwreck. Deep inside, I know the foundering of the self and the voices of the castaways of the East Indiaman, *The Berkley* foundering off the coast of Pondoland."

This fictional statement informs my life. I was born in England. My father was an Afrikaner. He studied medicine at Trinity College in Dublin, and then practised in England. My mother was Irish. They were married in Dublin. When Germany invaded Poland, my father decided to return to South Africa, with his family. Our ship docked in Cape Town, after a voyage of changing seas. A vast amphitheatre of clouds in the sky marked our entry into the southern hemisphere. I was eight years old. My last image of England was of guns erected on Westminster Bridge; a visit paid to the air-raid shelter of an uncle; a fitting for a gas-mask; and a vivid memory of Hitler's ranting speeches on the wireless. I was already a divided person.

My father took us to the family farm in the Eastern Cape. I was astonished at the brilliant light; the vastness of the landscape; the heat of midday; the citrus trees; the dark races; the intractability of the country. My mother was defeated. She was soon to discover that my father really was an Afrikaner. The veneer of the Englishman had worn off. She sank into a depression from which she never truly recovered. Their marriage collapsed. My parents were divorced, and I was finally reared in both Johannesburg and Cape Town.

Suffering a crisis of two worlds, I witnessed the battle between my parents in the arena of the Eastern Cape. The canvas was 'intractable' Africa. My mother wanted to return to England. My father chose to nurture his roots. The war in Europe decided the matter. So, we all stayed on.

Images of that first visit to my Oupa's farm remain. The old farmer would come into my bedroom to catch large bats — which frightened me — with his handkerchief. It was also an adventurous night-time ritual. I secretly enjoyed the thrill of the bats' arrival, and their subsequent capture. My Oupa always let the bats go free outside in the dark and humid night. A herd of ostriches disturbed me and my mother on one of our walks. This was another adventure. The landscape of cacti, thorn trees and aloes seemed to creep closer each day of that first Eastern Cape visit. The drought too was a new and mysterious enemy that I examined not only through the conversations held between my father and Oupa, but also in the dry soil, the caked mud about the citrus trees, and the equally dry and distant hills.

Cape Town also provided me with images that formed a young writer. I recall my childish fascination with an Indian snake charmer. The man always sat at the entrance to the Botanical Gardens. He played on a flute. Then, a golden cobra reared up in a menacing and thrilling dance. I spent many afternoons watching this spectacle. A small crowd always gathered. I added my pennies in appreciation of this show. I became aware that different races made their home in South Africa; blacks; coloureds; Malays; Indians as well as the English and Afrikaners. I had a sense of Cape Town's being fertilised by different cultures. Somehow, the idea of the Cape's being a halfway house between Europe and Asia set up vibrations within me even as a child. I knew that there was more to South Africa than the dour and hardy survival of my Afrikaner Oupa and his family. There were other elements as well.

I possess a very strong sense of 'The Journey to the East' myth. This is very much an interior vision. I think it is compounded of my early images of Cape Town, and my sense of rootlessness. I remain ambivalent in my relationship with South Africa. I am unable to identify with any culture here. I am not an Afrikaner. I am too distant from Ireland to claim any Celtic connection. I am certainly not English either, though I speak and write in that language. Even in my early days as a young woman spent in Sophiatown, when I helped Athol with *No Good Friday*, I felt no closeness to black life. I was a stranger in that world of political activity, the beginnings of theatre, and the emergence of black writers and journalists. Rather, I had to borrow a surrogate identity. I chose the East. I find a psychic correspondence there; textures that satisfy my need for ritual; images that are colourful and exotic; a sense of being a pilgrim. I know that it is my western consciousness impinging on India, an interior vision, that is the creative source. It has little to do with the 'real' India, as a recent visit to that

30

country proved. I noted then in my journal during a drive through Bombay:

> We drove through the streets of Bombay. To me, it seemed like an endless black location. The sea was just another watery aspect of the filth and humidity. This heat of India is totally different to Africa. It is a fetid heat that does not purify, but incubates and feeds more disease and misery for India. There is a terrible monotony to the weather which like the landscape is empty of meaning, or even change. Little energy is generated. It would be hard to write a novel, or a play in India.

Yet, despite my lack of identity or affiliation with any race group here, I cannot leave South Africa. The clash of cultures and the presence of inimical forces remain to challenge me. I will continue to write novels and poems. The seminal image of a castaway is intact. I travel often, yet returning to South Africa is always a complex experience. On my last trip home, I wrote a poem on the plane that crystallized these feelings. It reads:

> I witness the bare and savage Africa,
> Contemplate a destiny with stoicism
>
> In images of ultimate contradiction
> I refuse to turn my eyes away again.

These four lines of a longer poem state very clearly both my reason for remaining in South Africa, and for writing.

Nadine Gordimer

How did you begin writing?

Gordimer: At first I wrote as I'd danced as a child, very naturally and for my own amusement and pleasure and then slowly the other outlets for the imagination fell away and I concentrated more and more on writing. How much did the circumstances of being in the strange South African society contribute to it? Of course, with hindsight it was always a temptation to give more weight to this circumstance than I think was the truth because I began to write, as I say, in a very natural way and I began to write out of a sense of wonder at the mystery of life. The fact that I lived in a very strangely-organized society, a society grouped round the colour bar, I don't think I was even aware of when I first began to write. Whether you are born a white child in South Africa or you are born a black child — I have discussed this at length with black friends and with white friends — you accept the status quo. Children can't question; just as you're taught that you eat three meals a day and that you've got to go to bed at night, you know that this is the world made by grown-ups, and you have to accept it the way it is. When you're a white child in South Africa you accept at first the fact that blacks live segregated from you, that there are all sorts of activities in your life that they can't participate in. Then there comes a stage when, if you're going to develop into a rounded personality, and if you're going to begin to be a real human being, you begin to question this; you realise that this order of things is not God-given like the rise and fall of the sun, it is man-made, and then you begin to ask yourself why.

* This interview appears by kind permission of Nadine Gordimer and Chris Davies of Profile Productions. He is the producer of the filmed interview from which this is an extract.

How do you see yourself now as a writer?

Gordimer: To begin with I see myself, as an individual, as a white African. I'm not a European in the true sense of the word. I was born here; it's my home; I've lived here all my life, but that of course doesn't make me a white African. I feel myself committed to an indigenous culture here. I think it hasn't happened yet but it's something that one hopes will be allowed to happen — that there will be whites who will prove themselves acceptable in terms of our past to build a common cultural future with blacks. So from that point of view I see myself — yes — as an African, a white African. I am using a European language but then so are most black writers. Overwhelmingly they're using a European language and like me they are using European literary forms that derive from civilisations that have grown all over the world, so that one cannot separate what influence comes from where — what came from Greece, what came from Rome and in time one hopes one will not separate what came from Africa, from here. The cultural tragedy of the colonial period was that whites brought a culture from Europe, fossilised it here and didn't ever make the connection with an indigenous culture.

In South Africa, there was no written literature before colonial times but there was a very rich oral tradition and I would hope for a development in literature in South Africa that would bring together these two traditions, the one that was imported from Europe and the one that springs from the rich traditional culture. If and when that happens, and if black Africans allow it to happen, we would then have a truly new indigenous culture here and that is what I feel myself committed to.

What's the main purpose of your writing? Do you want to entertain, do you want to educate your readers, do you want to promote certain political ideas by literary means?

Gordimer: Well, I suppose there's always an element of entertainment. Every artist hopes to entertain, and knows that people will not read you, listen to you or look at your pictures unless you catch their attention. I'm looking at entertainment in a very broad sense. My own attitude to writing stems from that early sense people feel around about adolescence when they begin to wonder at life; they begin to think about where they've come from, why they're here and where they're going. For some people there's a ready-made answer in a religion or in a philosophy but I think the artist — it's in the nature of being any kind of artist — looks for his own answers and also of course interprets or tries to interpret those of others. For me it was really the sense of the mystery and also the chaos of life. Art is order.

Do you accept that whether you like it or not, as a writer in South Africa you do play a political role? The censorship committee, a government-appointed body, once accused you of exploiting the black-white dichotomy for political ends.

Gordimer: Well, I think that the censors were expecting me to become an apologist for the South African government's policies and I'm a writer; I'm not a propagandist. A writer cannot be expected to seek for balance if the balance doesn't exist. A writer deals with what is there in the society around him or her. The fact is it's proved in people's lives that there is no balance in South African society. The power is weighted on the one side, the oppression lies on the other. I can't invent a balance that isn't there, I can only reflect the imbalance that is there.

Stephen Gray

Writers in South Africa have been taking their bearings from the great, gruesome events of our history for many years: C Louis Leipoldt and the Second Anglo-Boer War; Sol T Plaatje and the 1913 Natives' Land Act; Walter Nhlapo and the *Mendi* disaster of 1917; Roy Campbell and the Bulhoek massacre; Donald Snowdon and 1922; Bosman and the gallows; Paton and 1948; Mphahlele and Sharpeville; Fugard at the Fordsburg Native Commissioner's Court in 1958; Plomer and the suicides of Ingrid Jonker and Nat Nakasa; Gordimer at the Fischer trial; Chris Mann at Pringle's reburial; Sepamla at Soweto '76.

Those who have been silent, have not been: they are as shaped by the feeling of stepping on a downward escalator as any others. We have all lived on the edge of apocalypse for many years. Our literature is riven with it; we are cursed, expectant, recording the momentum of collapse (too slow), dying, gone. Some to be remembered. Some on an upward path, really, meanwhile.

For we are, and throughout the century have been, all of us, suspended between African historical moments that should have coincided: we are post-colonial beings, but still we are pre-independent. As the torque between these appointments tightens, we make do, remain attentive, trusting in something bigger than us to cause the future to come true. An artist's role in all this slow movement is a small, supportive one, but look at what contortions we perform, trying to remain humane, integral, unmarginalised, coherent.

For myself, protest at this state of affairs is not a gesture, but a system of belief, a quiet and tenacious one, which is situated at the point where the way things are diverges into the way they could be. Or could have been. An act of memory in a society which has lost an internal dynamic of renewal can be allied to an act of provocation. (*Can* be.) Writing of a past that was different implies a future that will be, also.

I think that, particularly since Soweto, this sense of the possible power of some kind of revaluation has become a general belief among most writers in South Africa, in our theatres, and particularly in the once staid, now fomentingly active, departments of history, etc, on some of our campuses.

Because I am not personally courageous, I prefer to retreat into the past, but then, merely as a strategy, to use it as a predictive device. I don't believe that in South Africa today, you can't say precisely what you mean through the normal literary channels.

For me, this connects with another position. In the last decade South African literature studies have become considerably professionalised; the further back they track, and with more intricate and self-conscious systems, the more equipped we will be to go forward, soon.

In conclusion, I don't think:

That there is a useful distinction to be made between private and public, between art and society and between the individual and the people.

That any other writers can do for us what our own have, and do.

That as the radicals take over from the liberals we have lost much.

That, as writers, we have any choice but to take positions and work from there.

Mafika Gwala

I

Tracing The Steps

When I first saw something that I had written appear in print I was still in very angry mood. So much that I did not even firmly think I would continue to get published. Being a voracious reader, and having read lots of worthy literature — most of it banned — I told myself there was not much to be proud of. If I did write it would not be for the sole aim of publication. What mattered would be the spoken word. Whether it lay hidden under mats or got eaten by the rats would be a different story. But I wasn't going to be prolific for the mercenary publisher whilst knowing too well how relatively few of my fellow blacks had read as harmless a book as *Moll Flanders*, or *Anti-Dühring* for that matter. To try to discuss Zola, Brecht, Sholokhov, Kazantzakis, Frank Norris, or André Malraux (to mention a few) can sometimes invite trouble in black intellectual circles. People will want to stick to African authors, even though you are able to trace the literary influence in most of those authors. To blame it on Bantu Education is not enough; it can even be very misleading. The imperialist legacy behind the system that created Bantu Education cannot be left out.

I was a Ngoye drop-out, and so unsettled, especially since the national scene was bad. So many people that one knew were under banning orders. Others were being shunted off to join the likes of Nelson Mandela, Mbheki, Sisulu and others on Robben Island. Everywhere it was surveillance. It seemed that reading and cultural topics were the only things to sustain one. The only other unpublished black who kept me interested in writing was Mafika Mbuli. We discussed poetry, mainly. Already I had written batch upon batch of short stories which used to be read by a group of friends in a backyard room off Wills Road.

There weren't that many poems. Then an upcoming artist, Omar Badsha, introduced us to *The Classic* magazine. At first I was reluctant to send any stuff, perhaps unsure of myself. Omar insisted. Then I decided to give it a try. To my surprise *The Classic* accepted our efforts, Mafika Mbuli's and mine, on first try.

It was in those days that I came to know in person Nomafa Joyce Sikhakhane, the ever radiant but determined Nomzamo Mandela, Peter Magubane, Dumile Feni and other 'knowns' of the time. I drew inspiration. I remember it was the days that were to see active engagement of the Music, Arts, and Drama Group — MAD, whose live spirits were actor Benjy Francis (*The Blood Knot*) and Marge.

If one can venture to say it now, writing by blacks was just about emerging from the doldrums. Bannings, exile and death had robbed the literary scene of many writers. There had been, it seems, a vacuum, until along came Oswald Mtshali, Mongane Wally Serote and Njabulo Ndebele. I first met them in *The Classic*; also Webster Makaza of Pretoria and Meshack Hlongwane of Durban. These two were in short stories. I made contact with each of them, only to discover that they were also in my mood, so what continuum could we forge? Hoping it was only for the time being, we all withdrew from the demands of short story writing. Yes, all three of us, for Wally Serote had also had one short story published in *The Classic*. Some two to three years later Oswald Mtshali's first poetry collection was to receive rave reviews, to be followed by Mongane's the next year.

The writing that came with *Sounds of a Cowhide Drum* (Mtshali) and *Yakhal'inkomo* (Serote) was to carry an impact very different from that made by the writers of the late fifties and early sixties. Black writers and artists had decided TO TRACE THEIR LOST STEPS INTO THEIR BLACKNESS so as to plod better armed with ideas into the future. This tracing of steps unavoidably meant change in cultural beliefs and political perspectives. The change was being imposed by the situation prevailing in the country. It had come down on us, more markedly this time, that only the black man can liberate himself, psychologically and physically. He could no more trust in change of heart outside social, cultural and economic pressures.

During this jaunt in search of identity, my locale was Durban where I had grown up. Like most South African towns, it had something to keep one going — some kind of identity base — for remnants of South Africa's multi-racial character were still there. Vestiges of an undying past, so the old spirit persisted. Perhaps the reason for Durban's becoming the capital for Black Consciousness in the early seventies lay in its non-racial tradition. I only had to move into Grey Street or towards Greyville. Nearby the Shah Jehan cinema was the African Women's Hostel; and there was the African Churches area. There was the Bantu Social Centre on Beatrice Street. This was also Grey Street's shebeen area. The Lower Berea and Cannon Gate sector merging into Warwick's 'Casbah' also made one feel Durban was still home. On Leopold Street there were the herbalists' shops. We still have the masala spices and dried-fish smell in Victoria Street. And though the meat and fish market has shifted slightly, it still has the Asiatic bazaar. Though the Indian tailors have dispersed, the household names like Harribai, Solly Omar, Bhagwandas are still around.

Looking back, you realize it is here that you've watched people throwing their nuts around; here that you have asked yourself if you aren't being turned into a nutter; here that you've sought greater sanity. Then you also discover that, though in your early twenties, in this old city of Durban, you once rode on any bus, colour is now your bane.

The sixties were justifiably a period of anger and not much understanding between the races, whatever the term race means. One had to learn certain things. Well, now and then one would hear that some black or group of blacks had broken the rule of anger thus shaking some ideas out of other blacks. Though courage comes out of anger (in oppressive conditions) it cannot be mothered by it. Some very cool daring would appear here and there; followed by a Terrorism Act trial.

Each time one read of those deaths in detention it was like the ground was ripping open. There were days when one was visibly weak, peppered — as if one had petered out of ideas. Then there were days when one felt ineffably strong. But through all this, the anger sat, staring challengingly. And one brooded. Sometimes the brooding would raise the spirit; and hell broke loose. Somewhere in the inner theatre of the mind it was like slaughter — the pulling out of the innards. Maybe that's how Mongane Serote came to call his first collection *Yakhal'inkomo*. When I first saw the book I shared the same feelings.

The formation of the South African Students' Organization (SASO) expressed much of the slaughter feelings. SASO brought back the appearance of national organizations into the black struggle. The last of these had been the African National Congress and the Pan-Africanist Congress. SASO's successful launching through the formal adoption of a Manifesto and Constitution at the Second General Students' Council in July 1971 called for the formulation of a "way of life", an "attitude of mind", a "social outlook" or "world view" pertaining to the South

African situation. It all spelt one thing: consciousness.

As I found myself working with students and members of other Black Consciousness bodies my poetic life, if one may call it that, changed accordingly. The brooding was replaced by an understanding of hope. I have been striving to define that hope since then. Meanwhile, there were, as always, the usual signs of an impending State onslaught against Black Consciousness.

In July 1971 SASO invited the Malombo Band and the Serpent Players led by John Kani, Winston Ntshona and Nomsa Nkonyeni. The two groups spent the whole conference week with the students exchanging ideas. Ntshona and Malombo's Julian Bahul played the role of spokesmen for each of the groups, with John Kani and Abe Cindi being the chief craftsmen. That same year Barney Simon and the Phoenix Players had brought Edward Albee's *Bessie Smith* and Fugard's *Hello and Goodbye* to Durban at the invitation of Tecon (Theatre Council of Natal). Tecon had succeeded MAD. Most of the Tecon members had been students at the University on Salisbury Island. The leaders were Strini Moodley, his wife Sam and Saths Cooper. Strini and Saths were to be put in executive positions in SASO and the Black People's Convention (BPC) respectively. The most stimulating aspect of this cultural revival was that, following the demise of Union Artists, the African Music and Drama Association (AMDA), Crossroads and others, new groups such as Tecon (Durban), the People's Experimental Theatre group (PET), Mihloti (Johannesburg) and Serpent Players (Port Elizabeth) were bringing in a new message — the beginnings of resistance that was being experienced by the Black Consciousness organizations. Young blacks not only got bored with the old colourless effort but felt insulted by half-baked projects such as ALGIJEW'S PINA-CULO in 1972. To them Dorkay House in Johannesburg and the other social centres had been misused since the sixties. That was that.

Nationally, blacks were going through the synthetic phase of self-assertion — an accelerated process of national consciousness. In that way events following the ANC-PAC bannings were different from Soweto 1976, just as the latter came to differ from the period before the Freedom Charter.

It came as no surprise then that for their Third Annual Conference, SASO invited Njabulo Ndebele and myself to address students on the theme of "Black Creativity and Development". Interestingly, both our papers reflected an economic interpretation of history and political development, with culture as an inseparable aspect of history and politics. That very year, 1972, James Matthews, Oswald Mtshali,

Mongane Serote and Sipho Sepamla gave readings together at Turfloop University. Black Arts Studio, a BPC-initiated project, invited all South African black artists to a national exhibition of their works. In 1973, during Turfloop's Africa Arts Week, I was to read with Mtshali, Serote, Don Mattera, Phil Phetoe, Lefifi Tladi and Mike Dues.

With the demise of *The Classic* the vacuum was to be filled by such publications as *Ophir*, *New Coin*, *Purple Renoster* and *Bolt*. *Ophir* appeared to be the one most readily acceptable to blacks because of its lesser adherence to conventional English literary styles. Or was it that it had acquired an avant-garde approach to poetry? Of the main contributors to *Ophir*, black readers loved to read the poet-artist Wopko Jensma. I enjoyed Wopko; so did everybody with whom I discussed poetry of the day. Wopko's observation of the apartheid scenario was brilliant, and very open.

Wopko Jensma. For a long time I thought he was a black. After all we had discovered and again lost Howard Eybers to church ministry. So when I met Wopko one evening, edged against his self-withdrawal, I could only think of one thing: his white world was killing him, as if out to destroy him. Perhaps he had refused for too long to be the white he was expected to be. Another hurting thought flushed my mind. It was the gnawing feeling that with such cruel reality as we have in this country — and with worse to come — it was futile to engage in existentialist resistance against a culture of oppression.

In a book I had read in the sixties, Paul Robeson's *I Take My Stand*, I had discovered that black awareness was not incompatible with modern political beliefs. As Robeson found, it could rest on a sound ideological foundation. Besides, I had read and re-read Ralph Ellison. I had also read Peter Abrahams and Alex la Guma. Hence it did occur in my writing that, though 'blackness' was a unique phenomenon of the late sixties and early seventies, it was a variant of earlier experiences in the past struggles of blacks. This idea I was to reiterate time and again when talking to students. It is really disturbing to think that writing in this country still puts the writer in the position of the exile, if not worse. You are as good as exiled if, in order to remain loyal to your national conscience (that questions the starvation and poverty diseases surrounding you), you assume the role of an "invisible man". If I recall correctly, in 1967 the then principal of the University of Natal, Professor Owen Horwood, banned the campus magazine *Dome*, and together with it the Durban Students' Representative Council. Today he is the man who has a say on the difference between full and empty stomachs, and yet despite such power, some artists have stated categorically that their work can be apolitical. Speaking for myself I do not understand what "apolitical" has ever stood for. If someone came to me and said, "Your writing is political", that would call for my unswerving defence of whatever is "political" about my writing.

I say this in view of the offence taken by some very influential white writers and critics at some of the current black writing. Granted, they have the right to object according to the tenets of democracy. My question: what democracy? Does a democracy of inequality allow for natural rights to all? Is preferential treatment for pets (with extra-full meals and veterinary extra care) compatible with Jesus Christing? In the face of such reality there has been little endeavour by black writers to dignify their talk: simply because there is nothing dignified about the complacency engulfing us. Some expressions have exhausted themselves. I am reminded of a coloured youth who, arguing the success of Dr Chris Barnard with his school friends at the Mowbray Bus Terminus closed the topic by simply saying: "Chris Barnard is *Kruis Genade*". I had left James Matthews at his place; he had wanted to stay home that day, to write.

By the end of 1973 the upsurge of talent in the arts amongst blacks could no more go unnoticed. Music, painting, sculpture, literature thrived. New names gained national attention: Zinjiva Winston Nkondo, Nakedi Phosa, Fikile, Percy Sedumedi, Dikobe Martins, Shabbir Banoobhai, Nkathazo Mnyayiza, others. Later they were to include Neil Williams, Fhazel Johennesse, Mtutuzeli Matshoba and many more. What helped this process was the growing common consciousness amongst black contributors to magazines like *Ophir*. I was also sending poems to be included in the SASO Newsletter. Those poems were supposed to be purely black pieces -- part of the conscientization drive. Even then it was to dawn on me that there could be no 'pure' black. With the exception — a wild exception — of one or two, I have not included those poems in a collection.

On the very day we had spoken over the phone, about my going to Cape Town, Onkgopotse Tiro had been killed by a parcel bomb in Botswana. I was working on *The Black Review 1973* at Diakonia House in Braamfontein, and caught a train for Durban where I was to collect an air ticket to Cape Town from Tony Morphet of Natal University. On my arrival at my Hammarsdale house the next morning there was no greeting from my wife, but the question: "Have you heard about Tiro?" I balked, still nearby the door. "He's been killed."

Shit! I told myself. Hardly twenty-four hours since our conversation. He had even rapped about the Cape Town invitation, about taking black poetry to Whitey's territory: And jokingly I'd remarked that all of Southern Africa was "terry country". Further, I'd had to say how uneasy I was about the whole business of Black Consciousness and the controversies of liberal demeanour. Wally had also expressed some unease, but had urged that we go, to take what we could pick out of the experience.

That morning of the news — What? Tiro dead! — I went through one of my most painful moments. Right then I decided not to proceed to Cape Town.

At the Tiro Commemoration Service in the Regina Mundi Catholic Church, Rockville, my reason for more involvement with poetry became slightly clearer, though perhaps the haze still remains. I'm still wading through the mist. Nevertheless — if one has to put down the goings-on of the country more clearly, poetry is the best medium for this. When you face a truth and there is challenging need to express it, you can most emphatically capture it through poetry, because there is no way you can twist it about in a poem. You have to bring out the truth as it is, or people will see through your lies. It is also through poetry that you find, most soberly, that there has never been such a thing as pure language. That only academic fallacy can create and defend such abstraction. You thus cannot but be disturbed by academics who claim an almost sacerdotal authority over black writing.

My participation as guest speaker and delegate at the Black Renaissance Convention held at Hammanskraal in 1974, did affect my approach to writing and to the whole cultural spectacle.

To illustrate tradition and fallacy, I'll use this Convention. After much heated debate, mainly between the militants and the conservatives, delegates who served in collaborationist bodies were to be excluded from the proceedings. The meeting reached a stalemate. The elders would not vote for what they considered were radical motions; the young militants would not vote for what they considered to be compromise motions. Then the following morning the 'old guard' came into the hall in Afro attire, expensive stuff. This had not been the case on the previous day. Instead of gaining them acceptance from the young militants it had the opposite effect. There were a few young people in dashikis and dimbazas (Afro shirts) but the leaders were in the usual denims. The whole youth delegation got the cue. There was a rush to the rooms, as if by instruction. In a very short time everybody was in 'natural' working garb. Interestingly no caucusing had done it. Those kids followed instinct. The previous day's tension, accompanied by long-winded, 'moderate' speeches, showed we had little in common in our African identity alone. That morning the youth decided to refuse false compromise made on the grounds of African identity and the indigenous past. What also became more apparent was that those of us who had consistently warned against staying in the past had scored a point. For writers, the ghetto theme had become more realistic than the Muse's ventures into Swahili, Egyptian and Yoruba aphorisms. If we were to write on African greatness it had to be insistently linked with the present.

Writing in the vernacular has not achieved such a link. It has been subjected to another kind of academic take-over and is produced only for the school curriculum. Nothing has been published that is suitable for adults seeking education or entertainment, and the plays on radio and television are even worse.

Came 1976. By this time there had emerged a new character in the urban areas. Mass removals and the sprouting of peri-urban slums had resulted in split families. Members of families that had been forcibly removed would always want to go where security and proximity to the place of work could be found. In the slums, at the hostels, in 'resettlement' areas would be found the 'paper-carrier man' — ever shifting, spending nights at different places with friends or relatives. As the Hippos honked through the streets of black areas, there were blacks in those areas who had no fixed abode. This is perhaps how the poetry in praise of resistance and in praise of long established areas for urban blacks got into black writing. Long before 1976 blacks had been pressing home this reality of destitute people in the towns. My poems on Alexandra must have germinated from that.

1976 also saw the holding of a South African Writers' Conference at Wits University. I had been requested to do a paper for the occasion, which I did, but failed to get to the conference. What emerged from that meeting of writers, black and white, was to help us towards the formation of the *Staffrider* nexus that brought us to the first issue of *Staffrider* magazine in 1978. *Staffrider* was to publish my 1976 paper on "Black Writing in South Africa" in 1979. This nexus was the greatest thing to wire out of the black literacy and art scene. Contributors to *Staffrider* were from all the 'race' groups. Blacks freely contributed without fear of editorial censorship. Censorship is not confined to the censoring ordered or executed by the State. Some printers and publishers can be worse culprits, because they play the wolf in sheep's clothing.

Some of us had been detained after the State clamp-down on Black Consciousness organizations in October 1977. I had spent a hundred days in detention under Section 6 of the Terrorism Act. James Matthews had spent six months imprisoned under the Internal Security Act. We were not the only ones. One had to unscramble oneself in a very short period, with minimum side-effect. Amongst one's people there were still the festive mysteries common during December month. We were tied down, yet unknotting ourselves. At State level, more homelands were gearing for 'independence' as racism was being window-dressed for acceptance and respectability. Urban regulations were being tightened to rule out the paper-carrier man.

There had to be change of gear.

Writers of the *Staffrider* group included exiled writers like Mongane Serote, Mandlenkosi Langa, Amelia House, Daniel Kunene and Bafana Buthelezi. Geographically separated as the contributors have been, they had been experiencing, as part of the people, whatever damned repression the country went through. They did not start from the imagined — the abstract. They began with the concrete, with what they had seen of the post-Sharpeville period until the 1976 upheavals. They produced not some idealism of a mythified literary tradition, but a stretching of the English language so that it would accommodate their African background and ghetto ordeals. Which is why it is almost impossible to talk about literary style at this stage of African literature. Where would one start?

Style will come out of the common identity which no-one can disown. Poetry, to me, is so wide — complex, and many-angled. Yet there is, always, the viewpoint which produces distorted criticism of black literary attempts and can indeed become a general danger to aspiring black writers. Blacks thus fall back to Consciousness as an essential aspect of change in this respect. What we are writing today will carry different meaning in the future, but the validity of the present meaning will remain. How much remains will be determined by how we identify the forces at work throughout the country. By that time we shall find that language has grown and become enriched by that validity.

My first collection of poems only came out in 1977 although it could have been out the year after *Yakhal'inkomo*. The thing about it was that Black Consciousness tempted me, rightly, to want to be wary; and, perhaps erroneously, to want to calculate my impact. I do not regret the stance I took at the time. It was the correct one. Having moved and mixed in wider circles I had concluded that in a social situation such as ours, one always came to find people who were busily undermining sympathies for black artists; and if one did not tread carefully, a fall could be as slow as a climb. I had observed it with artists and musicians. The death of Nat Nakasa had been a terrible blow, a bitter lesson. Once I talked to Wally; we were getting drunk, or just about to get drunk. Wally stood up and shouted at a group of students seated in a corner: "Okay, Okay; I'm black and I'm proud. So what about it?" This was at Turfloop during Afrika Arts Week 1973. I was to hear Wally repeat these words many more times in future. That night he continued, quietly directing his talk to me:

"At least between us, my brother, we know why Black Consciousness. We are fighting the death of Nat Nakasa."

"And Can Themba," I added.

"Sure you've got it," he said, "And Can Themba. Those kids don't know that."

Later I was to discover that the death of Ingrid Jonker had brought the same feelings to James Matthews. James attended the funeral of Ingrid Jonker.

One could not afford to reify such people in one's writing just so as to create heroes. Neither could one try to lyricize too often, as this was dangerous. One would have to seek an approach which, from certain perspectives, would be desirable after blacks have achieved their liberation. Or rather, after Southern African society has become normal, open to all its peoples.

Rapping about oneself is not only tedious and full of self-trial; more, one cannot talk about oneself without diminishing something which one holds dear in one's writing. Writing about those miniaturized issues inside one's thoughts can make them run pell-mell. It's like choosing between glandular darkness and visceral dawn. There are fears that the positioning of one's mindset will be dismissed. Where does one draw the isogloss? From this focal point, I have chosen to talk about black writing as it affects me and other black writers — within our particular social context, and as that context's growth process is in turn affected by writers. Smoothly or tortuously. This way, hopefully, the problem of the black writer as a cultural worker in a social and artistic context that alienates him on the basis of class and colour can be probed more objectively.

My premise is based on the assumption that the chief South African theme has always been that of SOCIAL CONFLICT. For literature cannot be divorced from the life of a people. By black writers (novelists, poets, dramatists), the black is portrayed as a fully-fledged human being, with all the qualities that ought to make him a full citizen of his country, given all his capabilities of sacrifice and resistance. The black writer thus assumes a role in the social conflict; he cannot step out of it.

His is not a matter of choice but a necessity. He illuminates the contrast between the black and the oppressor, who may either be the fascist engineer (for Afrikanerdom) or the collaborationist black (for homelands rule).

II

Progressive Undoing — Writing As A Cultural Weapon

In a society where politics determine most aspects of our social consciousness through separate toilets, segregated transport, pass and curfew laws, the Immorality Act, unequal education — in short unequal rights based on skin colour — our speech and written language forms cannot but be highly politicized. In a divided society, words cannot be expected to carry the same value. Take the mythical notions of Afrikaner righteousness: Afrikaner superiority feelings of 'Kaffirhaat' continue to deny the South African black man his history. In the process it continues to destroy the Afrikaner's own true history.

We cannot write outside of our experience in a society where social deprivation is taken for granted. Though "all literature is propaganda but not all propaganda is literature", we find ourselves having to speak about our experience if we have to change it. Our critical attitudes towards racism, exploitation and inequality will inevitably dominate. It is total criticism of that inhumanity of man to fellow man that carries the hope of our regaining humanity for all.

We are no Messiahs. At a recent come-together attended by a few artists, one or two writers and several students, one student stated that blacks on this white campus had more respect for Afrikaans writers. At least, he said, they have something to fight against in their own community. English writers seemed to think there was nothing to fight against — as if all had been well with British colonial attitudes. As if asserting themselves against British South African prejudices and liberal demeanours was being ungrateful to their heritage. It is as if Olive Schreiner, Doris Lessing and Nadine Gordimer never existed on African soil, said one student, glooming irately.

We took it all in, pondered. And we got the cue. The total criticism of Afrikaner prejudices together with the highlighting of certain virtues of the 'volk', by such eminent authors as André Brink, Etienne Leroux and Elsa Joubert is very encouraging to the quest for a South African national literature.

It has not been easy to harmonize our black subject matter with the language forms of a dominant English culture. No one can objectively blame us if at times the culturally enriched English language has been stripped naked. One is reminded of how, at the height of cultural resistance by black Americans, Imamu Baraka (Le Roi Jones) advocated "poetry that kills" amongst blacks. And he found ready support. Likewise, in this country a choice emerges, heavy and demanding: bend or break. This is when the consciousness is irked. Questions crop up. Questions such as: what moral right does the academic have to judge my style of writing? What guidelines outside the culture of domination has he applied?

Most black writers of the seventies have shown themselves to be suspicious of technological progress. Yet to view technological advancement in critical spirit need not be disturbing, for technology has had its equal share of destruction of human nature. We have nuclear warheads, laser beams, nerve gas, defoliating agents, remote eavesdroppers — and more. When black women are forced by economic pressures into contraceptive methods that carry adverse effects, then there is reason to pause and think of the misapplication of technology for the more effective suppression of people who should have the right to decide against exploitation. Then you find yourself concluding that whatever the technological changes, our society remains unfree and, to large extent, set against change. You question every technological advance.

To me the Walk on the Moon seemed to be used to justify Vietnam; just as Dr Barnard's heart-transplant appeared to give most white South Africans a "Hands off!" attitude — that the outside world had no right to criticize this country's apartheid laws. Though one may hate to say it, every South African 'first' — technical, medical or economic — is a disturbing factor to the black. You hear it in the trains, in the buses, in the crawling transport queues, in the shebeens. Blacks have come to believe that 'progress' for South Africa prolongs the denial of their human rights.

South African whites can no more claim exclusive rights to correct English. The English language itself thrives on the adoption of foreign words and coinages. Besides, colonization and the imposed separation of races has taken care of what happens here. In our ghetto language there can be no fixity. The words we use belong to certain periods of our history. They come, they assume new meanings, they step aside. We have been Natives, Bantus, Plurals, Blacks, etc, yet all along we have been very African. Why, 'tsotsis' no longer like to call themselves by that name; and the term 'money' has been confined to meetings of small businessmen. We cannot make our language blindly try to follow

British or American expressions. We are bound to the demands of our own historical context, so that, while our English medium is being shaped by our history, 'command of the English language' becomes a myth of the first order. We have expressed ourselves accordingly. Black poetry makes sure that the centre of the 'white-culture-is-superior' myth does not hold. Yes, black poetry has saved the black man's day.

We cannot write honestly if we dismiss the things that we see around us: the voices that we hear, the facial expressions and gestures, the whole meaning of the social experience. No surprise then that South Africa's blacks use more or less the same verbal expressions, irrespective of the geographical distances between Durban and the other cities. Subject to the tendencies of a yet undefined 'back-to-the-people' movement, black poetic expression has helped to give the culture of the black a revived stimulus to resist a culture of white domination, so that both the black and white cultures become sub-cultures, part of a greater South African national culture. Since *Sounds of a Cowhide Drum*, black expression has gained renewed character — or should I say, the viable meaning of a growing national consciousness.

A G Ullyatt (*Contrast* 44, 1977) misses the point when he expects blacks to follow the traditional formalism of English language expression while seeking an alternative to conventional English culture. American English has not only withstood Oxford, but now poses a threat to Oxford English. According to critics like Ullyatt, all that is not Western-cultured in black English writing stems from the black writer's failure to grasp, or at least borrow, credit from the advanced state of the English language. But, there *are* times when the black writer's language has brilliantly described the black man's alienation. Then you discover that he or she has not explained that alienation. The Gaborone conference on *Culture and Resistance* in July 1982 highlighted the need for art not only to register resentment against social inequality and economic exploitation but also to contest these by creating wider social awareness.

Since the symposium on South African Art and Literature at the University of Cape Town in July 1979, it has been generally accepted amongst South African writers that every serious artist in this country has some allegiance to a socialist vision of some sort. Such vision finds open expression in the revamped but non-registered militant black Trade Unions, in the Students' Rights Movement, in the Black Consciousness bodies and in the national aspirations of those who seek constructive change. Predictably even the term 'class' is energetically replacing the term 'black' in the language of economic exploitation.

This steady process of transformation in consciousness is bound to come out more clearly in art works presently being produced by committed artists (art workers). A common movement is once more taking shape. Except that this time it will have gone a long way from the generation of Es'kia Mphahlele, Nat Nakasa, Richard Rive, Alex la Guma or Can Themba. Some older writers have written better than today's writers. We are learning a lot from them. We are also learning from the generation of Dumile, Ezrom Legae, Zondi or Omar Badsha. We have much to learn from the generation of Abe Cindi, Phillip Tabane or Kippie Mokoetsi.

Black Consciousness, I've been asked, what do I now feel about Black Consciousness? I can say I feel just about everything I shared with Black Consciousness adherents in 1971; but with varying degrees of stress here and low-key there. Black Consciousness was the opening of a new era of national consciousness. We needed a stimulus, a national urge.

At the second SASO Congress of 1971, which had Black Consciousness as its main theme, one had to point out emphatically that Black Consciousness was not an end in itself, since it was subject to the direction national consciousness would follow. Right through the hectic days it has remained an identity divided against itself — but with two class shades of different backgrounds. Although apartheid had separated the communities, Black Consciousness did bring Indian, Coloured and African together during the formulation of the homelands and group areas policies. But there were the collaborators, out to get a piece of the economic cake for themselves as a group separated from the vast majority of the black population. These status seekers even went to the extent of forming a Black Alliance to protect their position. On the other hand the rural workers, the semi-peasantry, the lumpen proletariat of the peri-urban slums and the urban workers who did not stand to benefit from collaboration, were also going through the experience of black awareness.

What made Black Consciousness backfire, which is something some of us had sensed all along, was that amongst the activists, the petit-bourgeois types in the ranks, some were only aware of their cultural alienation and dismissed the economic laws and historical processes that conditioned their position at that particular phase of the political struggle. Consequently, they have had to strive for recognition as leaders by using proprietorial feelings of a base nature. Base, since this bourgeois feeling of proprietorship is, despite the communalist rhetoric, condescending to the black worker, particularly the legislatively disabled migrant worker.

What has happened with some prominent protagonists of Black Consciousness is that they have refused to learn from the turbulent history of the twenties, or from historical perspective through the Freedom Charter, the Treason Trial into the Rivonia Trial. One could say they have failed to interpret the history of this country not only culturally, but politically and economically as well. Dialectically. Instead they have been tempted to think through their skins and their hearts.

By the middle of 1975 it had become evident to some artists that the overstress on indigenous context was the hallmark of petit-bourgeois mentality. These exponents of Black Consciousness have shown themselves to lack insight into the nature of power within a cultural liberation process. In the parallel trend, what the new black middle class cannot stomach about whites is the whites' role in the economy and consequent political domination; not their leadership. This status is not even contested, though coveted. It is ignored, though disliked. Some of our black community's leaders are so bourgeois that they will even fail to envisage any others leading the people except themselves. They are a choice split upon itself.

The collapse of the black collaborationist front over the new political dispensation for coloureds and Indians is going to affect the literary and plastic arts. In the process a new way in cultural resistance is a foregone conclusion. Already many artists and cultural operatives have come to accept the option of class analysis, particularly as the bourgeois element in the black communities has proved itself parochial. It sets a low ceiling to national expectation. This means that the language of the oppressed cannot always be lyrical, highly nuanced and frolicsome. Our language often answers to immediate needs and much African literature has answered to the boredom and the deprivation of those who are not free.

Only when Black Consciousness rhetoric has been utilized to forge a new reality, as part of conscious movement within a multi-racial South Africa that strives for a non-racial society, will it be viable. Right now one can unreservedly claim that there is nothing to be gained for blacks by continuing to mythify Black Consciousness. It has become a deviation from the path of national consciousness. That is, it becomes the politics of accommodation, convenience — not answering to the historical demand of social change.

Writing by blacks acquires political significance precisely because whatever they publish gains wide scrutiny from the State and from white academics. Blacks will often do the cheering or the jeering. Within such political significance, blacks discover that the English language also has its inadequacies. For instance, when whites talk of a 'middle class' there springs up the immediate question: middle between what?

Any change in black political beliefs and in their perspectives will unavoidably usher in new literary and artistic styles. We have seen how Mphahlele's African exile influenced his literary style. Given the odds against us, we have had to keep jotting down whatever needs to be taken note of. At the same time we are bound to live and answer to personal and collective responsibility.

What has been encouraging is to find that blacks are expressing themselves from a common experience. The first time I met Mongane Serote it was as if I had always known him since childhood days. The same happened upon first meeting with James Matthews, despite the age difference. As if we had marched together during the *Azikhwelwa* days.

All I've done is to suggest guidelines for understanding better: why the black upsurge in the arts? And also, why has this upsurge been subjected to misunderstanding at times? No suggestion remains absolute in time. Problems that hold us back call for collective concern. Take the problem of the writer as a member of a select few. To be adored as a writer or artist has often been proved to be dangerous, but a cultural worker's success need not be a self-elevating mechanism. Better if writers and artists are merely treated as cultural workers. One has seen how artists, novelists, poets can be so hero-worshipped that nobody notices their stagnation. Whereas to be regarded as a cultural worker is not only safer but it allows one social mobility.

Unless closely monitored, the cultural activism of Black Consciousness which, like Negritude before it, contains bourgeois overtones, can be a destroyer of class consciousness. Yet it is Black Consciousness which brought into focus the need for class discourse as an alternative to the bourgeois tendencies of thought produced by Bantustans. The validation of its function as 'a way of life' goes that far. Not beyond. Hence my statement way back in 1971 that it could not be taken to be permanent. I said that as apartheid became "more economic and militaristic in character than the racist and religious character of the pre-Verwoerd days . . . due to the emergence of the Bantustan reality", Black Consciousness had "of necessity to bind our identification of reality together with the pressing need to change our world outlook as a preliminary for a more constructive basis".

Black writing cannot be divorced from the struggle for a free South Africa. As Mongane Serote has said: "What direction the liberation struggle takes in the 1980s . . . that is the direction of the black South African poet". Let me add 'novelist or artist'. Our referential preferences are yet to claim freedom of their experiences in universality or the historical forms of the English language.

Geoffrey Haresnape

As an academic, literary critic, poet and editor of the South African literary journal, *Contrast*, I find the literary demands made upon me so diverse that it is difficult to know how to apportion the available time. In academe, my main interest over the years has been to win acceptance for South African English literature as the subject of serious study. When I wrote my MA thesis at the University of Cape Town in 1960 on "The Writings of Pauline Smith", this was rather a way-out thing to do. At that time, serious scholars either found places at good British or American universities to conduct their research programmes; or, if for one reason or another, they had to continue in South Africa, they tended to choose conventional literary subjects — "Walter Pater and the Concept of Style", "Image Patterns in *Astrophel and Stella*", etc etc. Guy Butler of Rhodes University and Guy Howarth of UCT were among the few professors at that time who would take a South African subject such as mine seriously. Throughout the 1960s this feeling against the inclusion of South African literature in university syllabuses continued. As late as 1969, Philip Segal, fine lecturer and one-time editor of *Contrast*, is on record as saying "... we cannot claim that it (SA literature) must be taught ... simply because it smacks of the local, for this is merely to assert a provincial and pointless cultural pseudo-nationalism". Many of us agreed with Philip that literary quality was important, but we did want to see a place for indigenous writing beside the works of the established tradition.

Writing in English from the African continent as a whole began to be taken more seriously in Great Britain and in America during the 1970s and the result of this for us was beneficial. For a few years now we have run courses in Southern African and in African Literature at UCT, and it is not considered to be freakish nowadays to choose topics from these areas for post-graduate research. This is a trail-

54

blazing field no longer, and one can expect the academic criticism produced to become more copious, subtle and sophisticated during the next few years. One danger which must be avoided is the promotion of too narrow a South Africanism in relation to its literature. Now that we have got our SA Lit. and Af. Lit. courses going, perhaps the time is ripe to have another look at Philip Segal's caveats in "The Place of South African Writing in the University".

Since 1975 my work as a literary critic has taken me three times outside the borders of the Republic. My special line of pursuit has been the early writings of Roy Campbell, William Plomer and Laurens van der Post. South African literature owes these three a tremendous debt for the collaboration which made *Voorslag* magazine possible. Their brief co-appearance in its pages during two or three months of 1926 led to a widening of our literary horizons and to an in-depth exploration of the colonial basis of our culture. Campbell, Plomer and Van der Post all saw that for our literature to be valid, it must look out towards the best and the most progressive in world literature. They simultaneously affirmed the importance of the local and the importance of the universal. Fittingly, and perhaps inevitably, their letters and manuscripts have been dispersed across the English-speaking world. I have had the curious and satisfying experience of reading Campbell on Ezra Pound on a hot Durban afternoon in the Killie Campbell Library; of reading Van der Post on Ingrid Jonker in an austere medieval library in a small university in the north of England; and of reading the Plomer collected by the University of Texas at Austin. Re-capturing their literary story has led to clues which criss-cross the globe. India and Japan have also proved to be part of the story. When I wrote up this research in a doctoral thesis and presented it to the University of Sheffield in England, few of my friends thought it a zany enterprise; the scene had changed radically from just twenty years before.

Poetry is my real involvement and love. My being excited about poems goes back as far as the first nursery rhymes I was taught:

There was an old woman tossed up in a basket
Ninety-nine times as high as the moon.

Rhymes like these meant enchantment, mystery — a kind of breaking out from the dullness of the particular time and place in which I was locked. When I grew older, I wanted to write poems myself. This provided for two contradictory impulses in my nature. First, I could try to show that I was a civilized boy, a reassurance I needed badly in my rooming-house environment. Second, it was possible to write comic or satiric verses which exposed what I considered to be too primly proper. Thus did poetry point me in the direction of 'respectability'; thus, at the same time, did it enliven me to 'respectability's' short-comings.

At one time I was an ardent rhymer. I loved verbal richness and formal stanzas. Soon I possessed sizeable wads of manuscript. People blanched when I visited them with my works. The realization came quickly. Who read long poems in outmoded forms? I was forced to accept that I was, after all, bound by time and place. Both poetic fashion and the harsh inputs of my particular society had to be considered. In recent years it has gone more slowly, often with a few lines worked and re-worked in the hope of bringing some image or combination of sounds into full life. I've found the tricky thing about poetry is that I can use the techniques of both the tortoise and the hare, only to find that neither guarantees arrival at the winning post of a successful poem. But as long as that repeated, restless impulse to make a poem keeps coming, perhaps I cannot complain.

What is poetry? I ask myself this question all the time. I find a formula which I think contains it, and then it slips away only to appear in some new form, or in a new range of subject matter. And yet I *feel* somehow that I know what it is — in my blood, in my nerve endings. Poetry's habit of putting a kind of stressful excitement on the whole organism is, I think, the reason why I am tempted to prepare lectures, listen to the children's homework, even wash dishes rather than work at a poem. But when I face it, there comes the sensation of being truly alive. Reading poetry too seems to demand that joy/effort.

Teaching poetry at university, I find that I have to fight off the influence of the established voices. Safe in their literary pantheon, many wonderful poets are all serenely chanting "our Horn shall be exalted". Sometimes it seems to me that their reputations have been gained at the expense of their true meaning. As respectable authorities in the imaginative kingdom, they tempt me to forget that writing a poem means going out afresh into dangerous places; that it is an activity which runs the risk of incurring unpleasantnesses like disapproval or misunderstanding. I believe that Boris Pasternak places the right emphasis when he comments that 'originality' and 'vigour' are the qualities which alone give value to a poem.

Many years ago, I used to visit the late Sydney Clouts in his Cape Town home. I was then in my 'prolific' phase. But Sydney did not mind that I was just a boy. He spoke fully and frankly, going into the whole business of being a poet. When he read poems — usually his own at that time — he became so energised that his eyes would seem to burn, strange and eagle-like, while the words throbbed deeply in his throat. I remember one particular visit vividly. It was on a fine night towards the end of summer. When at last I was due to leave and Sydney led the way to the bus-stop, his torch stabbing a pathway, we were intensely conscious of the stars, of the great bulk of Table Mountain looming up behind us, of the city lights in golden clusters and threads. Everything seemed to our excited senses to be speaking of one harmonious mystery.

I have since realized many times that this is what one wants in a poem — the vision. Whatever its subject matter might be, it is the conversion process that matters; the way in which the poem combines its disparate elements and becomes a single source of energy. As a would-be truth teller in our myth-ridden society, a poet must treat harsh themes. In many ways we have a system which bolsters the worst qualities in human nature — appetitiveness, exclusivism, naked prejudice, aggressiveness and injustice. As Sipho Sepamla remarks in *Da same, da same*, men here have "gotta big terrible terrible/some-wheres" in themselves. But I believe that a poem, if it is to be a good one, must somehow be an end in itself, or, to put it another way, must subserve its poetic purpose. There is a way in which the most vehement protest can fold in upon itself and be a poem as well.

Poems need hard work, yet they cannot be made to order. They must feed upon the day-to-day realities of social life, and yet they cannot be pressed easily into the service of pragmatic purposes. There are so many blind alleys cut short by blank walls. Yet when one occasionally breaks through, what a sense of freedom. . . .

Elsa Joubert

I was born in Paarl, to a conservative Afrikaans family. A certain amount of English was spoken in our home as my mother comes from Murray stock, but we were predominantly Afrikaans-speaking.

My maternal grandfather, a Dutch Reformed Church Minister, served as chaplain to the Boer women in the concentration camp at Aliwal North for a period of six months. As a Boland Afrikaans child who could lay claim to no great-uncles or *oupas* who had been in *die veld* with the Boers, this, however distant, was a connection of which I was very proud.

I remember the simple but very touching ceremony when we as young kindergarten children were handed our first copies of the Afrikaans New Testament and Psalms; and the eager way in which we could now recite in our mother tongue: *"Ek hef my oë op na die berge..."* instead of the more difficult and hardly known High Dutch.

Since early childhood I have wanted to 'write', starting off with nature poems and vague sentimental outpourings. I trained in languages and became a journalist. A love of travel took me on long trips through Africa, (impossible trips under present day conditions) and my first books were travelogues.

These experiences took me far beyond the confines of a typical rather late-Victorian Cape upbringing and homelife and a Stellenbosch University background where even World War II left us unbelievably untouched. Being physically beyond the frontiers of the country brought a new awareness and caused the vague unrest and uncertainty about the social and political anomalies at home to grow into something much deeper and more disquieting.

I felt the need to put this deep disquiet and increasing feeling of group insularity and self deception into words. But nothing I wrote seemed to say what needed to be said; I could do no better than soapbox oratory or cheap melodrama. Apartheid as a subject seemed to put *finis* to any literary attempt of mine.

Then came 1960. I was closely involved with Sharpeville in so far as my husband, a journalist, was literally on the scene. I remember well the night he came home — he was on night duty and I was becoming anxious at his being so very late — and he said to me, "Fifty-seven black people have been shot by the police. Nothing will ever be the same again in this country."

This brought things to a head in my writing. All other subjects seemed trivial and unacceptable. Limited as my capabilities were, I felt it vital, in the words of Eliot in *Murder in the Cathedral*, to "bear witness". The words "bearing witness" were key words in our conversations during those days. It was important to me that I should make the attempt.

A short account in *Die Transvaler* of 15 March 1961 gave me the story for which I was seeking.

In this story twelve whites were held captive by insurgents on a plantation in the north of Angola. Three times their execution was postponed because their captors were waiting for the captain to arrive. Three times during the course of that one hot day they were given the opportunity to delve deeper into themselves, to bear witness, if only to themselves.

I felt I could use these people to put into words my own frustration, my feelings of being of Africa but not truly African, part of this continent, but still, in so many ways, alien; my feeling of guilt, of helplessness, my awareness of cruelty and suffering. *Ons Wag op die Kaptein* (We are waiting for the Captain) was published in 1963. It has constantly been in print and this year, nearly twenty years later, it has appeared in an English translation, published by Hodder and Stoughton, translated by my husband, under the title *To Die at Sunset*.

In the late sixties and early seventies intensive travelling in Africa, especially Moçambique, Angola and Madagascar, offered material for more travel books, as well as a novel set in eleventh-century Tete, a story I once again used as an allegory for conditions in my own country.

But things were moving fast in Africa.

In 1973, after the publication of de Spinola's *Portugal e la Futura*, the Portuguese world in Africa came to an end. First of all Moçambique broke the ties, a year later there was civil war in Angola. In 1974 a bimonthly magazine offered me the assignment to go north to the South West/Angolan border and do a series of articles on the Portuguese white and mulatto refugees streaming over from Angola to South West.

It was a traumatic experience to watch the convoys of trucks, lorries, motor cars, bakkies, loaded with household goods, pets, foodstuffs, move slowly down southwards, in a slow cloud of dust.

These were not refugees seen on the screen from faraway places, these were people I had seen in their homes in Angola not very long before. Their lives had come tumbling down like a house of cards.

I knew then that the time had passed to set my stories in countries outside South Africa, or to use allegory. It was the here and now of our own situation, that in some way or other I had not yet faced up to in my work, that I wanted to write about.

I remember standing in the veld, seeing those refugees, speaking to them, hearing gunfire in the distance, and thinking: this is what it is all about. This is the Africa that is ours. And we have moved through Africa for so many years in such a blind, unseeing fashion.

I did not know where my search would lead me, but I started to gather facts. I wanted to know more, not about distant places, but about what was happening in my backyard, in the black townships, in the homelands, in the Pass Offices, in the law courts, in the witch-doctors' huts, in Groote Schuur Hospital waiting rooms.

I went to the Transkei, attended gatherings of the old men of the clan, visited schools, the *ilalis* or small settlements. In Soweto I spoke to many people, in Nyanga, Guguletu and Langa I visited crèches, churches, homes, had a session with a witch-doctor. I went north to Venda where I attended the rites and watched the dancing.

I did not know where it was leading me, perhaps towards a travelogue through my own country; I think that was closest to my mind. I recollect speaking to my publisher about it, saying we should know more.

And then the second major event: 1976 and the riots. Black people I had got to know well were deeply committed in the riots, their children were deeply involved. Their lives were disrupted, and torn asunder on many levels. June to December 1976 was a sad time for those of us standing by helplessly.

And then on Boxing Day 1976 the woman who was to become Poppie in my book, *The Long Journey of Poppie Nongena*, came to my home with the need to talk. Her need to talk was as great as my need to listen. And that was how we started working on the book. I knew at once: no travelogue, no allegory, but the stark truth, the story of this woman's life. This was where my study, my research, my travels in my own country had been leading to.

We communicated well, for her home language was Afrikaans, like mine. We worked hard; I checked and rechecked her story because no error, however slight, could be allowed to slip in and jeopardise the truth of the whole stark tale.

Writing the book brought me a kind of peace. It meant much to me to get to know the woman Poppie well, to be led into her life, step by step, to be introduced to a world that had been strange to me. I was the richer for it. Translating the book into English was a rewarding experience.

Douglas Livingstone

GIOVANNI JACOPO MEDITATES
(ON AN ALABASTER ADAMASTOR)

Upon my Bookcase sulks a gypsum Form.
Concussed, it bulks, that Hulk from Tartarus,
Whom Herakles clubbed to beach a Continent.
It seems, at Times, to shrug its muslin Cloak
While threatening Incontinence of Speech.

& then, one Day, its taunting Tongue appeared
To move. As in a Daze, I heard, aghast
The harshest Tones that ever rasped Man's Ears.
(The Accents haunt me still). He glared, & I
Was torn between the Poker & my Pen.

I

"Behold! A lexical Desperado
Has been reborn — that's me — about to do
Over-Due Derring-Dos, sans Derringer;
My Aim not too erratic; my cracked Brain
Not so *détraqué* it cannot attack.

One brims with Envy at their Frenzy — Those
Who beat their Breasts anent the Frontier Sins
Of Conquest, Exploitation. Earning Bread
From expiating ancient Faults chalks Scores
For Stints of Sanitation, rinsed in Print.

The Occident by Accident displaced
Due South looks longingly at West & North
Or East. Receded Tides of Empire left
A Wake: a Conscience-struck, bereft, pale-faced
Parched Populace who ache to hold their Own.

Now other Tides are in. The old Unconscious
Made Manifest is all that's left for Art.
Such Constructs test the Writer, force his Hand
To painful Dramas, Psychics, Rinderpest.
Some leave, of course, take Refuge in Disdain.

To celebrate a Fictive Art is no
Mean Feat. Its plangent Frivolities hunt
Delicious Deliquescence out the Spine:
Affront as you confront; Quick Fix of Ink;
In lieu of Guts: brief dangled Novelties.

A luminous Omneity transfixed
By Anatomic Candour, self-exposed;
Abysmal Chords within the Vertebrae,
Their Cadences unzipped; the half-closed Eye
— These are your blind Creation's bland Asides.

II

"Incurable Discrepancies between
Hurt Bard & World — damned tedious Debate:
Analysis or Synthesis — are null
& void. (The silly Pair breathe in & out).
Far stranger Strands compress the Poet's Chest.

Brief Intimations of a parallel
Or shadowed Universe still lark about
In early Dispositions of the Blood.
They do not lurk for long. Then Time, the Thief
Shows Goal as Way: 'The Way's the Goal — All's One'.

A great Tom-Buddha bares his Breasts at that:
'I think I therefore OM'.   His slit-eyed Gaze
Beams fatly back.   His Navel looks as if
Unveilings are in Store.   Droll Novels on
Nirvana give the Nod: *'We're* in the Know'.

As much as Devils, High Decorum tempts:
Among Apartheid's Aspects that revolt
Are Wraiths of Bad Art conjured up to show
Off Virtues on the Side of Angels, but
Such Phantoms are Companions to Ennui.

What Cabinet of Horrors lies below?
Here goes: See, some Retiring Place, twelve Paces
From Main Camp, with Hessian fenced about
— A Hadrian's Wall against marauding Claws.
(Against the Spiders there's no Guarantee).

The sultry Corners fingered by the Palms;
Planck's Constant warms the Text.   Becalmed, benumbed
By Sunstrokes on the Nape — what finer Bench
To con Relationships so often fraught,
Entangled by Penumbras, so plumped up?

III

"Who else do you write for if not each other?
The Mob hates your Cerebral Life — the Mob
of Starvelings, Racketeers.   You are but Wisps
Of History, of ignominious
Instincts, of fluctuating Certainties.

Reflect on your Infallibilities:
The Protest-Verse that serves as Masquerade;
Those vocal Critics — every second Year —
Bray New Directions for such Local Lays;
Grey Plagiarists rapacious in your Midst.

Your Chthonic Sol-Fa ('Sovieto'-Verse)
Is high-pitched racist Cant: the Over-Kill
Of Anti-Colonial Hyperbole
— Shrill Tits-for-Tat, siphoned off sharper Wits.
Tub-thumping drums in Place of Tribal Chants.

Crass Pathos, or your dull Apologia
— Your emptied Selves should image prior Gods —
You gulled grit-pitted Vassals of the Knee,
The Mirror's smashed, you genuflect in Vain.
You're ruled by ethnocentric Boerecrats.

Some Literary Friends of yours are stuck
In Jeans: nipped somewhere tight between Terrains
That start with Kerouac & terminate
Close to The Greening of America.
(A Transatlantic Mode is still *de trop*).

The absurd Parliament of Writer-Birds,
From Dawn to Dusk, discuss with Stridency
The Day's Affairs; & underneath them coil
A Choir of critical Suburban Cats:
Disharmonies progress from Myth to Lie.

IV

"Salacious as their Prospects are, None quite
So ravished by their Dreams of Anarchy
As your Politicos.   Their mottled Wattles
Swollen above Brass Necks too stiff to bend
To lend an Ear, & so to end must break.

Your Country's a hapless Microcosm of
The Horrors of Existence: Cruelty
& Concrete.   How not harp on Entropy?
The expected Cataclysms stultify,
So you make Artefacts instead of Art.

A Surrogate for Conscience is the Pen.
Some doughty Souls portray the secret Norms
Of private Life, while hoping to impose
These on the Body Public. Purblind Dolts:
Religion here is Property & Sport.

The Self-Esteem of the Unbuttoned throws
Out mournful Heroics to the Elements:
The bloody Martyrdoms from bloody Mayhems
Grow. Better to celebrate your Bourgeois
Interiors. At least, so many do.

While Science spells Obstruction for too much
That's Abstract, Truth, you say, is what you choose
To make of it. Mendacity's up front.
Remembrance fidgets on in Snapshots. Owls
Still bugle Iridescence at the Moon.

Your lilting Labials loosed in a World
Of Gutturals (where Ambiguity
Embraces Authenticity) demean
The Balustrades of Balconies anoint
By Pigeons. All's lost in small-mannered Rooms.

V

"Why are your Novels so politicised,
So pallid, blanched, so temporal? Just cast
About: the Servant in his Digs is Done
To Death, along with Trek Boers, Special Branch.
What happened to Romance? Look at your Grist:

Plain Discos where ignorant Barmies clash
By Night. The restive Wives corrupted by
The French (— a Jules et Jim Ménage would take
The Cake: Herself starred as the big Fromage).
Your Culture's truly rich — the Stuff of Dreams:

66

There's Gouda, Mussel-Chowder & Pink Wine
Sublimely swilled. Why Sex across the Line?
Such tired Depiction later Centuries
Will bluffly label Quaint. All that Conviction
Will strut its Stuff a Spell, get winked away.

The Freedom Individuals these Days
Require is: Eccentricity. The State
Demurs. Its Rôle: the dire Custodian
Of Refractory Matter, Critical Mass
('Or Else: it's Mushrooms, Firestorms, Megadeath').

& you have Mini-States — like: Outposts for
Your Oxbridge Imports to Natal. (To get
Rorke's Drift makes Travesties of Probity.
Those Vowels: they tend to flop when popped by Clans
Of triple-chinned Titanic Majesties).

Natal, Natal, you Femme Fatale encroached
On by Die Tweede Taal, reproachful to
Die Ou Transvaal — you hope a Dragon's Spine
Defines your Stance. O Happy Breed! You feed
The fattest, fastest Roaches in the Land.

VI

"Unravelled Fool, as soiled as any Navvy,
The Vessels of Research have you decked out.
The Ocean yields its Wares unyieldingly,
& then: burnt Shoulders in the Shower; your Hands
Sliced to the Quick by Wire, yearn after Ink.

In earning daily Crusts, there is not Time
— You bleat — to write, to read, to sleep, to eat.
Each Night's a geodesic Frustulum
Too shrunk for getting drunk, or happy Love;
& you've eschewed a Patron, slewed your Pen.

Coy Blunderer: the Doors & Floors you air
As Architectures of the Mind are skew.
Clapped Psalms about a windy Heaven's Ears,
Cracked Psalters, scrawled Graffiti on the Pews
— A Ploy of Flaws to play the Critics' Game.

You've strung my savage Thunders to your Lyre
Quite tunelessly, debunked my sleepy Murmurs.
Your Rigging's rigged, your bungled Jib's awry.
Your heartless Culpabilities include
The brazen Women cast out of your Ribs.

Congealed Foundling in a forgotten Mould,
Undeflected by Practicalities,
You battle nightly with Bottle & Muse;
Or, euphoric from the Euphorbias,
Stump past the Gentians to the Jackfruit Trees.

More than Parades of Schisms in Succession,
Your Specialisation wants Aesthetic
Correctives to your Esotericism:
You need a pristine Microchip that's spatial
— Capable of a new Configuration . . ."

                              *

I bowed before this Diatribe.   Then Rage
At all his Tribe engorged: "You Titans stormed
Olympus. Next Door: Mount Parnassus soars.
Now, Adamastor's Criticaster, yet."
I aimed the Poker at his phased-out Head.

"The Past wrought roughly with your Skull," I growled,
"Seduced by Thetis — duped — felled, uncouth Oaf
Who pose, forsooth, as Littérateur now.
You Charlatan in Tarlatan — Enough!"
With two "Hurrahs", I dealt the coup de grâce.

Don Maclennan

THE BLOODIEST OF ARTS

On my birthday in 1946 my father came home from the Vanguard Bookshop with an armful of poetry books, some of which I still have: Blake, Whitman, Keats and Shelley, Tennyson, Villon, Brooke, Spender, MacNeice, C Day Lewis, George Barker, Herbert Palmer, and *Modern Scottish Poetry*, edited by Maurice Lindsay, containing some poems by Hugh MacDiarmid, whom my father had known in London before the war. At the top of the armful, because it was the smallest book, was Palgrave's *Golden Treasury of Verse*.

At school I had already learned many poems by heart, and spent hours copying out my favourites in a small notebook. I suppose all poets start under the aegis of the poetry they know, and that is what tradition is about. That is certainly how I began writing poems — by imitation. In any case, who can invent something from nothing? Medieval theologians claimed that as one of the abilities of God. Yeats said, "Talk to me of originality and I will turn on you with rage. I am a crowd, I am a lonely man, I am nothing". What I'm saying is that 1946 was a watershed in the unconscious origin of my conviction that poetry comes primarily from other poetry, and not directly from life. This is probably what is lurking in the myth about Perseus slaying the Gorgon: there are some things you can only look at in a polished shield, some things which, when you look at them directly, turn you to stone or make you dumb.

Which means that poetry has everything to do with life, because the critical moments of life need poetry to transform them and make them human. It may even be the case that without poetry such critical moments do not exist, only a nameless void. The connection is intimate, the analogy strong. As a poem rides on its own melting, like a block of ice on a hot stove (says Frost), so a life deliquesces about the heat of its own convictions. As a fine poem is what it purports to be about, so a fine life is what it says it is or what it is trying to become. It is always a question of finding out who we are and how we ought to live, and nobody has the apodeictic answers, as Tess tried to tell Angel Clare.

How strange to have had as my adolescent *vade mecum* the complete works of Tennyson. To return to that time is to recall nightmares of the moated grange, despair, passivity, a smothered desire for life (with a capital F, as Milly says). How much easier my life might have been had I been urged to read the lucid, empirical prose of Bertrand Russell. As it was, getting immersed in and taken over by Tennyson was the closest I have ever been to madness, depression, and total failure. Out of it all, the only lines I keep as a banner are the cry of *angst* from the heart of *In Memoriam*:

> But what am I?
> An infant crying in the night,
> An infant crying for the light,
> And with no language but a cry.

Were I Pascal I would have that stitched into the lining of my cloak.

A while ago I used to wish that when I was sixteen I had met a serious, practising poet. I see now that it doesn't matter. Instead, Chris Copeman and I were sent by train each July to a farm at Schoemansdal, in the Zoutpansberg, to speak Afrikaans. In the long evenings, after *boekevat* and a last cup of coffee at the kitchen stove, Chris and I would go to our outside lean-to bedroom and take it in turns to read aloud from Palgrave's *Golden Treasury*. A flickering candle, dogs barking in the frosty, star-filled night, and half a mile away the night train thundering west to Mara. Chris read:

> Out on the lawn I lie in bed
> Vega conspicuous overhead.

That poem of Auden's, and Empson's

> I had overprepared the event,
> That much was ominous

seemed to us the most modern poetry possible.

Out of those gropings came five or six thousand lines of verse, which I burned before I wrote Matric. Had I known that mythical poet, he might have given me better reasons for burning my work. I was impatient, and I felt my work was totally self-indulgent, unconnected with reality.

Here's the problem. On page *ix* of the introduction to Nazim Hikmet's *Things I didn't know I loved*, the editor says, ". . . for Hikmet, only the kind of art that changes itself can change the world." The world's a big place. Hikmet spent a long time in jail. He loved Turkey. Did he change it? Did Yeats change Ireland, Montale Italy, Whitman and Frost America? Yes. They did. Turkey, Italy, Ireland, America and South Africa are their poets and their poetry.

Poetry is a necessary lie, a fiction, even a supreme fiction (Wallace Stevens). We ourselves are fictions. Poetry and we have creative and transformational powers. Poetry and Eros meet at every point. Poetry is "the lineaments of gratified desire" (Blake), and it is also a "flight before the truth" (Nietzsche). Poetry is an evasion of the given fact which redeems the given fact. It is important because it is always in opposition to unawareness, living death, misused chances to BE where we ARE. Rilke said, "Where you are a place arises." Poets are builders of the New Jerusalem or the New Bloomusalem. Poetry is opposition to the recurrent human failure to dare to be at all. So Hikmet is right — poetry is "the bloodiest of the arts", because you offer your heart to others and feed on it yourself.

The driving power of poetry is not discovery but re-discovery. Seferis says that ". . . to say what you want to say you must create another language and nourish it for years and years with what you have loved, with what you have lost, with what you will never find again." Poetry may have things to say that revolutionaries wish to suppress, because poetry can go on being revolutionary when the demagogues are already into the process of orthodoxy. Why else did Mandelstam and Akmatova have such a hard time in Russia, and Hikmet in Turkey?

Eliot said a wise thing:

> There is only the fight to recover what has been lost
> And found and lost again.

James Matthews

How I evaluate myself as a writer is a question that does not affect me overmuch. At most times, I am amused at the findings of critics who come to conclusions about matters in my works of which I am completely unaware. Of course I am concerned about my writing, but my ego does not stretch to the limit of placing myself on the same level as that of a Bessie Head or Alex la Guma and neither do I walk in the same street with the poets Mafika Gwala, Mongane Serote and others.

There are two or three stories that I feel very happy about — *The Park* and *Azikwelwa* — especially the latter. These two stories appear in many of the anthologies published abroad of stories from Africa and South Africa, and have always elicited a favourable response from people whom I presume to be reputable critics. Now I find that a local critic has stated that "*Azikwelwa* is a romanticised version of a political stance during a bus boycott. But it is successful in a way, in that he (James Matthews) deliberates on the motives of a 'coloured' as a person, joining the 'African' boycott."

My first story was published in the late fifties and my output has been rather meagre up to the present time: a collection of short stories — *Azikwelwa* — published in Sweden in 1962, to be followed by a novella the following year, also brought out in Sweden. Then there followed a period of not producing any work because of my having taken offence at being told by a well-meaning person that I had turned into a very fine coloured writer. I was too wrapped-up in the race issue to realise that, in a way, he was paying me a compliment as I was writing about things that affected me very much — my environment and those around me.

The collection of short stories only surfaced in English in 1974 when it was published in South Africa under the title of *The Park and Other Stories*. The novella still has to appear in the language in which it was written.

I write, at times, but I am not filled with the mystique of being a 'writer'.

All my earlier writings published in newspapers and magazines, although not overtly political, contained strong streaks of social realism leavened, at times, with humorous overtones.

My stories began to show more political awareness with the publication of *Azikwelwa* as I was beginning to move out of my surroundings, or rather the atmosphere of my surroundings, into an atmosphere of a more political nature.

I was (to a certain extent) trapped in my environment and could only relate to the situation as being 'Us and Them' — the 'Haves and the Have-Nots'. The 'Haves' were not only white. In my ghetto-background those whose houses had electricity, a box-like radio and a car that moved were part of the 'Haves'.

My involvement in producing stories of a political nature also focused the State's attention upon me with the result that I was unable to obtain a passport to attend a writers' conference held in Kampala during the early sixties. I was only able to procure a passport in 1980 when I attended the Frankfurt Book Fair.

Some of my brother-writers left the country — the leaving was not always of their choice — and in my case a paralysis set in. It would be more honest to say that I was fearful of the wrath of the State. I was plagued with a period of sterility; sterility of the spirit and not so much of creativity.

1972 became too much for me. The Dimbazas, Ilinges, Sadas and Limehills. Dying children — starvation, their sickness. The uprooting of people; the harvesting of crops of crosses, the only fruit the land would bear. Detention and the deaths in detention. It became too much for me.

The mirror became a reflection of condemnation. I was not unaware of what was happening. The newspapers were filled with it. I could write but was not doing anything about the situation. I felt physically ill.

I wrote. It was not prose. Critics hyena-howled. It was not poetry, they exclaimed. I never said it was. I was writing expressions of feelings. I would find it extremely difficult to write poems of love or praise of nature. Neither would I produce lines so finely polished or use metaphors and metre — art for art's sake. I would feel like a pimp using words as decoration for my whoring.

Expressions of feelings became easier to handle. Perhaps they were abridged short stories. In 1976, I found myself (like many others), resting in detention. My spell inside was not very long but it had its compensations. I produced another collection of expressions of feelings.

To quote a critic: "James Matthews does not rise above the level of the protesting poet in *Cry Rage*, though there is some improvement in *Pass me a meatball, Jones.*" As I have stated before: the carping of critics I find very amusing.

I feel that what I do write, the majority of the oppressed who read, understand. I must also stress that the oppressed are not necessarily coloured black. My expressions must be seen as those of a black in a white-dominated society. The militancy in my lines should be understood. I am not asking the oppressor to lighten the lash. I am expressing my rage. There would be no need for expressions of black militancy in a just society. What I am writing about is the vileness of oppression based mainly upon racism.

I am not a poet, neither am I a 'writer' in the academic sense.

Es'kia Mphahlele

MY EXPERIENCE AS A WRITER

I was fifteen when I began high school at St Peter's Secondary School, Rosettenville, one of Johannesburg's southern suburbs. This was January 1935.

There was a sense in which boarding school protected one from the vulgarity, the squalor, the muck and smell of slum life such as Marabastad was — a Pretoria location (I still feel 'location' gives ghetto life a more distinctive character than the fancy name 'township' does today). At any rate during term time. The reading bug had already bitten me, so I spent hours of free time reading in the school library: Dickens, R L Stevenson, Walter Scott, Edgar Rice Burroughs (I was once thrown out of class for reading a Tarzan book during a free period), Conan Doyle, Baroness Orczy, Pearl Buck, Quiller Couch, Buchan, and so on: from Tarzan and mystery thrillers to the sublime.

Back in Marabastad I had rummaged through a lot of junk literature donated by some suburban families and dumped on the floor of a store room attached to a community hall that bore the sign MUNICIPAL LIBRARY. After ploughing through boys' and girls' adventure stories (all about white kids!), through ghost stories, after throwing aside astrology books, I had one day stumbled upon Cervantes's *Don Quixote.*

In the early years of the war I was at Adams (Teachers') College, my next boarding school; I read more of the same stuff, adding to the list titles like *Gone with the Wind*. I was also an avid reader of *Outspan* which during the war ran thrilling hunters' stories, mystery and real-crime stories about John Dillinger, Pretty Boy Floyd, Baby Face Nelson, G-Man Purvis and so on. As I was an irrepressible movie-goer who had evolved from the silent days to the talkies, I read everything I could lay my hands on about the art and techniques of the cinema.

A story well told: this became in time an obsession with me. I retold a folk tale for a school contest at Adams and took away the

75

first prize of ten shillings.

During my first job at Ezenzeleni Blind Institute in Roodepoort (near Johannesburg), a trade school that overlooked a valley and stood serenely on one of the many ridges around, I started to write verse. Chunks of long talkative verse, a compulsive lyricizing of my immediate external nature. The impression had been left in our minds at school that poetry must be about trees, birds, the elements. We had never been taught poetry as well as we know how today. We had a compulsion to memorize in my school days, and it was a joy to recite and listen to the grandeur of Shakespeare on campus and during school debates. These debates were more an exercise in rhetoric than in the method of argument. The spoken word or phrase or line was the thing, damn the dialectic. So I was writing verse out of a book as it were. There was no one an apprentice could go to for advice on techniques, or merely to show a manuscript. It was a shot in the dark.

In the years that I worked at Ezenzeleni I lived in a location on the western edge of Roodepoort town. It was no less slummy than our Marabastad. Just another heap of rusted tinshacks. The same dusty pot-holed streets, the same communal taps, streets flowing with dirty water and littered with children's stools; the same mongrels that accentuated the would-be stillness of my nights with their howling as I sat up late studying privately for the Matric Certificate (I had only the Junior Certificate and the two-year teachers' diploma). Sailing along the night air was also the incessant hum of location life. It was a hum that seemed to suppress the bellowing, screams and shrieks and street singing that would finally burst into an orgy with a reckless fury and abandon come Saturday night. Like the people of Marabastad, my Roodepoort people were hurting, even in the process of creating their own fun, their own little nook of pleasure.

The war was raging in Europe and North Africa, Marabastad was being bulldozed, Jan Smuts was sending troops to snuff viciously the municipal workers' strike that had burst into rioting in an African hostel adjacent to Marabastad. But Roodepoort West location was still standing in its rusted stubbornness, stretching out its lease of life till the Nationalists would blast it away during the sixties.

On those Roodepoort nights, when I had had my fill of geometrical theorems and algebraic equations and graphs and Shakespeare and Milton and the Boston Tea Party and Bismarck and the Black Hole of Calcutta, when the stench of night soil choked the night air from the wagons passing by, I would try to relax, seek refuge in the workshop of mind. I would listen to the stories milling around in the workshop, looking for words to give them form. Before I knew what I was doing I had embarked on the great adventure of story-telling. I had in earlier years fallen in love with the printed word; now it was an obsession, aching for articulation by no other person than the present narrator. The story had found me. I had never read modern short stories before and, as I recall, I turned out pages and pages of free-wheeling narrative episodes.

I'm one of hundreds of writers who first came to English as a working language, a learning language, a political medium of communication in a multilingual society, rather than as a native tongue. Thus studying English, either in a formal or non-formal situation, has enhanced my writing ability. While my general reading was for pleasure, it was also for learning the language. My books are full of markings that trace the paths of a mind obsessed with idiom, the well-chosen word or phrase, the exquisite narrative and descriptive line. So private study, which took me through the University of South Africa for the BA, BA Honours, and the MA, and the teaching of English in high school after Roodepoort, afforded me ample opportunity to re-educate myself in the English language via its literature.

I was reading the Scottish and English ballad for Matric when I became enthralled by its story-telling manner. Its brooding mood accentuated by the refrain and the supernatural element, its economy of language, its dramatic 'leap' to clinch the violent happening — all these features reinforced in me an intuition about the mechanism and spirit of the short story. And my life in Marabastad, Roodepoort and later in Orlando, provided that atmosphere that breeds violence, death, deprivation.

It was by mere accident that I came across an educational pamphlet brought out by Julian Rollnick's African Bookman Publications, Cape Town. I nervously put my writing together in a packet and mailed it to Mr Rollnick. He promptly sent me back the verse and said he wanted to publish six of the ten stories — a pick from a bunch I had been accumulating for six years. *Man Must Live and Other Stories* (1947) was Rollnick's first try in fiction publishing.

In the early fifties I was going through a number of literary experiences that were drastically to change my social attitudes and my writing style. I was introduced to Nadine Gordimer who immediately took an interest in my writing. She agreed to look at my stories. The discussions that followed and my initiation into Nadine's own craftsmanship in the genre gave me new insights into what I was engaged in.

I began to read the Russians: Gogol, Chekhov, Tolstoy, Gorky. Their mastery of the short story, especially that of the first three, blew my mind. By accident I discovered the Afro-Americans. Fanny Klenerman, the *grande dame* of Vanguard Booksellers in Johannesburg, had titles by Richard Wright, James Baldwin, Langston Hughes. Wright's volume of short stories, *Uncle Tom's Children* contained the kind of violence and brutal truths about white racism that struck a common chord in me, even as they tore me up inside. I also discovered Ernest Hemingway and William Faulkner, Carl Van Vechten's *Nigger Heaven*. I discovered English translations of Flaubert, Boccaccio, Rabelais. Hemingway and Wright taught me economy of language and the impressionistic concreteness of image, Faulkner taught me resonance, the Russians the totality of craftsmanship.

On the advice of Nadine, who was impressed with the story, *The Suitcase*, I sent it to *New World Writing*, an international anthology published in New York. The story appeared in this collection in 1955. The late Langston Hughes read it in New York and wrote me a flattering word of appreciation, sending me at the same time his first book of poetry, *The Weary Blues* and a book of short stories, *The Ways of White Folks*: the beginning of a long friendship. Later in the decade when I was investigating South African fiction, I was to be most favourably impressed by William Plomer's work. Over the years as I corresponded with William he wrote me commentaries on every book I published in England until the last one before his death. Yet another friendship I have valued immensely has been that of Martin Jarrett-Kerr, member of the Community of the Resurrection and critic. He also has monitored my writings all along. Martin, before his return to England, had been one of the few European patrons who came regularly to our theatre and music performances in Johannesburg.

Drum magazine was launched in 1950, and had by 1955 established itself as a vibrant monthly for black writing and the black urban proletariat. Names like Can Themba, Bloke Modisane, Casey Motsisi, Todd Matshikiza, Richard Rive, Peter Clarke, Arthur Maimane, Henry Nxumalo became *Drum*'s regular literary furniture. I had myself published the first story in *Drum* in 1952. I became its fiction editor in January 1955, staying on till I left for Nigeria in September 1957. *New Age* and *Fighting Talk*, the two leftist papers of the decade, and Ronald Segal's *Africa South* also featured Alex la Guma, Rive and myself. Although we were not at school in the fifties, although we had diverse interests and intellectual pursuits, even as journalists, we shared this much in common: we had found a voice. And because urban blacks in South Africa have so much in common with urban Afro-Americans, almost to a man the writers of the fifties had more than just a dip into

78

American culture: journalism, imaginative literature, jazz, innovative prose styles. There was in our styles a racy, concrete, nervously impressionistic idiom, often incorporating the grand Shakespearean image. Nxumalo, who had come to *Drum* already an experienced journalist, did not fit into this stylistic pattern.

For my part I was, as a result of all these influences, learning to be much less sentimental in my view of character, much less didactic in tone, more concrete and incisive in dramatization and idiom. I was also trying out the same discipline in my creative writing as my UNISA mentor, Professor Edward Davis (now deceased) was putting me through in my English assignments. A notorious taskmaster, but a man I admired for his sparkling intellect and critical acumen.

Exile. In 1957 I moved from one vibrant literary scene, where new things were happening, into another: West Africa. I had the privilege of working with writers like the Nigerians Wole Soyinka, Chinua Achebe, Christopher Okigbo, J P Clark; the Ghanaians Kofi Awoonor, Efua Sutherland, Ama Ata Aidoo, the Gambian Lenrie Peters. There was abundant theatre activity, and the artists were most prolific. Independent commercial publishing was thriving, books found their way to the stalls of the open-air market square where food and miscellaneous goods were sold.

When I worked in Paris (1961—3) and was organizing writers' and artists' centres, literary and educational conferences in Europe and Africa, I rubbed shoulders with Léopold Sédar Senghor, Sembene Ousmane, Bernard Dadié, Birago Diop, Aimé Césaire, and other French-speaking blacks from Africa, the French West Indies and islands of Oceania, Madagascar.

After *Down Second Avenue* (1959) and *The African Image* (1962) I was again writing short stories. This genre had been for us in South Africa a condensed form of prose that required a few broad but incisive strokes or flashes to get the 'message' across. The writers who were creating out of a rural sensibility had been writing novels and lyric poetry that depicted the intrusion of Western-Christian values and customs into a non-aggressive pastoral humanism. The works of Thomas Mofolo, Sekese, Sol Plaatje, John Dube, A C Jordan, H I E Dhlomo, B W Vilakazi, B M Kgaketla fell in this tradition. The more intensely urban were using the short story and reportage as a way of coming to terms with their anger, as a response to the immediate pressures of deprivation and racism.

This was no longer my milieu in West Africa and France. In Kenya and Zambia I would experience only the residual effects of a colonial presence that was receding. I was having to write out of new discontents or remembered hurts which I knew would still be the lot of those I had left behind. The element of immediacy had gone. I was among people whose discontents had reference to other historical roots, although they merged with mine at the point of Europe's colonial entry. But the discontents I found called for other responses than those demanded by racial confrontation and contemplation. My novel, *The Wanderers* (1972), was an attempt to reflect the fragmented passage of a South African black through a continent fragmented by a colonial history but trying vaguely to grope for a sense of unity on the grounds of that very shared history.

When I was waiting for something to be born in fiction I took to poetry, but more importantly to literary criticism. The revised edition of *The African Image* (1972) and *Voices in the Whirlwind* (1972), plus other essays that appeared in journals, are examples of these waiting intervals.

In all the nine years I was in America, I could not feel the country, grasp it, couldn't pick up distinctive smells of places. So I gave up trying to spin something out of an American-inspired imagination; except, again, to express myself on Afro-American life, thought and literature. As long as I refused, consciously and unconsciously by turns, to dissolve into the American landscape and milieu, so long was I going to continue to avoid using the American experience as novelistic or poetic material. Africa would continue to be my literary beat. And although *Chirundu* is about a Zambian episode, I try to capture some of the essence of Africa in general, of the African agony. It seemed to me that a 'decision' to forget the South African experience, or to allow it to recede into the background would amount to a rejection of Africa as a whole, to lose faith in it. Such has been the measure of my pan-African sensibility, my awareness of Africa's history, my exposure to its anger and frustrations, its joys, its wisdom and humanism. West Africa kindled this awareness.

A return to South Africa would have to be the resolution of my identity as an African teacher and writer. The one has often accused and justified the other by turns, and similarly they have wept over and gloried in the other.

For the last decade I have been debating in my mind the function of literature in the present-day world and the individual writer's role in relation to this function. The writer expresses himself out of a sense of compulsion and according as his sensibility conducts him. Ideally he wants to communicate thought and feeling both as a cultural compulsion and as an act of language.

At the level of function where we contemplate the uses of literature for the individual reader and evaluate his responses, and for the writer himself, there are no violent disagreements. There is a kind of consensus about what actually happens between writer and reader. But on what literature actually does and should do to and for society, for community, there is a wide range of claims. We hear words like 'commitment', 'revolution', 'art for society', 'art for my sake', 'bourgeois art', 'elitist art', 'words must act like bullets' and so on.

The claims for literature's social role have often been expressed in moralistic, apocalyptic and transcendental terms. In some realm of our responses to it, it is supposed to be a civilizing agent, supposed to spark in us revolutionary zeal and even trigger the bullet for us. As it is an art process, and all creative forms of expression called Art are supposed, in the tradition of German idealism, to be a meeting point between Mind and Nature and to reconcile them, it is taken on trust that literature belongs in that lofty realm. How does Art do this? God will take care of that.

I should hope that my writing increases the reader as much as it increases me. The larger public and institutions can do what they like with it, short of debasing it, twisting it to endorse their own immoral positions. If my works turn out not to please and increase future generations, I shall not be alive to care. I'm content with approval of what I'm doing *now*, my own gratification from what I have created, the conscious effort I make to achieve directness, clarity and richness of expression — when this has been realized: these will suffice for *now*. I am conscious of being an African writer speaking to Africans. T S Eliot's notion of a world intelligence as an audience is too ephemeral for me to cherish.

It would be a comforting thought to share fully the transcendental view of art, even only privately. But I'm preoccupied with grassroots responses to literature, and am often too cynical to allow my mind to dwell on those possibilities that only live in the intellect.

And yet I feel outraged enough to curse those who censor literature (other than self-serving pornography) in South Africa and elsewhere. I care enough about the banning of books *per se*, mine or other writers', to want to howl up and down the streets and incite the reading public to wage a crusade against acts of censorship. South Africans are generally apathetic about the literature they are forbidden to read or circulate or possess: part of a more serious malaise that blunts sensitivity so that the violation of human freedoms is spoken of as 'routine checks' and accepted as such.

In the collective sense in which we speak of literary products, books, censorship today would be the only reason for caring now about what will be available and acceptable in the future. Because rather than censor our own thoughts as writers, we should consider creating undaunted, believing that if the future generations are going to be the true judges, cause for indictment should be anything but self-censorship. Intellectual dishonesty is already an act of self-condemnation.

I used to worry that because of our separate racial lives blacks and whites do not know enough about each other fully to portray character across colour and racial lines. I'm too cynical now to care any longer: blacks never asked for apartheid.

Finally, it is an exaggerated claim for literature that it can spark a revolution. There are surely more immediate irks that incite a revolution — all those irks that arise from a sense of deprivation and loss. People expect to be incited by the language of everyday usage, not the heightened form of expression and metaphor of the kind that make imaginative literature. By the time a writer has done composing a play, a poem, a story as a vehicle of political agitation, the revolution is under way. Literature may record, replay, inspire an on-going process. As an act of language that renews, revitalizes, it is a vehicle of thought and feeling that should increase by reliving experiences. Literature is forever stirring us up. This is its own kind of revolution.

Essop Patel

TOWARDS REVOLUTIONARY POETRY

> I viewed civilization as a curse. I felt a burning hatred for the thousands of years of oppression against my predecessors. I realized that the feelings of all those people buried together in ditches were once the same as mine.
>
> Ali Shariati

I

There is nothing perverse in that the majority of the contemporary black poets have consciously and deliberately jettisoned the inhibiting concept of *art for art's sake*. In a revolutionary situation the poet has no desire to be shackled by liberal aesthetics. Mahmoud Darwish, "the Lorca of the Palestinian resistance movement", declares:

> . . . it is essential to reject the rose
> That comes from a dictionary or a volume of poetry.
> Roses sprout from a peasant's arm, a worker's grip;
> Roses sprout on a warrior's wound,
> On the forehead of a rock.

II

South Africa, today, is a country of politically oppressed, economically exploited and socially segregated people. It is a historical consequence that the oppressed, the exploited and the segregated are the *people of colour*. Historically, there has been settler occupation, enslavement and the destruction of indigenous cultural values. There has been white domination, subjugation and the undermining of African

83

cultural progress. Now, there is apartheid, racial tyranny and dismember-
ment of modern black literary tradition, primarily because of censorship
and banning of writers. Throughout the course of history there has
been an intense black struggle: resistance, protest, defiance, national
consciousness and recently the escalation of the revolutionary thrust.
It is against this background that the black poets are writing. The
black poets share a common experience with the people. In the poem,
In this World, my Sister, Nthambeleni Phalanndwa concludes:

> No more turning back
> I have seen enough of the veld
> Where our lives are not our own.

It is in the last line that Phalanndwa invokes the poet's and the people's
experience: "Where our lives are not our own", implying that *our* lives
are manipulated by powers beyond *our* control, namely, the white
oligarchy. It is immaterial whether the poet writes in the first person
or the third person. The pronoun 'we' sustains a communal bond; it is
at the same time the voice of the poet as well as the voice of the people.
Even when the poet uses the first person, it is not the assertion of the
individual regarding his individuality: he articulates the collective
experience and communal spirit through the 'I'. For Lewis Nkosi says,
"The artist in Africa is a man alienated neither from his community nor
the world of nature which sustains him". And the Russian poet Yevgeny
Yevtushenko writes:

> There only those are born poets
> in whom a proud civic spirit dwells
> . . . .
> The poet is the image of his own age . . . .

Thus, the black poets invest their hopes, their aspirations and their
commitment in *solidarity* and not in *individuality*. Jean-Paul Sartre
rightly said that the writer should address himself to his contemporaries,
and not to posterity. In essence this is the trend and the thrust of
contemporary black poets in South Africa. For James Matthews inti-
mates the *immediacy* of his 'declarations' in *Cry Rage!*

> I record the anguish of the persecuted
> whose words are whimpers of woe
> wrung from them by bestial laws.

84

III

In the eighties, black poetry must develop its own dynamism. It is apparent in the historical process that change is inevitable. In the light of increasing polarization it is likely to be a cataclysmic change:

> in the sun
> we, the roaring rage of smouldering voices
> bursting through the rock of the volcanic mountain
> deafening the ears of the world.
> (*Fragments in the Sun*)

To vary René Depestre's aphorism: There can be no liberation without an authentic revolution. The forces of oppression and the forces of resistance are invariably locked in a series of confrontations. And the inevitable result is the mounting revolutionary zeal to bring about an authentic change. We note that the dilemma of many of the Third World countries was that the revolution was primarily a social, political and (to a limited degree) an economic one. For an authentic revolution there has to be an aesthetic revolution. Only then will there be a cultural liberation. The word revolution does not necessarily connote total destruction. It has to be understood in a wider context. In terms of literature, revolution implies the rejection of bourgeois literary concepts which undermine the development of the black writer. In most of the Third World countries cultural revolution followed the socio-political revolution.

In South Africa, the liberation struggle and cultural liberation are parallel processes. This is because Black Consciousness provided the initial impetus in the rejection of art as an aesthetic indulgence. Once the black poet freed himself from Eurocentric literary conventions, then he was *free* to create within the context of a national consciousness. The black poet's starting point was the articulation of the black experience. It is the movement towards the development of revolutionary poetry.

In constructing an *African* aesthetic the poet readily draws upon ancestral spirits, traditional rites and identifies himself with Africa. Within the realm of spiritualism Ingoapele Madingoane informs:

> in the ancient language of mankind
> i heard the spirits talk back to me.

Njabulo S Ndebele explores ritual in the poem *The Man of Smoke*:

GOGOM GOM . . . . GOGOM GOM . . . .
Alleluya! Alleluya . . . .
. . . .
They kneel before the face of smoke
they cry, they shriek,
they breathe in gasps
they say a wind must enter them
. . . .
rising to sing and dance and clap hands.

In the poem *Words to a Mother* Mafika Gwala establishes his nexus
with the African continent:

I was a cosmic ray in your wombed dreams;
I lathed through the orbit of your dreams
Mother Afrika.

And Madingoane says:

i am africa
i am the blazing desert yonder
a tall proud grain amidst the sand

The black poet is not an interpreter, but in essence he is an innovator.
He synthesises ritual, magic, language, music and the rhythm of Africa.

IV

The principal criticisms levelled against black poetry are that it is
sheer protest, and secondly, it lacks universality. The initial impulse to
write a poem may be nothing more than a political cause (possibly with
social ramifications) and readily stigmatized as 'protest poetry'. The
black poet should strive to discover the appropriate metaphorical
metamorphosis, then the poem will indeed transcend its mere declara-
tory function — the poem will move beyond protest.

It has been suggested that black poetry is too parochial and lacks
universality. In a changing revolutionary climate the black poet cannot

afford any individualistic indulgences. Pablo Neruda writes, on reflection, "The world has changed and so has my poetry". Thus, he wants his poems to be functional, that is:

> useful and usable
> like metal and cereal
> that waits for plowshare
> tools for the hand

The functional aspect of black poetry does not necessarily detract from the universalizing force of a poem. It is possible to elevate a socio-political experience to a universal plane. For Jacques Roumain writes:

> As the contradiction among the features
> create the harmony of the face
> we proclaim the oneness of suffering
> and the revolt
> of all the people on all the faces
> of the earth
> and we mix the mortar of the age
> of brotherhood
> out of the dust of idols

V

Black poetry, today, is dynamic and alive (unlike white English poetry which is comatose). Black poetry is developing in a continuing process of confrontation. In South Africa there is revolt at all levels of human existence — social, economic, political, cultural and artistic. This includes the revolutionary aesthetic. Mbulelo Mzamane says: "The poets, in the service of the revolution, have the function of articulating the people's aspirations, sustaining their spirits . . . ." Barry Feinberg, in introducing the anthology *Poets to the People: South African Freedom Poems*, writes: "The revolutionary poet concretizes the dreams of the people for a better life; the liberation movement fights to make these dreams a reality".

Thus, the poet must be committed. It is out of commitment that the poet will inspire the Azanian perspective. The poem must embody both commitment and affirmation. The committed voice of Mazisi Kunene affirms:

> They were breaking the long ropes of the night
> Setting the world loose, turning it at will to their east.
> I saw them unafraid, as the earth hurled into a void;
> And I knew then the vision of a new era is born of the nightmare.

Alan Paton

How do I regard my role as a writer in South Africa? When I am actively making a book, whether a novel or a biography, I am not thinking of my role at all. I am enjoying the making of the book, and I am trying to make it as good a book as possible. Will my book lead to political and social change? I have no idea. I am not making the book with any intention that it might be an instrument of change.

What am I doing then, when, for example, I write a novel? I am trying to write a story which will be true if not factual; it will have a shape, it will have a beginning and a middle and an end; it will be a narrative. If it teaches any lesson, if it spurs men and women to greater endeavour in pursuit of goals that they believe to be good, if it cries out and protests, that will be because I am that kind of person. But I must first and foremost obey the rules of the craft, which I have set out at the beginning of the paragraph. There is however another aim that is fully permissible, and that is to want to tell the reader about the strange and beautiful and tragic country where I was born.

These rules are very strict, and if they are not obeyed, the story will be flawed. Protest must not be allowed to destroy the art of the writer. Nor must moral considerations. This is a much greater danger for black writers than for white. Many black writers would argue that if a novel is not a novel of protest, it is totally irrelevant. One can readily understand this argument. One can hardly expect a black writer to escape a deep involvement. Literature can never mean the same to the ruled as to the rulers, nor to the conquered as to the conqueror. There is however a great deal of evidence to show that the white writer is less and less able to avoid involvement.

Can protest and art be happily married? There is a superb example of this, and that is the dramatic sketch *Woza Albert*, with its rich accompaniment of humour. Indeed some black critics thought it was too funny, and that one should not laugh in such bad times. Another example of a happy marriage is J J R Jolobe's superb poem *The Making of a Servant.*

I shall give one last example of the great difficulty of marrying protest to art. I went to see, in the company of a leading British critic, a play by a black playwright. It was long and its tensions were unrelieved by either tears or laughter. When asked his opinion, the critic said, "It's tough and it's sincere, but it's not theatre." This caused considerable anger, and he was told "This is our theatre, and that's the way we like it, and we don't want western theatre here."

I do not think it very profitable to think too much about your own role as a writer. In any case there is a special breed of beings who will do it for you, and they are called the critics. I am the last person to generalise about critics, for some of them have given me great praise. But some I am sure *do not understand* the book they are reviewing. Others exhibit what I can only describe as *venom*. Some dislike the *style* of the writer, and are more or less inflamed by it. Shelley maintained that the harsh criticism of *Endymion* in *Blackwood's* brought about the early death of Keats, though this assertion is not generally believed.

Malcolm Muggeridge told me that he does not read reviews "on principle". Our South African writer Braam de Vries told me that he is utterly indifferent to a bad review, and looked surprised when I asked him, "Are you sure?" I know another South African writer who was so devastated by a review that she had no heart to write again.

I am sometimes invited to some conference where my writing will be discussed. I do not go. The thought of being compared to Nadine Gordimer or André Brink, to my advantage or to theirs, absolutely appals me. A writer is, more often than not, a private creature, but the moment a book appears over his name he is a public creature, and must expect hard blows. It is, I think, the sneering critic who is the most wounding, but it is he and not the writer who will assess the writer's role. Let me say in conclusion that I *want* to have a role in the country, but it is not for me to say what I think it is.

My last task is to say what my response is to recent developments. I assume this is a political question. I alternate between hope and despondency. I ask myself whether it is in our human nature for the conqueror to accept the conquered. The Norman conquerors of England eventually became part of the country, just as the country became part of them. In 1982 Englishmen can make jokes about the Conquest. We in South Africa, black or white, are far indeed from being able to laugh about it. White South Africans are even now searching — the best of them — for ways to undo their conquest. Black people are searching for ways to undo it also. The magnitude of the task is impossible to exaggerate.

Olive Schreiner wrote in 1906: "This is not a nation that can safely be hurried." This is an epigram, and cannot therefore be taken as a final statement. But of its truth one is immediately aware. It raises also a second question: Does this epigram mean that the nation will therefore inevitably be unsafely hurried? The epigram seems to reveal the wisdom of this strange and gifted woman, but in the fifteen years that she was yet to live, the wisdom became obscured, perhaps even destroyed, by her growing melancholy and hopelessness, not only about her own country but about the world itself, whose civilised nations, with their great literatures and their music and their art, had become embroiled in the most terrible war in human history. One could say of Olive Schreiner, that if anyone took the role of a writer seriously, it was she. She was one of our prophets, but the end of her life was tragic in the extreme. I have been called a prophet too, but I am also a stoic, and alas, she was not.

I have just finished reading Phyllis Lewsen's superb biography of another prophet, John X Merriman. One of her closing sentences reads thus: "He saw deeply into the future, and the problems he identified seem even more insoluble today."

It makes you think, doesn't it?

Richard Rive

THE BLACK WRITER IN SOUTH AFRICA

Because of the worsening political situation in South Africa, group polarisation is accelerating and the individual is constantly forced to define and redefine his position. The writer, especially the black writer, is no exception. Personally I have been forced into the position of having to call myself a black writer: I have recently been writing articles on black literary development and I have produced an auto-biographical work called *Writing Black*. In spite of this seeming emphasis on ethnicity, I do not see myself as being in the process of abandoning my non-racial stand. It becomes a matter of definition and clarification.

I see 'black' as politico-economic rather than ethnic. When I call a literature 'black' I imply that that literature emanates from a people who are unenfranchised and discriminated against because of the colour of their skins. Such a literature must differ in texture and quality from that emanating from a people who have the vote, suffer no discrimination and are in a power position because of the colour of their skins. If this were not so, it would imply that external forces play hardly any part in the moulding of creativity; that the writer does not create out of experiences surrounding him; that there is therefore a common reaction regardless of the diversity of the forces at work.

The writer who cannot vote, who carries a pass and who lives in a ghetto, must necessarily write qualitatively differently from the writer who can vote, does not carry a pass and lives wherever he pleases. If one of the objects of literature is to record and interpret experience (individual as well as collective) then the literature of the 'have-nots' must differ in theme and texture from the literature of the 'haves'. So that no matter how sincere and motivated the white writer is, he is writing about the subject of racial discrimination, whereas the black writer is writing from within the subject of racial discrimination. There is no doubt that the barriers causing this are artificial, but the differences will remain until discrimination, especially constitutionalised discrimination, is removed.

These differences were highlighted recently by two situations. The first was the decision by Johannesburg PEN to disband because it found that its non-racialism had become untenable. The second was the decision taken by the influential African Literature Association of the United States to deny membership to anyone resident in South Africa, regardless of colour, on the grounds that all who live here are in some way or another collaborating with the apartheid regime.

Both are primarily gestures intended for a wider audience. As such they are understandable as a temporary expedient, but they remain short-sighted and retrogressive.

In the case of the first situation, the decision by Johannesburg PEN may be condoned as a necessary measure to counter hostility outside of literary circles. The establishment, in its place, of the blacks-only African Writers' Association fills the gap partially, but if its exclusive composition becomes a permanent one, the step must prove counterproductive. One cannot exclude any writer from the struggle against oppression. No matter what sophistry is employed and how pragmatic the motivation behind such a move, if one strips off the verbiage then what remains is a concerted move to debar other writers on grounds of colour. Of course the writer forms part of his society and cannot be divorced from it. But amongst other things, he is the articulator of that society. As such he is required to think ahead and his position may be well in advance of the society of which he is a part. He has no alternative. The direction he takes must lead to truth; that is why no genuine writer in South Africa can be a supporter of racial or any other forms of discrimination. No matter how unpopular that road, he cannot deviate from it. He cannot sacrifice his destined role on the altar of temporary expediency. And if he remains on the right path the price he pays is severe. He is under attack from both the authorities he opposes and the people he is leading.

Is it necessary to reiterate that the writer who excludes any other writer from his association on grounds of colour is as guilty as that other writer who voluntarily accepts his exclusion for what he believes to be the greater good? Whereas it is possible to understand and appreciate the invidious position in which the black South African writer finds himself, the decision taken recently by the African Literature Association of the United States to exclude all resident South African writers seems to lack an understanding of the writer's position in this country. To claim that the stand taken is necessary, since any South

African writer by virtue of his living in his native country is guilty of collaborating with the authorities, is as absurd as accusing all resident American writers, including those belonging to the African Literature Association, of collaborating with the Reagan administration.

By virtue of living in any country one is bound to collaborate somewhere along the way. There must be some forced working within the system since to do so may, in certain circumstances, be a matter of survival. Certainly we are guilty if living in a Group Area, carrying a pass, working at inferior jobs reserved for us at a discriminatory wage rate, is collaborating. We certainly do not do so willingly since no man voluntarily and felicitously collaborates in the processes of his own humiliation and degradation. We collaborate only where we have no alternative. Where we do, we avoid and often actively oppose that which emasculates. We certainly do not willingly and consciously contribute towards the maintenance of an apartheid-mad regime. We realise that when our actions become too overt we could face batons, tear-gas, arrests and bannings. But through all this we maintain our belief in our cause and the rightness of that cause. If we seem to collaborate on the surface, we do so sullenly while we catch our breaths.

There are some amongst us who, in their extreme bitterness, accuse those exiles who have now become our accusers, of opting out of the immediate struggle and fighting our battles from the safety of Canada and the United States. I do not count myself amongst them since I believe the fight to be on all sides, both here and abroad. I do not believe that anyone should be denied his contribution because by remaining in South Africa he is collaborating, or by remaining in exile he is collaborating in our continued oppression.

I can see the African Literature Association resolution only as a gesture to display its antagonism towards the South African victimizer, albeit at the expense of the South African victim. But it also stems from a sad lack of knowledge about what is happening in South Africa and is a decision taken by those who have possibly been too far removed from the struggle in time and distance. Indeed there are some who must mount the battlements and others who must record the events. And in order to record the events as truthfully as possible, in order to keep alive international pressure, in order to tell the world that so it is, it is necessary for some to be physically present. The writer who chooses to remain behind (or is forced to remain behind) and records from the humiliation of daily discrimination, is to be supported, not hounded out of international forums and branded as a collaborator. Collaborators are those who co-operate traitorously with the enemy. It will indeed be difficult to find any writer in South Africa of any colour who fits such a definition.

The writer in South Africa needs international support, not international opprobrium, in his attempt to maintain a climate in which real change becomes possible. The African Literature Association might feel that it does not need the support of the South African writer in its fight against discrimination, but the South African writer desperately needs the support of the African Literature Association in the fight against apartheid.

Karel Schoeman

REKENSKAP VAN 'N GETUIE
(THE ACCOUNT OF A WITNESS)

As skrywer voel ek my nie geroepe of verplig tot openbare verant-woording nie: die boeke wat ek skryf, moet vir hulself kan spreek sonder angsvallige pogings aan my kant om hul te onderskraag. Om van tyd tot tyd by jouself te besin, kan seker geen kwaad doen nie, maar openbáre besinning is 'n ander kwessie, en 'n aktiwiteit waarvoor ek bowendien geen besondere aanleg besit nie.

Dat ek my nou enigsins huiwerig aan openbare besinning waag eerder as om dit oor te laat aan dié van my mede-skrywers met groter selfvertroue, of groter bedrewenheid in openbare optrede, is omdat ek voel dat daar in hierdie bespreking van bewustheid en betrokkenheid in die Suid-Afrikaanse letterkunde ook 'n stem gehoor behoort te word wat in Afrikááns daaraan deelneem, hoe stamelend dit miskien is; want Afrikaans is nie net die taal van die huidige Suid-Afrikaanse establish-ment nie, hoeseer dit so voorkom en in hoe 'n mate dit in die oordeel van 'n groot aantal Suid-Afrikaners met onreg en onderdrukking vereen-selwig is. Die taal kan ewe goed gebruik word om protes teen die optrede van die establishment aan te teken, om kritiek daaroor uit te spreek of om vrae daaroor te stel en vraagtekens daarby te plaas, en ek dink dat dit heilsaam is om af en toe aan hierdie feit te herinner.

Ná hierdie omslagtige inleiding moet ek die onderwerp onder bespreking egter op negatiewe wyse aanpak en beken dat die huidige modewoord 'betrokkenheid' vir my 'n onding in die letterkunde is, in elk geval in die sin waarin dit gewoonlik gebruik word, ook in Suid-Afrika. Die aard van die maatskappy waarvan ek deel uitmaak en die verhouding wat ek daarmee het, is nie van primêre belang nie, want wanneer dit kom by skryf, is dit die skrýf wat primêr is, en alle ander faktore is bysaak waar jy alleen oor die papier geboë sit. In die skeppings-proses, hoe nederig en eenvoudig dit miskien ook is, luister jy in eerste instansie, dink ek, na 'n innerlike stem, 'n innerlike ritme —

jy rig jou volgens 'n innerlike ingewing of gesig, sou mens miskien selfs kan sê, en jy sit nie vir geval jy dalk vergeet by jouself en fluister dat jy 'n blanke Suid-Afrikaner in die vroeë tagtigerjare is nie. Dit wil natuurlik nie sê dat tyd en omgewing in die skryfproses van geen belang is nie, want jy is die produk van albei en word deur albei gevorm en beïnvloed. So kan jy jou in hierdie besondere geval nooit losmaak nie van die feit dat jy deel is van 'n verdeelde maatskappy gekenmerk deur protes, geweld en onregverdighede, en selfs al sou jy die besef doelbewus probeer ontvlug, sou die ontwyking in sigself ook 'n reaksie op die situasie wees.

Indien jy as méns begaan is oor wat jy daagliks óm jou waarneem, sal jy jou natuurlik by geleentheid afvra of dit wat jy as skrýwer doen wel genoeg is en of jy nie miskien méér behoort aan te pak nie; maar dit is 'n versoeking wat na my mening weerstaan behoort te word, hoe begryplik dit ook lyk. Jy kan nie gaan sit en skryf met die bewuste voorneme om te protesteer, te ontbloot of aan te val nie. As jy dit doen, sal die eindproduk betoog of propaganda wees, en op hierdie vak miskien ook baie knap en geslaagd, maar kúns sal dit nie wees nie, létter-kunde sal dit nie wees nie, hoe beskeie dan ook. Jy gaan sit voor die papier om te skrýf, en dit is al.

'n Sekere selfverwyt sal dus bly, 'n gevoel dat jy te kort skiet, 'n gevoel van onvolkomenheid en skuld — om jou boekies te skryf, om jou versies te skryf, om in jou werkkamer voor die papier te sit, kan in hierdie situasie tog nie genoeg wees nie, voel jy, nie náástenby genoeg nie. Ja, miskien ís dit ook nie; maar die feit dat jy 'n sekere gawe besit om boekies of versies te skryf, beteken nie noodwendig dat jy met veel welslae enigiets anders sal kan aanpak of uitvoer nie, en terwyl 'n blote gebáár ook sin en waarde kan hê, is gebare helaas nie altyd in ooreenstemming met die goeie wil of goeie bedoelings wat daartoe aanleiding gegee het nie.

Dus terug na die werkkamer, terug na die geduldige papier; terug na die één soort werk waarvan jy weet dat jy dit met 'n sekere mate van welslae kan verrig, wroegend en onwillig terug na jou privaatwêreldjie terwyl die situasie onveranderd buite jou vensters voortduur, besig met jou harsingspinsels terwyl jy droom van die gróót dade van protes wat jy sou wil verrig, die vlammende woorde van aanklag waarmee jy die land aan die brand sou wil slaan sodat die gloed aan die horison van ver weg sigbaar is. Maar dit is helaas ándere beskore, en die enigste wapen wat jy het, die enigste wapen wat jy waarskynlik ooit met enige effek sal kan hanteer, is woorde; en jy buk jou dus oor die papier en skryf verder.

Vir vele wat hierdie uiteensetting lees, sal dit seker nie naastenby genoeg wees nie, want daadwerklike betrokkenheid is vandag die slagspreuk. Daar is egter baie maniere waarop betrokkenheid uiting kan vind, hoe power en ondoeltreffend sommige daarvan na verhouding ook lyk. As die skrywer oop staan vir wat óm hom gebeur en waarlik besorgd is daaroor, sal dit in sy werk neerslag vind, hoe indirek dit miskien ook mag gebeur.

Die stille stem kan soms verder dra as die luider krete, en 'n besinning oor beginsels kan moontlik oor 'n wyer gebied en vir 'n langer tyd sy geldigheid behou as die uitbeelding van aktualiteite wat, hoe aangrypend ook, aan verbygaande gebeure en instellings gekoppel is.

Weerstaan die versoeking om ook betrokke, aktueel of sinvol te wees, om vir jou tyd te skryf en getuienis van jou betrokkenheid in jou skryf-werk af te lê, om iets voort te bring wat tot jou tydgenote spreek. Kyk, luister, neem waar; neem in jou op, verwerk; slaap daarmee in die nag, word daarvan wakker. En vergeet dan daarvan wanneer jy weer voor die papier gaan sit, en skryf soos oordeel en besinning jou ingee, want onvermydelik sal hierdie dinge ook êrens in jou woorde klink en met jou geskrif verweef wees, ook al is dit nie onmiddellik herkenbaar nie. Op jóú manier is jy ook besig om getuienis te lewer van wat óm jou gebeur; op jóú manier is jy ook besig om te getuig.

Deur diegene wat in hul daaglikse lewens náder deur die wantoe-stande in hierdie land geraak word as ek tot dusver, sal my redenasie waarskynlik verwerp word as die poging van 'n blanke Suid-Afrikaner om uit sy veilige en bevoorregte posisie sy gewete te probeer sus. Dit is 'n reaksie wat ek kan begryp en waarmee ek simpatie kan hê; maar tog hoop ek dat diegene wat hierdie besinning end-uit gelees het ook sal probeer om te verstaan en my goeie bedoelings sal aanvaar. Voor-lopig is dit ongelukkig al wat ek het om aan te bied — dit en my geskrifte; en ten slotte is dit in sigself geen onaansienlike gawe nie. Om getuienis van onreg te lewer is nie noodwendig minder geldig as om die met dade te weerstaan nie.

THE ACCOUNT OF A WITNESS

I do not feel myself obliged or called upon as a writer to justify publicly what I think; the books I write should speak for themselves and not need any anxious attempts on my part to support their intent. It is one thing periodically to reflect by oneself upon the state of affairs and quite another to make public statements. I have in any case very little talent for the latter.

That I nevertheless tentatively attempt a public statement rather than leave it to fellow authors of much more confidence or greater experience in public debate is because I feel that an Afrikaans voice should also be heard participating in this discussion of awareness and involvement in South African writing, no matter how faltering that voice may be. For Afrikaans is not the language only of the present establishment in South Africa, however much that may seem to be so because of its identification in the minds of many South Africans with injustice and oppression. This tongue can be used equally well to protest against the actions of the establishment, to criticize or question them, and I think it is salutary that people be reminded of this from time to time.

Having given this lengthy introduction, I now feel myself compelled to approach the whole matter in a rather negative way and to confess that I find the word 'engagement' rather modish and something of a misfit in a literary context — at least, in the sense in which it is commonly used in South Africa and elsewhere. The nature of the society of which I am part and my relation to it is not for me as a writer of primary importance, for in the act of writing, it is the writing which comes first. Everything else becomes secondary when you sit bent over the sheet of paper. In the creative process, no matter how unassuming or modest, you obey essentially, I think, an inner voice, an inner rhythm — you might even say that you were led by an inner prompting or vision. You do not sit muttering to yourself all the time that you are a white South African of the early eighties, just in case you might forget.

This does not, of course, imply that the times and your environment are not of great importance in the creative process, because you are yourself the product of both, shaped and influenced by both. In these circumstances, you can never free yourself from the fact that you are part of a divided society, marked by protest, violence and injustice. Even the attempt to flee from this knowledge would in itself be a reaction to the situation.

As a human being who is disturbed by what happens around you every day you would naturally ask yourself on occasion whether what your writing accomplishes is really sufficient, or whether you should not attempt more. However understandable this impulse may be, it is to my mind a temptation to be resisted. You do not set about writing with the conscious purpose of protesting, exposing or attacking; the end-product of such a purpose could only be expostulation or propaganda. On this level it may be very accomplished and successful, but it will not be art or literature, of however unassuming a kind. You go and sit before the sheet of paper to write, and that is all.

A certain self-reproach will therefore remain, a feeling of inadequacy and guilt — for surely it cannot be enough, in a state of affairs such as this, to remain in your study and write your little books and poems — not nearly enough. Well, perhaps it isn't, but the fact that you have a certain talent for writing books and poems does not necessarily mean that you could be equally successful at anything else. And although the mere gesture towards something can in itself be meaningful and valuable, gestures are, alas, not always expressive of the good will or intentions that provoked them.

Therefore, once again, back to the study, to the long-suffering piece of paper; back to the one job you know you can accomplish with some degree of success; you may be reluctant and full of remorse, but nevertheless, back to your own private world, while outside your window the situation continues unchanged. You busy yourself with the creations of your imagination even while you dream of the great deeds of protest you would like to have performed, of the flaming words of accusation with which you had hoped to set the land ablaze, so that the glowing horizon would be visible from afar. But that, alas, is for others; the only weapon *you* have, and the only one you would probably ever be able to handle to any effect is words. So you bend once more over the paper and write on.

Many who read this exposition will no doubt find it highly inadequate, because today's slogan calls for active participation. Being involved, however, can find expression in many ways, however poor and ineffectual some of them may seem, compared to others. If the writer remains responsive to what is happening around him and feels real concern, it will manifest itself in his work, no matter how obliquely.

The quiet voice has sometimes greater carrying power than the strident one, and reflection on principles may perhaps range wider and retain more lasting validity than the depiction of topicalities, which, moving though they may be, are nevertheless tied to transitory events and institutions.

Resist the temptation to be 'involved', topical or 'meaningful', to write for your time and to make your writing the witness to your involvement, to insist on proving something that would speak to your contemporaries. Watch, listen, take note; absorb, digest; sleep with your observations and wake to reflect on them. And then forget about them when you are in front of your writing paper, in order to write as your judgment and inspiration lead you, because these things too will inevitably resonate somewhere in the words you write and they will be enmeshed in the texture of your writing even though they may not be obviously and immediately apparent. You too are bearing witness to all that is happening around you.

Those whose daily lives have been affected much more deeply than mine by the oppressive conditions of this country may well reject my argument as another attempt by a white South African to salve his conscience from within his safe and privileged position. I can understand such a reaction and I can sympathise with it, but still I hope that people who have read all I have written here will also try to understand and accept my good intentions. Unfortunately this is all I have to offer at present — this, and what I have written elsewhere, in itself, after all, no mean offering. To bear witness to injustice is not necessarily less valid than to oppose it with action.

100

Peter Wilhelm

In the ideal world it is probably preferable that writers do *not* comment on their work and critical responses to it. Publication marks the point at which the work passes beyond the writer's private control: after that, revision or recantation must appear faintly ludicrous or, even, a deliberately presumptuous intervention between the reader and the text, flawed though it may be.

Sometimes, however, one does wish to respond to responses; at the risk, of course, of being told that the confusion and ambiguity start with oneself.

An easy example: in my story *LM* I chose to identify the narrator as "Peter". My motive was to indicate that I, the writer, and "I", the narrator, felt a common sense of engulfment/entrapment by the recorded experience. But the obvious conclusion which many drew was that *LM* was autobiography. It was not; but my point was over-subtle, and therefore flawed. I have learnt, in any case, to tolerate that kind of linkage.

Nonetheless, it might be helpful if I stated, as clearly as possible, certain premises of my fiction.

The word most commonly used to describe my work is "bleak". Allied to that, "pessimistic", "disturbing", "macabre", and "depressing". One reviewer, in particular, felt compelled to write (of my collection *At The End Of A War*):

> Wilhelm depicts a bleak, precarious world where man is essentially an isolated suffering victim, either of the political system, or of his own impulses, or of sheer accident. Over this universe, apparently abandoned by God, Wilhelm presides as an ironic, almost sadistic puppeteer, consigning characters to unhappy endings or delivering dismissive shorthand judgments.

His conclusion:

> The experience of this collection is perhaps best summed up in the pregnant quotation of Antonio Gramsci in his *Prison Note-books*: "The old is dying and the new cannot be born; in this interregnum there arises a great diversity of morbid symptoms." Peter Wilhelm is in his best work the relentless and disturbing recorder of those symptoms.

There are sweeping assumptions here, as well as the critical failure to distinguish between author and narrator. To condense, *another kind* of literature and society is indicated as preferable: and one senses the lingering, at several removes, of the assumptions of the Great Tradition; which means, effectively, a nostalgia that renders the present, our present, marginal. The critic reaches into the past and dreams of a future; and both are unreal.

Every age is an interregnum; but it requires a dissociation from effective life to perceive it as such. The dissociation can register in language which is charged with certainties: a 'good' morality, a 'progressive' Marxism, a religious 'affirmation'. The contemporary writer, however, is probably being dishonest if he confesses to much more than a sense that the grids do not fit. That can make for some difficulty for the reader, but since the numbers of the literate are declining in any case, the risk seems worth taking.

A scientific metaphor might make this plainer. In any experiment the interaction of the observer with the observed influences the outcome. There is an energy interchange between a distant star and the eye of an astronomer. A vista of receding perspectives presents itself: character and plot are not neatly sealed off for inspection.

Within this relativistic continuum, the serious writer, I believe, must address himself to the issues of conflict, and the decay of order or decency: why is it preferable to do or say one kind of thing than another? is any outcome of an action truly predictable? and so on. I *suspect* that what we are trying to do is create, or recreate, a mythic basis upon which action can be, in some sense, fulfilling, recorded or judged.

It is a difficult struggle. To say, therefore, that my "world" is "apparently abandoned by God" and that I "consign" various fates — "unhappy endings" -- is simply not pertinent. Contemporary physics and cosmology suggest that the origin and nature of being are inexplicable. The world is mysterious and dangerous; in it art and love occur

102

not without intense labour and the probable intervention of grace.

An American writer whom I very much admire, Thomas M Disch, said this when challenged about the 'bleak' nature of his work:

> What sort of criticism is it to say that a writer is pessimistic? One can name any number of admirable writers who indeed were pessimistic and whose writing one cherishes. It's mindless to offer that as a criticism. Usually all it means is that I am stating a moral position that is uncongenial to the person reading the story. It means that I have a view of existence which raises serious questions that they're not prepared to discuss; such as the fact that man is mortal, or that love dies ... The radical solution shouldn't be easier to achieve in fiction than in real life.

Note that Disch speaks of "stating a moral position" which is uncongenial to some; not of having no moral position.

Of course, the rebuttal can come back: what *is* your moral position? One had better edge into that cautiously. Obviously, for a variety of reasons, a turbulent society such as ours is unlikely to produce literature of, say, Elizabethan qualities (though life was as "precarious" then as now). It may produce no literature at all, or literature that is marginal in the historical perspective that we cannot have. No one can choose to write great, or for that matter 'bad' literature: we simply cannot know. We have to go on the life around us; and, who knows, the tiny fragment of time we experience may gain a retrospective lustre from the work it casts up.

But, for the present, one is up against the facts of violence and instability; and the profound psychological damage caused by the philosophical basis of our society. There are the real counter-balancing terrors of repression and resistance: there is the more hidden but equally real destruction of personal relationships, not least in the corrupting unhappiness of our rulers.

Time after time I have found myself compelled to write out an event or ending which I would far rather not have occur. But the experience of these matters is a pressure in the work which I can't avoid: and I sense the same pressure in other writers. Obviously it *would* be possible to write out different endings. But this, I think, is where the writer and the critic can easily part company. What might be called the sense of an appropriate ending is something that only the writer can feel: he can certainly choose something less painful to himself or his reader — and sense the work going dead on the page.

Fairly recently I have encountered a recurrent image in my work; that is, I only became completely aware of this image once a certain number of stories containing it had been published: it was not 'put in'. It is that of a dead child. Why? Why return to such a sad and final image?

I feel — in retrospect — that it was forced upon me. It certainly contains, for me, a number of arresting implications though it is, finally, beyond any statement I can make about it.

It is life and innocence irrevocably cut off. It can reveal ultimate loss in a relationship. It can question the very right to exist of any society that tolerates such deaths where they are not accidental — ours, for example, during and after 1976, but not ours alone. It should make us doubt the sanity of our regressive tolerance for violence; the death toll of any war, for example, includes the unborn children of those killed on the battlefield. I could go on.

Phrases like "life and innocence", "regressive tolerance for violence", and so on seem to demand further explanation; a statement of that "moral position" perhaps. But there I can only point back to the fiction where, opposed to the forces of negation, I have placed characters who, while not heroic, seek to find and live out the requirements of love, compassion and healing. Such a search is never easy, its outcome never less than ambiguous. But the characters are there.

CRITICAL ESSAYS

The Motif of the Damaged Child in the Work of J M Coetzee

JOAN GILLMER

Dusklands, *In the Heart of the Country* and *Waiting for the Barbarians*,[1] J M Coetzee's monologues of self, each of which forms a distinct facet of a consistent whole, are, for the most part, painfully ugly exposures of the spiritual plight of the West; yet they are achieved with such linguistic skill, imaginative intensity and audacious invention that they command respect. The fictional worlds they present, often with jolting immediacy or hallucinated disjunction, are, whether in American suburbia, the African hinterland, on an unlocalized frontier or stone desert at the heart of nowhere, all countries of the mind, territories of "Empire" where sustaining traditional mythologies have been subverted by the "master-myth of history" (*Dusklands*, 28) and where "the voice of the doubting self, the voice of René Descartes [drives] his wedge between the self in the world and the self who contemplates that self." (21) Thus fragmented and isolated, the "alienated *doppelgänger* rationality" (21) that governs these regions, convinced of the otherness of life and turned helplessly against itself, ravages the earth and its natural offspring and launches attacks upon the "Vietnam" that lies within. "Vietnam, like everything else, is inside me, and in Vietnam, with a little diligence, a little patience, all truths about man's nature." (15)

This insight offers itself to the narrator of the first section of *Dusklands*, Eugene Dawn, mythographer and exponent of psychological warfare. Anxious to retain the approval of his superior, an anti-self named Coetzee, whom he regards as a "failed creative person", yet compelled at the same time to disobey him as he struggles in his writings to fashion a "core" for himself, Dawn, whose chronic alienation from self, world, wife and child has become extreme, approaches the point of psychotic breakdown. He broods obsessively over his collection of photographs of the war, three of which he describes as showing, firstly, the act of violation of a tiny woman or child by a bulky U S Air

107

Cavalry sergeant, secondly, a group exhibit of three severed heads, and thirdly, the opaque, dark eye of a brainwashed prisoner in a tiger cage. He is aroused by these pictures to a pitch of nervous excitement which, together with the shocking inappropriateness of the provisional title he has assigned to the first picture ("Father Makes Merry with Children"), points to the presence of powerful links between these images and an underlying vortex of extreme anxiety and emotional turmoil. After an attempt on his son's life, and his subsequent treatment in a psychiatric hospital, he discovers that his photographs have disappeared:

> My photographs are gone. I had photographs of the worst of my tormentors before they were stolen from me. I will not forget them. I will not mistake them. I will identify them before the judgement seat. I will see them in hell. I try to dream them up as I used to in the old days, but I no longer sleep the same kind of sleep, and they will not come. (50)

One makes the inference that the tormenting images in Eugene Dawn's war photographs are either, as his wife supposes, responsible for the condition of his disordered consciousness, or at least reflect it in a significant way. It will be suggested in this essay that they represent the stigmata of "alienated *doppelgänger* rationality", that they are indices of cultural decline, and that variations on these images and their metaphors recur and expand throughout the three books, lending coherence to the series of monologues and helping to articulate something of the dilemma of the artist who finds himself as Magda says in *In the Heart of the Country* "alone in the historical present". (120) Seen in this light, the severed heads and the eye staring back from the tiger cage become emblems of the detached intellect, which, when divorced from bodily and emotional experience, looks out upon the world with a freezing camera eye, destroying the natural equilibrium between thought and feeling, reason and imagination, just as the propaganda services to which Dawn and Coetzee belong are planning to do in Vietnam. That the picture of the violated girl/child represents an integral part of the same psychic complex, and that all three images are symbols of a state of mind Blake called "Single vision & Newton's sleep",[2] will be adumbrated later.

This kind of deformity of human experience is shown developing in the course of Jacobus Coetzee's narrative of his journey to the land of the Great Namaquas two centuries earlier. Confronted by his own failure to order and control the irrational impulses of instinctual life, personified in the tribal Hottentots, he is forced to reject the consoling eighteenth-century myth of the dignity and virtue of man in a state of nature, and falls into sickness and delirium from which he recovers by withdrawing into himself, casting off all attachments, and learning to play the game of minimal survival. Imitating the "Zeno" beetle, which feigns death and allows its legs to be pulled off without wincing, he represses his sensuality, as well as his rage and anxiety, and survives in the form of a diminished selfhood:

> There had been legs, metaphorical legs, and much else too, that I had been prepared to lose. In the blindest alley of the labyrinth of my self I had hidden myself away, abandoning mile after mile of defences. (103)

No longer sustained by a sense of Christian destiny, he conceives the task of finding his way back to civilisation as a game or contest played against an indifferent universe:

> In each game the challenge was to undergo [an alternative invented] history, and victory was mine if I survived it. The fourth game was the most interesting one, the Zenonian case in which only an infinitely diminishing fraction of my self survived. . . . (105)

Thus, when Jacobus Coetzee, "tamer of the wild", (82) makes his second journey to the hinterland to take revenge upon the Hottentots and the four servants who have defected, he has become a different man. His style has altered. He is detached, abstracted, with a developing historical perspective and a sense that the interior has become a void, a desolation before which his imagination fails. This time the European and the aboriginal man do not ride out to meet each other peacefully, breathing in unison. The savage does not approach; and Coetzee gives orders to the Griqua soldiers to destroy the Hottentot village. The deaths of the former servants are described in horrible detail with a brittle control of the mixed feelings they arouse, but the rape of a child is reported with a numb matter-of-factness and a clumsy circumlocution which emphasize the speaker's failure to respond or intervene. In this way the image of violation becomes linked with the idea of failure to protect childhood innocence, both as a concomitant and a perpetuator of the alienated vision in which experience is transformed from raped interior to observed exterior. Through the deaths of the servants and the tribal Hottentots who had previously punished and expelled him following his attack upon their children, Coetzee asserts his own threatened reality, but finds himself despairing that there is no longer any resistance to his omnipotence. He is totally enclosed in an egocentric vacuum, estranged from his own humanity, listening to the conflicting voices of his theoretical speculations, afraid there may be nothing "outside".

In opting for rationality and the detached eye as his stratagem for survival in an anarchic world, Jacobus Coetzee has not only abandoned "mile after mile of defences" (103); he has also surrendered to oblivion those elements of human nature that are traditionally ascribed to the nurturing feminine principle — qualities such as love, mercy, forgiveness, intuition and creativity[3] — as well as the memory of the timeless vision of childhood. This, in part at least, is the metaphorical significance of those images of violation and injury of women and children which appear so enigmatically and apparently so gratuitously in all the monologues.[4] In the desiccated mythographic terms employed by Eugene Dawn, this state of mind is described as a condition in which the patriarchal sky god no longer lies with and impregnates the mothering earth but cohabits incestuously with the goddess of *techne*, sprung from his own brain, the goddess who has no inner space, no means of entry to the interior life, and who grapples the impenetrable world to herself with "the gun and its metaphors [as] copulas". (18) One draws the conclusion that the human child, deprived of its natural mother, is cast out of the infant paradise into the fallen world of the time-bound ego, where it is prematurely exposed to the severity of the father's power and learns the lesson of rebellious violence.

Images of diseased, mutilated or otherwise disabled children suggest just such a blighting of human and personal potentiality. When the ironically named Eugene Dawn, having abducted his five-year-old son from his wife's care, finds himself in no mood to cope with the child's "irrational behaviour" and feels him to be nothing but a burden, he seems to discover why he is still unable to feel happy or liberated, and recognizes his own self-hatred:

> I know and I know and I know what it is that has eaten away my manhood from inside, devoured the food that should have nourished me. It is a thing, a child not mine, once a baby squat and yellow whelmed in the dead centre of my body, sucking my blood, growing by my waste, now, 1973, a hideous mongol boy who stretches his limbs inside my hollow bones, gnaws my liver

with his smiling teeth, voids his bilious filth into my systems, and will not go. I want an end to it! I want my deliverance! (40)

The attempted rescue of their son by his wife, assisted by law officers, provokes a desperate reaction and as his knife pierces the boy's back he feels with amazement that he has been struck "a terrible blow", that he is beginning to be hurt, and, as he falls, he recognizes the smell of the carpet on which he used to lie as a child. The unconscious identification between his own child and the child he once was is complete. Pain and violence passing from father to son demonstrate a tragically fated pattern as well as an intermingling of murderous and suicidal impulses that threaten the very existence of the self.

Dawn's fantasy of the hideous mongol boy is matched by Jacobus Coetzee's nightmarish vision as he lies, suffering from severe hunger and the effects of a peri-anal abscess, in a Hottentot hut:

A child strayed into the hut and stood at my bedside pondering me. It had no nose or ears and both upper and lower foreteeth jutted horizontally from its mouth. Patches of skin had peeled from its face, hands, and legs, revealing a pink inner self in poor imitation of European colouring. (88)

This, too, besides suggesting the idea of minimal survival, is a horrific portent of violence to come. There is the physical violence which Coetzee inflicts on the mischievous Hottentot boys who have removed his clothes from the river bank, even biting off the ear of one of them in a paroxysm of fury; and there is the metaphorical violence with which he attempts to obliterate the experience of his own senses (all save the eyes)[5] in his retreat to civilization after he has been robbed and driven off by the outraged adults. Their accusation, "Do you not know how to play with children? ... You have mutilated this child" (97) seems to point to the irony of Dawn's caption to his first photograph: "Father Makes Merry with Children".

In the symbolic dimension invoked by such controlling metaphors lies a clue to understanding *In the Heart of the Country* and *Waiting for the Barbarians*, since they too project the same "submerged mind of Empire" albeit with the differing perspective of the protagonists' sex, setting and situation. The disturbingly powerful monologue of Magda, an Afrikaner spinster immured on her father's isolated farm, is arguably the best of Coetzee's three works of fiction, perhaps because of its emotional intensity but surely also because of the tight control of the language with its peculiar double effect, as of the blending of two voices: that of a wild kind of imagination and that of the self-critical intellect of the writer. Without any distinct memory of her true mother, this deprived and immobilized woman is locked into a restricted existence of attendance upon her remote father and conventional exchanges with the servants. Grotesque and barren in her own eyes, a "thin black beetle" full of self-loathing and self-mockery, her dark thoughts are obsessed with her exclusion from her father's love.

Jealously, she imagines her father's connubium with a new, greedy, sensual wife or his infatuation for the coloured labourer's childish young bride. Though a reluctant inheritor of her progenitor's masterful language and speculative bias, she nevertheless has access to the world of emotional experience that the patriarchal intellect has despised and repressed. As representative of the feminine principle, however painfully distorted, and as custodian of the creative imagination, she is all inner space, "a hole crying to be whole" (41), a black widow in mourning for the uses she was never put to. It is she who uses the phrase "childhood rape" in connection with the fate of the "daughters of the colonies. . . . Wooed when we were little by our masterful fathers, we are bitter vestals, spoiled for life." (3) She also understands the one-sided effect of this upon her own consciousness:

> My father is the absence of my mother, her negative, her death. She the soft, the fair; he the hard, the dark. He has murdered all the motherly in me and left me this brittle, hairy shell with the peas of dead words rattling in it. I stand in the empty kitchen hating him. (37)

As a "poetess of interiority", she is able to enter her childhood again, recalling a time when, at the feet of an old manservant, she had "drunk in a myth of a past when beast and man and master had a common life as innocent as the stars in the sky". (7) Retaining some vague sense of a lost golden age, she aches to "form the words that will translate [her] into the land of myth and hero" or carry her from "the mundane of being into the doubleness of signification". (4) She also relives in vivid imagination the child-trauma, the vast helplessness and rage of a child's loneliness and pain: exclusion from the parental bedroom, physical violence provoked by importunate demands for attention, the loss of innocence, the splitting into self and little ghostly watcher, the fall into the black vortex. It is her version of the rape:

112

I am hit . . . . The blow does not hurt but it insults. I am insulted and outraged. A moment ago I was a virgin and now I am not, with respect to blows. (57—8)

Such probings of the interior for explanations of the self only leave her possessed by violent and horrible fantasies of parricide, rape by the servant, and death. Spoiled for life and ruined for love, she finds herself incapable of resolving conflict with her father in a "true agon with crisis and resolution" (62) and turns, in her reach for transcendence, to a dream of a burning bush that will resist her metaphysical conquest, and listens to her voices from the sky. Forming letters on the ground with white-painted stones, she attempts to spell out in a new language of true exchange, unlike her father-tongue of "hierarchy, of distance and perspective" (97), messages to the sky gods, poems at dusk expressing her yearning to become a medium, a median, a bridge between. She arranges her last remaining stones in the shape of a woman lying on her back, in the attitude of the earth-mother awaiting the sky god. What were no more than abstractions in Eugene Dawn's mythographic analysis of the problem of "Vietnam" have here become spontaneous images of the naive imagination, pointing, in their crude way, to the conjunction of masculine and feminine principles, the reconciliation of contraries, the union of self and world that the West has lost but true poetic vision still commands.

But no epiphany ensues. Knowing herself solitary and God-forsaken, a castaway of history, Magda finally puts to herself a choice that confronts a literary artist for whom nostalgic poems about *Verlore Vlakte*[6] no longer serve to communicate his own voice: either crazily to trust the symbols of the mythic imagination or to "yield to the spectre of reason and explain myself to myself in the only kind of confession we protestants know". (137)

If the ruthlessly depleted humanity of Jacobus Coetzee, the psychosis of Eugene Dawn, and the murderous fantasies of Magda offend the susceptibilities of decent, respectable readers (who are also, perhaps, waiting for this phase of history to pass), the liberal humanism of the elderly Magistrate who is the narrator in *Waiting for the Barbarians* may seem more reassuring; but he, too, must make the journey to the interior where all complacencies are tested. While the symbolic dimension is here more plainly hinted at in the setting (a frontier outpost at no particular time and in no particular country, merely somewhere in the northern hemisphere where winters are severe, spring begins to arrive in March, and the barbarians beyond the limits of imperial order are mounted pastoral nomads of a Mongolian type not unlike the Tartar hordes which overran the classic civilizations of the past), the metaphors of alienated vision and childhood rape that one has come to recognize in the two former works are more fully elaborated and their inter-relatedness has assumed a different configuration. Where formerly it was typically a father-figure who directly harmed the child, now it is the representative of a new regime of Empire, operating under emergency powers with a vision more alienated than any before, who interrogates under torture both father and daughter, destroying the natural bond between them.

The detached eye of Colonel Joll is not only shielded from the light of the sun by the dark lenses of his new-fangled glasses; it is also veiled from the gaze of the Magistrate, who sees himself reflected in them and will later come to recognize, with rage and hatred, his anti-self, the other side of Imperial rule. This darkened vision, belonging to a "new science of degradation" (108) in which Eugene Dawn's morbid passion for exploration without penetration of the interior has come to full flower, extends its mastery even over the traditional truths of human experience, which are forced to conform, in pain and outrage, to the shape Joll believes and wills them to have. The tireless interrogations that achieve this purpose have left a barbarian girl simultaneously orphaned, crippled and semi-blind, and hence reduced to beggary and total dependence upon the questionable goodwill of the Magistrate, who inherits the problems Joll leaves behind. Subconsciously identified with the image of a hooded child in a dream sequence which weaves a thread of a more lustrous texture into the fabric of the monologue, this passive figure, with her mutilated feet and peripheral vision, is seen as the "key to the labyrinth" in which the narrator has lost his way. Through his involvement with her, he is compelled to experience the involuntary power of emotions that have been consigned to oblivion, to become aware of unconscious guilt that motivates his obsessive concern with cleanliness and his compulsive rituals of purification, to examine the threadbare ideals of civilized conduct that sustained him before his authority was challenged, and eventually to recognize that a state of emergency really does exist, despite his longing to resume his tranquil life of cultivated pursuits and "placid concupiscence". (9) Though much of what lies at the heart of the labyrinth remains ambiguous, the mythic treatment of the barbarian girl/dream child image points toward a possible resolution of conflict and does permit a momentary release of natural feeling.

When the Magistrate takes the crippled barbarian girl under his protection, and develops his "inexplicable ritual" of washing, oiling and rubbing her damaged feet and the rest of her body and then falling into blissful trances and spells of dreamless sleep, he becomes obsessed by the desire to discover what her torturers have done to her and notices that, besides the obvious injuries to her feet and eyes, she has a "phantom criss-cross of ridges" (31) under the skin of her buttocks. It seems to him that the marks on her body are signs that must be deciphered. He also feels driven to recover an image of her as she originally was before being abused, an image which he is convinced is hidden somewhere in his memory:

> ...I must believe she was unmarked as I must believe she was once a child, a little girl in pigtails running after her pet lamb in a universe where somewhere far away I strode in the pride of my life. Strain as I will, my first image remains of the kneeling beggar-girl.
> ...I find it impossible to believe that once upon a time I imagined the human form as a flower radiating out from a kernel in the loins. (33—34)

The explicit suggestion here that the image of unblemished childhood forms part of some lost paradise of the imagination is not only a pointer to allegorical values in the Magistrate's story; it also evokes an echo of Magda's "land of myth and hero".

Though the association between the barbarian girl and the hooded faceless child building snow castles in his recurring dream is still unconscious at this stage, he begins to ponder the quality of his relationship with her: the indirect eroticism of his compulsive rituals, the failure to penetrate her inwardness which has its counterpart in his physical impotence with her, the baffled anger which he realises may correspond to what her torturers felt as they hunted the secret she seemed to conceal. At this point, he appears wonderingly to sense that it is some violence done to the experiencing self, some hitherto unquestioned belief in the otherness of life that links him with her torturers, makes her body (like that of Eugene Dawn's goddess of *techne*) seem impenetrable and compels him to try to obliterate her image by dwelling upon its ugliness and featurelessness:

> Thick-headed and confused, angry too, I try to look into myself but see only a vortex and at the heart of the vortex oblivion. (47)[7]

It is the same blankness that obscures both the image of the barbarian girl as she was before the interrogations and the face of the hooded child in his dream.

Patrolling the threatened frontier between rational mind and intuitive self, he dreams again and sees that the child is building a fort of snow, a detailed replica of his own walled town, complete with the square in which he stands; but it is empty. He wants to say, "You must put people there", and immediately, as though she has heard, she turns her hooded face towards him. For a moment he is afraid of disappointment, but "no, she is herself, herself as I have never seen her, a smiling child, the light sparkling on her teeth and glancing from her jet-black eyes. 'So this is what it is to see!' I say to myself." (52) The recovery of the lost image of the barbarian girl as she once was, which is what this must surely signify, coincides with the appearance, face to face, of the smiling child in the dream, offering a glimpse of the reconciling vision of innocence which is the work of the mythic imagination. The dream itself encodes a message, an intuition of a need to fill the empty inner space and restore a vision of full humanity, though the dreamer fails to interpret it. Still puzzling over the unknown script of some former civilization, he misses his opportunity to learn from her the living language of the barbarians. Still unable to determine whether it is the fact of her stigmata or the image of her former wholeness that fascinates him (and doubtless hoping to revert to the familiar routine and myopic tranquillity of the past) he undertakes the perilous journey across the limits of Empire to return the barbarian girl to her own people and the world from whence she came.

This venture to the interior, officially announced as an expedition to restore goodwill, is construed by Joll as "treasonously consorting with the enemy". (77) He launches a punitive campaign against the barbarians and has the Magistrate placed in solitary confinement in the barracks hall, formerly used as the interrogation room where the girl had suffered her ordeal and her father had been provoked to the attack which led to his death. Here the Magistrate's mind begins to dwell shrinkingly upon the details of the scene, recognizing it as a paradigm of broken relationship and sensing its reference to a universal condition:

> Somewhere, always, a child is being beaten. I think of one who despite her age was still a child; who was brought in here and hurt before her father's eyes; who watched him being humiliated before her, and saw that he knew what she saw. (80)

116

Concentrating for hours on end on this figure of the father who knows he cannot protect the child he loves, he enters into a new and painful kind of knowledge, the father's "knowledge of condemnation". (80)[8] Together with this insight, the Magistrate's detention as an enemy of the state and the open declaration of hostility between Joll and himself precipitate a gradual collapse of ego defences as he learns what it is to suffer enforced solitude, to live in a body that is hungry, naked, unwashed, and damaged, to feel pain, to discover that escape into "freedom" means only starvation, and to undergo the ultimate *sparagmos*, or scattering of the self, covered in nothing but a woman's undergarment and made to endure a ridiculous parody of the archetypal death upon a tree. Now totally discredited, an "old clown" begging his food, regarded as too harmless to be kept a prisoner any longer, he wanders about the town, sensing the general failure of hope, the spreading conviction of living in a time of the end, that only the children do not share.

The dreams that accompany his experience of disintegration are of two kinds, the first being the phantasms of nightmare in which, for the first time, the crippled barbarian girl replaces the dream child in the square. She huddles in the dusty wind, showing her painful misshapen feet which grow into protean images of forgotten fears and griefs. The dreamer tries to comfort her, to carry her across the seemingly endless barracks yard. "There is no hope of reaching the other side, but I plod on carrying the girl, the only key I have to the labyrinth." (87) The other dream follows upon his public denunciation of Joll for "depraving the people" which is rewarded with the vicious hammer blow that injures his face. This time the girl is fully identified with the original dream child and has become a nurturing soul figure, as simple, stylized and reassuring as the other was ambiguous. With her empty snow fortress now metamorphosed into a clay oven and her hair braided in barbarian fashion beneath a gold-embroidered cap, she smiles and holds out to him a freshly baked loaf of bread. Capable at last of a spontaneous response to her creative love and generosity, he feels a surge of gratitude and opens his arms to embrace her. While the dream fades, he feels his saliva run and recognizes his own urgent need of nourishment. It seems significant that when, shortly after this, Joll forces him to interpret the unknown archaic script on the poplar slips in his archaeological collection, he "translates" them as letters from a father to a daughter.

As Joll's campaign against the barbarians fails and the garrison abandons the townsfolk to the imminent threat of invasion, the old civil servant takes up his responsibilities once more and prepares to withstand a siege, or at least to survive the coming winter. He takes stock both of depleted stores and of augmented self-knowledge. This knowledge is a "knowledge of condemnation", a recognition of the wrong turnings that have delivered him to the heart of the labyrinth. Above all, he remembers with shame the hypocrisy of his protection of the barbarian girl, seeing himself as a false seducer in whom envy, pity and cruelty have all masqueraded as desire, and acknowledging that she can never be restored to her former state, that his responsibility can never be discharged. In this way he approaches the awareness that he and the hated Joll are two sides of the same imperium of time-bound consciousness, a fallen world of ego-mastery where the principle of entropy implacably prevails. Indeed, one may agree that if Joll's fashionably darkened vision, breaking faith with the wisdom of the fathers and compelling the mysterious body of life, with instruments of torture, to declare its secrets, has depraved the people and defaced the human image, then the Magistrate's "lugubrious sensual pity" (135) has marred it by default. Brooding over its scars, forgetting the image of the lost original, he has corrupted the imagination, denied the freedom of the indwelling spirit, and betrayed the poet's vision of what Blake termed "the human form divine,/Love, Mercy, Pity, Peace." As Magda once complained, "There has been no transfiguration. What I long for, whatever it is, does not come."

Yet, her dream of a burning bush and his dream of a smiling child seem to promise otherwise and to assert their permanence in the timeless world of the mythopoetic imagination. In the last dream of the sequence, the dreamer, experiencing a new anxiety, a fear of harming the child as a fierce wind blows him towards her across the square, finds it dispelled by a momentary vision of her face, "the face of a child, glowing, healthy, smiling on me without alarm". (136) As winter sets in and the town becomes inured to the anxieties and deprivations of permanent crisis, the first fall of snow brings out children to play in the square and to build a snowman, not perfect, not even quite complete, but fully equipped with eyes, ears, nose and mouth, and the narrator feels an inexplicable joy at the sight. On another occasion he imagines the return of the barbarian girl, no longer hampered and half-blind, but riding at the head of a troop of horsemen as " a forerunner, a guide, pointing out to her comrades the lay of this foreign town where she once lived. Then, [it seems to him] everything will be on a new footing." (152) Like T S Eliot's Marina, restoring lost images of a first world, this daughter of the primitive muse brings a promise of regeneration and a reminder that in the world of mythic art the unreturning time of history yields to the recurrent cycle of the seasons and mundane reality is transfigured by the timeless vision of the dreaming imagination.

An analysis of this kind suggests that the horrifying pictures of war which govern Eugene Dawn's vision of hell have not only developed into a diagnostic metaphor of a spiritual sickness, endemic in our times, in which the manifest symptoms are separation from self, incomplete vision and acceptance of a violated image of life; they have also been allowed to grow into an allegory of the artist's task. In the midst of the medley of voices which communicate Jacobus Coetzee's rejection of the primordial self, Dawn/Coetzee's experience of the war of self, Magda's bitter knowledge of the rage and desolation of the excluded self, and the Magistrate's purgatorial recognition of failure to protect and unite with the intuitive self, one hears, too, the voice of the author who knows that language is itself a copula, alienating the world from the experiencing mind in the very act of seeking to grapple them together. What he seems to be discovering is that the artist who obeys the inborn images of dream and looks "through, not with the eye" may recapture something of the unfallen vision of the child within that irradiates and unifies the life of art. That Coetzee's monologues both symbolize and demonstrate the growth of this insight may be one measure of the seriousness of his literary vocation.

NOTES

1   Coetzee, J M *Dusklands* (Johannesburg: Ravan Press 1974), *In the Heart of the Country* (Johannesburg: Ravan Press 1978), *Waiting for the Barbarians* (Johannesburg: Ravan Press 1981). Page numbers in brackets refer to these editions.

2   In a poem in a letter to Thomas Butts, 22 November 1802. *The Writings of William Blake*, Volume 2, edited by Geoffrey Keynes, 3 Vols (London: 1925) p209. Coetzee's portrayal of alienated rationality is reminiscent of Blake's idea of "Single vision" by which he means the restricted ego-consciousness of the isolated individual who broods upon his own abstractions and loses all sense of an infinite and eternal reality perceived by the inward eye of the poetic imagination.

3   In the initial euphoria of his "freedom" Jacobus Coetzee exulted "like a young man whose mother has just died". (101)

4 Peter Wilhelm, whose writing often reflects a concern for psychologically damaged children, places an image of a similar type near the centre of his short story, "At the End of a War" in *At the End of a War* (Johannesburg: Ravan Press 1981).

5 "Only the eyes have power. . . . As the other senses grow numb or dumb my eyes flex and extend themselves." (*Dusklands*, 84)

6 Literally 'desolate plains'.

7 It appears that what Magda was able to remember of this "vortex", he has repressed.

8 It may be recalled that failure by a father-figure to protect a daughter is depicted in Jacobus Coetzee's account of the rape of the Hottentot child. (109)

Coetzee's Idylls:
The Ending of *In the Heart of the Country*

PETER STRAUSS

It must have been difficult for Coetzee to find an ending for *In the Heart of the Country*. Magda says at one point: "I want my story to have a beginning, a middle, and an end", (43)[1] and the novel enacts her failure. She makes beginning after beginning, she is constantly initiating action, but the consequences of her acts of freedom always have less to do with the acts themselves than with the trap she was in in the first place. It is one of the conventions of the novel that Coetzee's writing of Magda's story should be conflated at almost every point with Magda's living of it, and it is plain that her problem will repeat itself for him. Aristotle's ideal of a plot which is a whole in order to represent an action which is a whole depends on the ability to read events in that form -- a capacity which is given or subtracted by the historical moment and which the novelist, however wilful the games he believes he is playing, is powerless to fake successfully. Coetzee is kept from finding a straightforward end to his story by a philosophy of action — he takes Sartre's neo-Cartesianism as his starting-point — which is hyperconscious of beginnings and less confident about consequences. It is as though the concentration on the moment of choice, the bareness of that choice in such a scheme, makes it impossible to see the world as a place *containing* freedom, as opposed to a place in which acts of freedom are occasionally made; it is as though all the freedom were used up, as it were, in the initiation of action, to which the world is unable to give an adequate reply. Magda longs for the retribution which will turn her life into a story, but nothing happens which would make her existence that real — all that happens is that the same structures reassert themselves, possibly in shifted forms but never in forms which bear the trace of her action's meaning. Both Magda's story and the philosophy which Coetzee chooses as the basis of his novel's structure reflect the white South African's sense of impotence. There is nothing arbitrary about either.

Coetzee solves the problem of the ending by abandoning the narrative perspective which sees a situation in terms of time and action — he shifts to a different co-ordinate, as it were, adopting the voice and optic of the idyll, the perspective of the eternal present:

> There are poems, I am sure, about the heart that aches for Verlore Vlakte, about the melancholy of the sunset over the koppies, the sheep beginning to huddle against the first evening chill, the faraway boom of the windmill, the first chirrup of the first cricket, the last twitterings of the birds in the thorntrees, the stones of the farmhouse wall still holding the sun's warmth, the kitchen lamp glowing steady. They are poems I could write myself. It takes generations of life in the cities to drive that nostalgia for country ways from the heart. I will never live it down, nor do I want to. I am corrupted to the bone with the beauty of this forsaken world. If the truth be told, I never wanted to fly away with the sky-gods. My hope was always that they would descend and live with me here in paradise, making up with their ambrosial breath for all that I lost when the ghostly brown figures of the last people I knew crept away from me in the night. I have never felt myself to be another man's creature (here they come, how sweet the closing plangencies), I have uttered my life in my own voice throughout, what a consolation that is, I have chosen at every moment my own destiny, which is to die here in the petrified garden, behind locked gates, near my father's bones, in a space echoing with hymns I could have written but did not because (I thought) it was too easy. (138)

* * * * *

In *The Theory of the Novel* Lukacs defines the idyll as an illegitimate attempt to give narrative the quality of lyrical experience. "In lyric poetry, only the great moment exists, the moment at which the meaningful unity of nature and soul or their meaningful divorce, the necessary and affirmed loneliness of the soul, becomes eternal."[2] The idyll is the attempt to transfer this experience to the epic, to expand the lyrical moment to the world of events and actions. The peaceful glow which it casts over life is a 'purely artistic' solution; it involves looking at the world of men as though it were nature, and hiding the real conflicts and tensions, the actual discords between soul and world which rapidly make themselves felt in the realm of time and action. It is an attempt to invest the passage of time with the sensation of eternity which in our age can belong only to the rare moment. In short, it is a distortion of the epic mode and thus exacts a price — the price being that such a production is incapable of taking itself absolutely seriously.

Thus it makes sense to put the question whether the ending Coetzee found for *In the Heart of the Country* is a faked resolution. The passage itself confesses as much — "(here they come, how sweet the closing plangencies)" — but we need not leave it at that. Nor need we take the view that would undoubtedly be Lukacs's. For one thing — few of us having been able to remain as stubbornly Aristotelian as he was — we will get further with this novel by regarding it as an interfacing of writing modes than as the representation of an action. Moreover we are not dealing with a whole text which is an idyll, but with one that chooses the idyll as an element, and uses this mode at least half ironically.

On the other hand, Coetzee has not snatched the idyll out of the empty air, whether we accuse him of some sleight of hand or not. Looking at the ending we realize that this novel, which is so frenziedly concerned with the question of action, has been haunted with the presence of the idyll throughout. If we wish to understand what Coetzee is doing when the voice of his novel takes its last twist then we need to plot his siting of the idyll within the mental topology constructed by his novels.

From this particular passage we can see that for Coetzee the perspective of the idyll relates to time and change and action as poems (or hymns) do to narrative. Also that it can be used to reflect the dying away of action and of the struggle to construct meaning, into the self-directed irony — "what a consolation that is" — of impotence. That it is linked to nostalgia. That the woman who has made it a matter of pride to live her life as narrative treats the idyll with scorn, yet is at the last moment uncertain whether that exhausts the matter.

*　*　*　*　*

In the Afterword to the narrative of Jacobus Coetzee in *Dusklands*, a section which mimics to perfection the myth-building stream of South

African historiography, so that students frequently take it for real, there is a passage which is directly reminiscent of Magda's ending:

> Their huts of curved wattle branches have given way to mud houses with corrugated iron roofs made in Benoni. Yet even these are capable of picturesqueness: smoke drifting up from the wood-stove, pumpkins on the roof, the naked bottoms of children, etc. There is a principle of stability in history which refines from all conflicts those conformations likeliest to endure. The quiet farmhouse on the slopes, the quiet huts in the hollow, the starlit sky.[3]

Of course, there is a difference. The nostalgia of the ending of *In the Heart of the Country* is real, however bitterly felt to be an evasion by the voice that speaks it, whereas what we have here is a dishonest and self-flattering sentimentality. Would-be scientific phrases — "There is a principle of stability in history" — phrases which could have no substance even if that were seriously intended; talk of social configurations as though they were natural evolutionary growths; the combination of various appeals to the reader (the appeal to a wise, life-accepting tough-mindedness and the appeal to the sentimentality of the social father); the bland masking of the true relations of domination and subjugation under the 'neutrality' of a concept such as configurations — the passage leaks bad faith from all its edges.

Coetzee is dramatizing the availability of the idyllic vision as an ideological tool.

And in *In the Heart of the Country* we are made to feel how such ideological maskings are not at first the work of willing historians, that they are made in the first place by the way human beings register their society in their raw experience — in that the exchanges in Afrikaans between master and servant are blatantly explicit dramatizations of the master-slave relationship and its effects on the reality-sense of the participants[4] — and at the same time they are totally satisfying poems of nostalgia, with the eternal 'rightness' of litanies.

* * * * *

This sense of the treachery of the idyllic vision, whether nostalgic or utopian, will be one of the factors present in Coetzee's attitude when-

124

ever it is invoked. Yet the yearning is presented with such power — the descent of the gods to fill her world with their ambrosial breath is desired with such intensity by Magda, her feeling of exclusion is so painful to her — that it is given a certain dignity. It is an ever-present factor in human experience. In her case it cannot simply be equated with the weak-minded evasion of a mealy-mouthed historian;

> . . . for the comfort of my dark days, the consolation that keeps me from closing my eyes, folding my arms, and rocking myself forever into vacancy, is the knowledge that from me and from me only do these flowers draw the energy that enables them to commune with themselves, with each other, in their ecstasy of pure being, just as the stones and bushes of the veld hum with life, with such happiness that happiness is not the word, because I am here to set them vibrating with their own variety of material awareness that I am forever not they, and they not I, that I can never be the rapture of pure self that they are but am alas forever set off from them by the babble of words within me that fabricate and refabricate me as something else, something else. The farm, the desert, the whole world as far as the horizon is in an ecstasy of communion with itself, exalted by the vain urge of my consciousness to inhabit it. . . . Would that I had never learned to read. (48—49)

Now there are passages like this in Samuel Beckett, in *Watt* for instance. But there are differences. Watt's mild ecstasies (which he will be railing against furiously the next moment) are expressed in a lyrically cadenced style which is *seductive* in a way Magda's is not. The rapture of being presents itself as a *temptation* to Magda, which her pride as a representative of consciousness teaches her to resist, and which she knows could lead nowhere if pursued. From her point of view the appeal is treacherous, but she does not, as Beckett's characters do, project a sense of malicious deception onto the universe. For Beckett the dream of 'being' is merely a trick of the organism, just one more of the dirty tricks that are played on man, or that he plays on himself in spite of knowing better. It is true that Coetzee, too, has written the above passage in the form of a trap: it is Magda's consciousness which excludes her from 'being', but 'being', without her consciousness, would not be there at all, so it is doubly impossible. Yet the desire is a serious, crucial reality to her, not a contemptible distraction.

There are sets of polar oppositions in Coetzee's work which enable one to see various concepts or images as corresponding to each other. Here 'being', excluded by consciousness and language — in particular, the book — is the primeval paradise (though it must be remembered that in the last lines of the book it is described as a "petrified garden"); it is the kingdom of heaven which is easily available and yet, due to some freak of the human constitution, absolutely unattainable. As such it is comparable to the wilderness which the colonizer in *Dusklands* destroys, or rather excludes himself from even as he attempts to win it for himself. This exclusion, so the book suggests, was already pre-ordained in the colonizer's technology, and this technology already implied in the invention of the book, and that in writing, and that in language — to look at it that way, consciousness in itself is enough to exclude man from being. And, moreover, absolutely.

Yet this absolute division of consciousness and being is intertwined with a mode of thought where the dichotomy is relative. In *Dusklands* the Hottentots live psychologically in the wilderness, they live what the colonizer excludes himself from. Yet a second optic is introduced whereby the Hottentots are also conscious beings, so that they too are excluded. It is only the colonizer's conception of things (we think) which makes the Hottentot into the other, into the possible self who would not be excluded. Yet some reality must correspond to the distinction he feels, or why would the presence of the Hottentot act on him in so maddening a fashion? Perhaps it is a matter of degree. Perhaps the Hottentot, without measurement, without the book, without the gun, is *relatively* unalienated?

I suspect there is something logically indefensible about this way of thinking which mixes absolutes with relatives, and it certainly allows Coetzee to play a range of tricks on the reader, to shift his ground treacherously (and at times, I think, a little too neatly, too easily). But on the other hand this overlapping means that Coetzee's novels never become simple metaphysical games, detached from the concerns of ongoing life — political concerns, for instance. It means that his novels are not simply a critique of the human situation but a critique of western civilization.

These things work much more indirectly in Beckett, insofar as they work that way at all. There is a kind of gaiety in Beckett's petulance, the energy and gaiety of detachment, or unconcern — rather fey. The prison of hope shows itself to him only as a wispy, insubstantial distraction, like a fly buzzing round his head. That gaiety is not available to Coetzee, though he offers something different in its place. It is a matter of the fundamental set of the will: will to detachment or will to involvement. Beckett is easier to take than Coetzee.

* * * * *

The human world, as seen with the eyes of the idyll, presents itself as a vision of peace that is clear, simple, self-explanatory, visible. Yet it contains the element of the impossible, the inconceivable, which Magda situates in her world of stones and trees. It is a death-world, and near the end of *Waiting for the Barbarians* the old Magistrate rightly acknowledges his fantasies about slipping off to join the fisherfolk or the barbarians as reflecting a death-wish:

> The children never doubt that the great old trees in whose shade they play will stand forever, that one day they will grow to be strong like their fathers, fertile like their mothers, that they will live and prosper and raise their own children and grow old in the place where they were born. What has made it impossible for us to live in time like fish in water, like birds in air, like children? It is the fault of Empire! Empire has created the time of history. Empire has located its existence not in the smooth recurrent spinning time of the cycle of the seasons but in the jagged time of rise and fall, of beginning and end, of catastrophe. Empire dooms itself to live in history and plot against history. One thought alone preoccupies the submerged mind of Empire: how not to end, how not to die, how to prolong its era.[5]

Of course, on one level the Magistrate is simply a decent old man longing for peace. And of course any peace he could conceive of would still be an imperial peace. But the fact that he can recognize this and recognize its inadequacy is due to the element of the impossible, the inconceivable, making itself felt in the idyllic vision. The idyllic vision is an intuition of what lies outside the world which has been structured by the thought-patterns of a society. It enables the Magistrate to understand the nature of Empire as reasonable thinking could not have enabled him. It is a necessary tool of thought.

The basic mode of *In the Heart of the Country* — and of Coetzee's novels in general — is fundamentally opposite to that of the idyll. Yet the idyllic vision is present and the novelist maintains a careful responsibility towards it, as something able to imprison the mind as

127

nothing else can and also uniquely able to press a mind beyond itself, to press it to move outside its own strictures. And of course the idyllic permeates the whole book as an extremely austere lyricism, hidden inside Coetzee's extraordinary prose style, that style forever on its guard against itself. The idyllic, lyrical, is not the main focus of *In the Heart of the Country*, but it is an essential element. No wonder he lets us taste it, even if with bitter suspicion, at the moment the book closes.

NOTES

1   Coetzee, J M *In the Heart of the Country* (Johannesburg: Ravan 1978). Bracketed page references in the article are to this edition.
2   Lukacs, Georg *The Theory of the Novel* (London: Merlin Press 1971) p63.
3   Coetzee, J M *Dusklands* (Johannesburg: Ravan 1974) p123.
4   I am thinking in particular of the way the servant addresses the master or mistress in the third person, as for instance "die Mies" — as if to deny his own participation in the master's experience of subjectivity. But the very rhythm of the exchanges shares this exemplary quality: all formulae seem regulated by the degree to which the speaker is required to mask out aspects of himself.
5   Coetzee, J M *Waiting for the Barbarians* (London: Secker and Warburg 1980) p133.

Waiting for the Barbarians:
Two Sides of Imperial Rule
and Some Related Considerations

W J B WOOD

This novel joins J M Coetzee's previous two as part of an ongoing concern to exorcize the ghost of colonial and imperial consciousness. What distinguishes it from its predecessors is that it takes the liberal humanist position into account, for this is what the old Magistrate can be seen to represent. Coetzee presents the Magistrate's predicament in such a way as to make it profoundly moving and disturbing, especially to anyone with liberal humanist proclivities. Yet, cogent as the insights are into the consciousness of this master who serves Empire, I feel bound to question the central diagnostic proposition Coetzee offers us concerning him -- and it is one which the novel is very carefully intent on enforcing:

> I was not, as I like to think, the indulgent pleasure-loving opposite of the cold rigid Colonel. I was the lie that Empire tells itself when times are easy, he the truth that Empire tells when north winds blow. Two sides of imperial rule, no more, no less.[1]

As a strategy this can be accepted, but as diagnosis it deserves to be challenged. For exorcism of a more fundamental and far-reaching kind than that of imperial consciousness seems to me to be involved here — exorcism of the ghost of Descartes. The presence of the Magistrate in Coetzee's third novel extends the critical quest that begins with *Dusklands*,[2] but *Waiting for the Barbarians* also reveals the extent to which that quest is circumscribed.

A useful starting point from which to explore this line of inquiry is the one given us by Coetzee's title, which translates the title of one of Constantine Cavafy's finest poems and discloses their common ground. The reader is implicated in the imperial view of the 'threat' of barbarian invasion, only to be surprised and dislodged into new insight into the relation between these supposed antagonists. Either work would prevent an established conception of imperial civilization from ever being quite the same again. But it is the differences between these two writers, in stance and disposition, that interest me as much as the affinities. They both address their art to related socio-political contexts — and they span the African continent geographically and historically (deriving from the Alexandria of 1898, and from the Cape Town of 1980). This makes their corroborative testimony, exposing a long-standing conception of Empire, most striking. But to read Cavafy's poem in the context of the rest of his work is to realize that his ironies at the expense of Empire are those of a man who *is* "liberal and humanistic in his thought",[3] which, in fairness to Coetzee, we are hardly likely to accuse him of being!

The commitment and concern from which proceed these salient critical insights into the consciousness that is bound up with the politics of Empire are developed in Cavafy's poem *The Retinue of Dionysus*. It begins with a poetically charged evocation of a sculpture of the god and his retinue by a clearly gifted artist, then it proceeds to this conclusion:

> . . . And as he works
> his thoughts turn now and then
> to the fee he's going to receive
> from the king of Syracuse:
> three talents, a large sum.
> Adding this to what he has already,
> he'll live grandly, like a rich man,
> he'll even be able to enter politics
> — what a marvellous thought:
> he too in the Senate, he too in the Agora.[4]

The poised and pertinent irony of the close does not simply expose the sculptor for being in the fee (in both senses) of the king of Syracuse, and invite a superior contempt for such base and commercial motives. We should be struck by the fact that this artist proves a sell-out to the conception of power represented by the "marvellous thought" of public office and recognition. What, conceivably, can life offer that is greater and finer than this? — wonders the sculptor of a statue evoking

> . . . the god leading his retinue
> in divine glory, with power in his stride.

130

Against the sculptor's view, Dionysus represents a conception of power that proceeds from within, and which is not externally derived or dependent. He does not lead his retinue by exalting himself at their expense, by dominating in order to exploit. In the name of *this* conception of power, potent and creative, we are invited to contemplate capitulation to the conception of power that is possessive, self-assertive, materialistic and exploitative — all the attributes of power, in fact, that Coetzee ascribes to colonial aspiration and imperial decadence. Coetzee's art and insights, however, permit no such distinctions regarding power, and likewise preclude any such affirmation.

What seems to me to be at issue here is a reconception of how Mind is constituted, and a revaluation of the Body as a source and means to knowledge. Are Mind and Body interactive twin poles from which conjointly we derive our being, or are they to be accepted, in Cartesian fashion, as distinct and divided, with Mind reigning supreme in its control over the subjugated Body? The Cartesian legacy promotes the desire to master a world which has become the object of an all-contemplating Self. It is when life is consequently experienced as uncreative that the myth of Dionysus would seem to have something in particular to offer us.

It is one thing for a Greek-speaking white African poet, at the turn of the century, to invest the myth of Dionysus with this kind of significance, but the interest and relevance of the line I am taking is considerably strengthened and reinforced by the corroborative testimony of a living black African writer — and one whose intellectual and creative attainments are extensive and substantial — Wole Soyinka.

Empire, in Cavafy's poem, can be seen to have striking affinities with the condition of the kingdom of Pentheus in Soyinka's play *The Bacchae of Euripides*.[5] In both cases the state is ripe for insurrection; both writers perceive the threatened political crisis as subserving profound human need that has been neglected or suppressed, and both aim to dislodge traditional modes of perception and established values. Both recognize that the apparent threat from without is symptomatic of the source of the problem which lies within. Pentheus, as a man and as a ruler, is cast in the same mould as the imperial potentate who needs and desires to possess, to dominate, to exploit. For him, civilization means that society, like the self, must be well ordered and controlled — from above. The structures of state, as of consciousness, are hierarchical and oppressive. He sees himself as a reasonable, enlightened and just ruler, but exhibits intellectual pride, arrogance, inflexibility and symptoms of a passionate but repressed nature. The state, which in his eyes safeguards a just, cultivated and prosperous life, becomes increasingly experienced by the people as narrow and oppressive. What clearly has struck Soyinka about this Greek drama and its mythology is that it recognizes profound human imperatives that lie behind political discontent: economic exploitation of the peasants is not all that is at stake. More radically subversive for Pentheus is the resurgence of the cult of Dionysus.

The advent of this godhead is not the external threat to law and order that Pentheus insists it is — the work of anarchists and infiltrators, given over to barbarities, licentiousness, perversion and irrationality. It is up to Pentheus whether or not the god need appear. He does not come because he wants to; he can only appear in response to sufficient need. But Pentheus is bound by fears which he fails to confront, and so he is shown to be responsible himself for precipitating precisely what he most dreads. What he fears, and fails to value, is the Body. A liberating insurrection becomes necessary; Pentheus becomes the sacrificial victim who fulfils the very ritual and prophecy that he wilfully opposed and denied. The god comes again in Cavafy's poetry, again in Soyinka's play. These are writers who resist the wedge driven between Mind and Body by reconceiving how they relate. They do not capitulate, as does Coetzee, to the intellectual imperatives, or the logic, implicit in *Cogito ergo sum*.

* * * * *

In Coetzee's novel, the barbarians are actually encountered: sought first by the Magistrate as the culmination to his relationship with the tortured barbarian girl, and then by Colonel Joll's forces intent on their crushing defeat. In some important respects, barbarians are found to be humanly better equipped than their 'civilized' imperial counterparts. They are self-possessed, in a very literal and positive sense — not self-divided nor in bondage to mind-forged manacles. They suffer neither the self-doubt of the Magistrate, nor are they prey to the self-assertive compulsions of a Colonel Joll.

In this way the barbarians serve to reveal not what is inimical to Empire so much as what ails it: in misconceiving the barbarians, Empire misconceives its own nature and condition — which must doom it to the disaster course it so much dreads. *Dusklands*, in its suggestive network of connected contexts, offers just such an analysis in terms of a colonial past and neo-colonial present. Colonel Joll can clearly count

Jacobus Coetzee among his forbears. But what are we to make of the old Magistrate in the light of this analysis? He poses questions which Coetzee's two preceding novels do not undertake to answer — does he suffer from the "malady of the master" as well?

In *Dusklands*, the "malady of the master" is that he asserts power and authority over those who are subject to him, not as he supposes, for their sakes so much as for his own: without someone to assert power over, and without some externally derived means of doing this (a gun, a system of technology, a certain socio-political structure), the master has virtually no Self to assert, no power, no authority. This truth compels him to assert himself and his power most desperately and destructively if confronted by his true nature and position. If we accept this analysis, we can certainly see that Colonel Joll, his understudy Mandel, and the regime they serve are evidence of this malady in a severe form. We must surely also recognize that the Magistrate's fundamentally different temperament and impulses constitute resistant immunities, and that it is precisely for want of these that Colonel Joll is susceptible to this malady. (The Magistrate survives; the Colonel finally cannot hope to.) In the very terms of this analysis the Magistrate must be seen as 'other' and contrary to the Colonel rather than allied to him. The effect the Magistrate finally has on Mandel and Colonel Joll is significantly analogous to that which the Vietnamese have on U S strategy (the testimony of Eugene Dawn), the Namaqua on Jacobus Coetzee — the barbarians on Empire. It is the effect that only a difference in kind, not merely in form or degree, can account for.

At the very outset we can find evidence to challenge what the novel seems intent on preparing us for. The Magistrate is nonplussed by the Colonel's sun-glasses, something he has never before seen, but is perceptive in gauging their significance. He notes that they are not removed indoors — they are not worn simply for the practical reasons given by the Colonel: they satisfy the Colonel's vanity and reveal the store he sets by youthful appearance. The manner in which the Colonel seeks to impress the Magistrate speaks of his need to reassure himself; the Magistrate does not need to cut a figure for his own or the Colonel's sake. The Colonel is not literally blind (the first thought to cross the Magistrate's mind) but figuratively speaking, particularly beside the Magistrate, he is. He treats the Magistrate as an object at his disposal. But we find that the Magistrate, on the contrary, does not regard the Colonel in this way: his impulses reach out, he is prepared to be open to what is different and other. He stands in relation to the world beyond the Self on terms altogether different from those of the Colonel. He has

133

the inclination to perceive more than merely what he needs and wants. We find him accordingly endeavouring to engage with the Self behind the mask the Colonel offers him — but this mask is one which the Colonel cannot afford to drop. In fact he might be said to be trapped behind it, which again is not the Magistrate's case. Their exchange about hunting is revealing: the memorable hunt for the Colonel is one which yielded "a mountain of carcases [that] had to be left to rot." (The Colonel's aside, "Which was a pity", can only mean he regrets that the meat could not be turned to more profitable account.) But for the Magistrate, the insights and the excitement afforded by a nocturnal fishing expedition with the native folk "is an experience not to be missed." (1)

The moment the Colonel sets to work on the two prisoners, the old man and the boy, the Magistrate senses the uneasy and problematic nature of his predicament. The point is quickly reached where, as the Magistrate says, "I grow conscious that I am pleading for them" (4); and, more disturbingly still, "I begin to plead my own cause." (5) Required by his office to support the Colonel, he is by nature humane and must therefore deny his nature or the Colonel's authority. In the Colonel's eyes the Magistrate is not defending people; he is defending barbarians. We note the terms in which he attempts to explain to the prisoners and justify to himself the Colonel's actions: "His work is to find out the truth." (3) The Colonel supposes this to be true, but the real truth begins now to dawn on the Magistrate. He begins to subject himself, as much as the Colonel and the Empire which they serve, to critical scrutiny.

The tension between Self and Office engenders in the Magistrate profound doubt about both, as we are to see from now onwards. Throughout this period of crisis he becomes incapacitated in both the public and personal areas of his life. Yet finally we are also to see that he manages, at extremely painful physical and psychological cost, to resolve his dilemma and recover a measure of self-possession.

But this begins to move beyond the more overt concerns of the novel: the course the novel intends to chart is clear enough — the Magistrate is not a man apart from his socio-political context as he might suppose or his mode of life might suggest. What might appear to distinguish him from the Colonel, we are meant to realize, is of minor account beside what they share. The point gets reinforced as we find the Magistrate's own conscious thoughts tending this way: attending to the tortured and terrified boy, the now self-doubting Magistrate finds this thought surfacing in his mind: "It has not escaped me that an interrogator can wear two masks, speak with two voices, one harsh, one seductive." (7) That the reader is being pointed in the direction of the two sides to imperial rule is obvious enough. Yet to me this idea seems to consort awkwardly with the particular human context given. From the boy's perspective the Magistrate may indeed be seen in this light. He has not the opportunity which, for instance, the barbarian girl is to have, to perceive that the Magistrate's attitude is different. If, however, we are not content to look upon the Magistrate (or the human possibility to which the character points) with an external and objectifying eye, we cannot be satisfied to find in him simply another version of the Colonel. Adequate perception and understanding must surely depend upon inter-subjective relatedness and responsiveness — the very thing we see the Magistrate prepared to attempt and the Colonel always intent on avoiding. Coetzee's refusal to concede the possibility of the mutual responsiveness of two subjects, his insistence that the Self can only ever make objects of the selves in the world beyond it, has striking affinities with Sartre's analysis of how selves relate.[6] And it is this affinity that has led me to think that Coetzee's work is testimony not so much to a truth about Empire and the legacy of imperial consciousness, as to the legacy in alienation that is our Cartesian inheritance.

I hope it is clear that I do not regard Coetzee's critique as untrue: it is part of the truth, but offered as a whole and satisfactory truth, it will not do. That his art should itself suggest why, is a measure of its distinction. Where Coetzee would seem concerned to stress, as in the scene referred to above, that in the Magistrate we have no real alternative to the Colonel, there is evidence in support of a divergent view. The Magistrate responds humanely to the boy, whom *he* regards as a *subject* whose suffering and fears affect him; he therefore attempts to do what little he can to alleviate them. His stance allies him increasingly with the *enemy* of Empire. This is to say that, although a liberal humanitarian may, through insufficient awareness (or innocence), acquiesce in a role of complicity with a regime represented by a Colonel Joll, he can nevertheless constitute as real a threat in his own way to such a regime as the barbarians can in theirs. They *both* precipitate a similar response from the regime, a response having similar significance in either case. The Colonel and his like are as blank about the barbarians and the threat they pose (they naively suppose them easy prey) as they are about the Magistrate and the qualities he possesses (to them he is a negligible and contemptible relic from the past); but there is no need for the reader to adopt their view in either case. Indeed, the Magistrate can be said to represent something in that past which ensures him a part in a future denied to the Colonel and Mandel.

Addressing Mandel, the Magistrate presses home:

> Forgive me if the question seems impudent, but I would like to ask: How do you find it possible to eat afterwards, after you have been . . . working with people? . . . I am trying to imagine how you breathe and eat and live from day to day. But I cannot! That is what troubles me! . . . He wrenches himself free and hits me so hard in the chest that I gasp and stumble backwards. "You bastard!" he shouts. "You fucking old lunatic! Get out! Go and die somewhere!" (126)

Neither Mandel's nor the Colonel's kind of power has any defence here. When the Colonel faces the Magistrate for the last time, caged behind the glass of his official imperial carriage, he is in retreat from the barbarians, the frontier-folk, and the Magistrate's gaze. Can we really regard the Magistrate as liable to a similar fate? Even within the confines of his context, the Magistrate struggles with himself, his manhood, his office, and all that he is subjected to — if he is resistant to anything, it is to settling for such security, comfort and power as the Colonel's undeviating stance would otherwise offer him. His struggle concerns changes in self-awareness. However we may qualify such headway as he makes, the struggle that he sets up, and is set up in him, testifies to a capacity for life that is creative rather than exploitative.

But the lack of fuller progress in the character is also meant by Coetzee to reveal that the Magistrate is as "infected" as the Colonel. My own view diverges to the extent of saying that the Magistrate deserves to be regarded as a *truth*-loving opposite to the Colonel, who epitomizes the denial of truth and creatively continuing life. Indeed I think you could say of the Magistrate as was said of the barbarians, that he, too, constitutes "a kind of solution"!

* * * * *

My case, and Coetzee's, can rest upon a look at a key passage that occurs just before the proposition concerning the "two sides of imperial rule". Let me give it fairly fully:

136

I wander down the wide road down to the lakeside. The horizon ahead is already grey, merging into the grey water of the lake. Behind me the sun is setting in streaks of gold and crimson. From the ditches comes the first cricketsong. This is a world I know and love and do not want to leave. I have walked this road by night since my youth and come to no harm. How can I believe that the night is full of the flitting shadows of barbarians? . . .

I pass the ruined fields, cleared by now and ploughed afresh, cross the irrigation ditches and the shore-wall. The ground beneath my soles grows soft; soon I am walking on soggy marshgrass, pushing my way through reedbrakes, striding ankle-deep in water in the last violet light of dusk. Frogs plop into the water before me; nearby I hear a faint rustle of feathers as a marshbird crouches ready to fly.

I wade deeper, parting the reeds with my hands, feeling the cool slime between my toes; the water, holding the warmth of the sun longer than the air, resists, then gives way, before each stride. In the early hours of the morning the fishermen pole their flat-bottomed boats out across this calm surface and cast their nets. What a peaceful way to make a living! Perhaps I should leave off my beggar's trade and join them. . . .

Calf-deep in the soothing water I indulge myself in this wistful vision. I am not unaware of what such daydreams signify, dreams of becoming an unthinking savage. . . . Without exception they are dreams of ends: Dreams not of how to live but of how to die. . . . What has made it impossible for us to live in time like fish in water, like birds in air, like children? It is the fault of Empire! Empire has created the time of history. Empire has located its existence not in the smooth recurrent spinning time of the cycle of the seasons but in the jagged time of rise and fall, of beginning and end, of catastrophe. Empire dooms itself to live in history and plot against history. One thought alone preoccupies the submerged mind of Empire: how not to end, how not to die, how to prolong its era. . . . A mad vision yet a virulent one: I, wading in the ooze, am no less infected with it than the faithful Colonel Joll. . . . (132—133)

The Magistrate's state of mind is self-critical, self-disparaging, inconclusive in its grasp of what his experience means. His attempts to think about it are to conclude: "I think: 'There has been something staring me in the face, and still I do not see it.'" (155) What this self-deprecation really derives from is the author's view of his creation. For Coetzee, the Magistrate's failure to distil from his experience an adequately conscious grasp upon it in the Mind, means that he (a caveat for the reader!) is trapped where we find him at the end — "feeling stupid, like a man who lost his way long ago but presses on along a road that may lead nowhere." (156) We may recall here a thought dropped like a pebble into the pool of the Magistrate's mind by the author with no apparent effect there — the ripples are meant, however, to wash up something on the shores of the reader's consciousness:

> '... perhaps it is the case that only that which has not been articulated has to be lived through.' I stare at this last proposition without detecting any answering movement in myself toward assent or dissent. (65)

There is a point to be taken here; but need it be taken at the expense of a figure who fails not for want of trying? Above all, need it be taken at the expense of non-conscious responsiveness to life, the knowledge and experience in the Body which feeds the Mind? We are meant to find, in the passage cited, that associated with this incapacity in the Mind is an unfortunate susceptibility in the Body: a capitulation to feeling and sensation made to seem regressive, debilitating, futile, and responsible for trapping the Magistrate where he is left. "Pleasure-loving" is what he is made to convict himself of being. Coetzee's culminating indictment of the Magistrate is that he indulges in wish-fulfilling dreams: "Without exception they are dreams of ends; dreams not of how to live but of how to die." He, as much as the Colonel, stands convicted of resisting the changes necessary to life's creative continuation. The Colonel is dedicated to rigid perpetuation of Self in service of an Empire whose motto could be "eternal dominion". Empire's vision is "mad" because it is uncreative, anti-creative. Similarly, the Magistrate's is a pathetic and hopeless case. Thus Coetzee.

The solemnity of this somewhat puritanical judgement on the Magistrate that we are invited to share astonishes me. But it helps us to locate a dilemma in which Coetzee places himself. Accepting entirely as I do the assumptions here about the necessity of creativity and the attendant judgements on the Colonel and his regime, I find that Coetzee takes a stance that denies the way out of the impasse which he rightly diagnoses. And at the root of the trouble is what prompts this sort of thing: "I, wading in the ooze, am no less infected . . . ." This image is meant to colour our response and betray him to us; surely something in his creator seems to be betrayed instead. The image is meant to highlight the regressive nature of the character's sensuous susceptibility to experience. (How incessantly, in Coetzee's work, the experience in the Body becomes a source of feelings of pain or disgust, can hardly go without remark.) But surely this sensuous susceptibility *cannot* be viewed in this light? Without it, the Magistrate would not have been responsive to the suffering of the two prisoners in the first place, nor moved to pick up that lantern; unthinking feelings were what prevented him from putting it down once it began to shed some light on a truth hitherto unsuspected by him — these are not the responses and reactions of an essentially self-indulgent person resistant to being carried beyond the bounds of what is known and pleasantly possessed.

The responsiveness of the Magistrate to the natural world around the lakeside is love, and knowledge, of a world beyond the Self. The same is true of his responsiveness to the excitement of the native fishing expedition: it is to a mode of life that is different, other, beyond the bounds of the known self. When the Magistrate recalls with affectionate nostalgia his past and his youth (and we note no bitterness or resentment when he contemplates the children; whereas we recall the Colonel's concern to preserve his youthful appearance), he is not trying to preserve the Self against all odds. He clearly experiences his age in a continuum with his youth. Some reluctance must, quite naturally and healthily, be felt when contemplating a happy youth that now is past — I can see nothing pathological in this! -- but the point here is that we find that the Magistrate *still* takes pleasure in that landscape: the present pleasure in the walk recalls the fact that he has *always* loved the place he has grown up in. To know and love this world is not to be a victim of self-centred love that is a spurious construct of the Mind. And such love and such knowledge come from the Body.

But, and I take up the final point in the passage, such experience is momentary, true enough. The question is, do we confine ourselves solely to a sequential time-scale? A related question is, to what extent have we the capacity to live (in a full and intense sense) in the present? It is through the conscious Mind that we know time as sequence — that we are located in historical time; through the Body we know time in the present, which in a sense is the time experienced by fishes, birds and children. Coetzee would seem to embrace the position that plays one conception off against the other; yet surely we live, and know, by virtue of both, and should therefore think accordingly? Herein lies the significance of the Magistrate's capacity to live in the present — a capacity that has to do with the sensuous susceptibility Coetzee wants us to disparage and deplore. Herein lies the only possibility, so far as I

139

can see, of experiencing life in terms *other* than those which can fatally enclose man — yet this possibility is precisely what the novel wants to warn us against.

The tension that I have shown to exist between Coetzee's art and his more conscious intention is evidence that it is not only Empire or colonial consciousness that is divided against itself in such crucially important respects. This is why I began by submitting that perhaps a ghost other than that of Empire needed exorcizing. In his time Descartes's thought was a liberating factor in an intellectually stultifying climate, but the kind of power he released and the possibilities he may be said to have opened up, have brought with them consequences that, in turn, engender the kind of impasse to which this novel testifies. The kind of reconception and revaluation necessary to dislodge the limits set by a Cartesian legacy would therefore seem to me to be along the lines indicated in Cavafy's poetry, or Soyinka's work, rather than in Coetzee's. Nevertheless, *Waiting for the Barbarians* must be recognized as raising profoundly challenging issues — as stimulating for its diagnostic thrust as for its revealingly symptomatic testimony.

NOTES

1   Coetzee, J M *Waiting for the Barbarians* (Johannesburg: Ravan Press 1981) p135. All bracketed page references are to this edition.
2   Coetzee, J M *Dusklands* (Johannesburg: Ravan Press 1974).
3   Cafavy, C P *Complete Poems*, translated by Rae Dalven (London: Chatto and Windus 1968) 18—19.
4   Cafavy, C P *Collected Poems*, translated by Edmund Keeley and Philip Sherrard, edited by George Savidis (London: Chatto and Windus 1978) 19.
5   Soyinka, Wole *Collected Plays 1* (Oxford: Oxford University Press 1977).
6   See Wood, W J B "*Dusklands* and 'the impregnable stronghold of the intellect'" *Theoria* 54 (May 1980) 13—23.

Tamar and After:
A Glance at Dan Jacobson's Recent Work

SHEILA ROBERTS

Dan Jacobson claims that in his career as a writer he has gone round the course twice, implying that he has been defined and has seen himself as, first, a South African writer, but then has become merely a writer, unclassifiable, or regarded broadly as British.[1] His early novels and short stories, up to and including *The Beginners* (1967), were all set in South Africa or were about South Africans. But *The Rape of Tamar*, appearing in 1970,[2] certainly seemed to point to a new direction for Jacobson's talent. Yet while I would not want to challenge the author's own assertion that with the composition of *Tamar* he moved away from being a South African writer, I would like to point to preoccupations in *Tamar* and in Jacobson's later work that seem to me to derive from political insight and from a way of perceiving that have been moulded by South Africa.

Of course the biblical story of Tamar's rape by her brother Amnon is curious enough to arouse the interest of any story-teller. Although the whole of 2 Samuel 13[3] is devoted to the story of the rape and its aftermath, the narration is ambiguous and incomplete, the most mysterious part being David's decision not to punish Amnon according to the dictates of the law for his offence against Tamar — the king's only legitimate daughter and his favourite child.

Other inexplicable facets of the biblical story are why, following the rape, Amnon turns against Tamar with hatred and throws her out of doors;[4] why Tamar goes to her brother Absalom for redress instead of to her father; and why Absalom takes two years before deciding on revenging the harm done to his sister. Then there is the inscrutable biblical narrator, Yonadab, friend to both Amnon and Absalom, a figure that must have appealed immediately to Dan Jacobson in its suggestion of subterfuge, voyeurism and devil's-advocacy. In *The Rape of Tamar* he becomes another in the long line of observers, always

141

vaguely guilty, in Jacobson's work: the unnamed narrator in *A Dance in the Sun*, Michael in the short story *Beggar My Neighbour*, and Timothy Fogel of *The Wonder-Worker* whose passion for observation creates in him a desire to become that which is observed.

Yonadab is observer, gluttonous for intimate information, and thereby betrayer. He is first-cousin to Timothy Fogel and brother to Josef Baisz, protagonist of *The Confessions of Josef Baisz* (1977).[5]

Apart from the several mysterious elements in the story of Tamar's rape, elements that taxed Jacobson's ingenuity as novelist, there is the presence of David in the background, a king who looms large and very powerfully. It is in the matter of David's ploys for power that I see *The Rape of Tamar* as relating to Jacobson's previous South African work and his later, ostensibly un-South African, writing. All of Jacobson's fiction (with the possible exception of *The Beginners*) examines the nature of power and powerlessness. In fact, I don't think it is too wide a generalisation to say that all South African fiction of any seriousness deals explicitly with those states. The possession of power, its use and misuse, has been the tormented interest of writers from Schreiner through to Coetzee: it is the sole preoccupation of all black writers.

Only a writer fascinated by power ploys, as Jacobson has been, could have detected the buried political significance in the Bible story and introduced these subtly and ironically in a reconstruction of Yonadab's narration. As Jacobson knew, David was a man in a vulnerable position. His uneasily united Israel and Judea was a provincial country, tiny in relation to the empires and metropolitan powers of the time. David's kingdom was still in the process of building a foundation from which to define itself. In *Tamar*, Yonadab says:

> . . . The kingdom itself has only been recently established, and therefore has not long been in a position to buy, pillage, or receive as tribute the treasures of its more sophisticated neighbours and predecessors. But we have done our best, and anything you may see of value and fine workmanship inside our houses, in any material from wood to gold, or from earthenware to lapis lazuli, is likely to be not 'ours' at all. All we have that we can really call our own are legends, tall stories, grandiose claims . . . . (14)

In writing the description Jacobson puts in Yonadab's mouth, was he not perhaps prompted by a sardonic awareness of the provincial country he himself was born in? On the one hand South Africa defines itself, as it has done for over three hundred years, in relation to the cultures of Britain and Europe, a self-definition that results in a comparable self-deprecatory stance in which nothing local has any value — only the imported product has worth. On the other hand, it has striven to recreate itself, especially since 1961, and to redefine itself according to its perception of itself as a white western African country with mores, laws, monuments, rituals, legends and tall stories, all strictly its own.

In David, Jacobson creates a man of cunning, one whose intelligence is sharpened to an understanding of his people and exercised in establishing not only the outward appearance of his capital city but also his kingly presence, the activities of his throne room, and the business of state. We see him slowly fashioning what he, in time, will be able to call his own. But the mere fact of conscious creation establishes a studied, artificial quality to David's behaviour. He stage-manages the day-to-day enactment of government and manipulates the tone and mood of state functions. After days of smooth, undisturbed business, David will engineer a disruption, an outburst of rage, or an unexpected announcement. Thus the effect of a possible 'show' on other more peaceful days is made so much more compelling for participants and onlookers alike.

The pre-arranged insecurity of his officers, courtiers, and subjects is one manifestation of David's determination to maintain and assert power. Another is his insistence on his sons' submission to him, not singly, but as a group, a group that derives its being and welfare from him:

> ... he made a point of being unfailingly generous towards them, [Yonadab explains] giving them houses, farmlands, flocks, servants, women, titles, everything they asked for. Except power. Except the satisfaction of knowing where they stood with him. Except freedom from his insatiable demand for love and admiration. (18)

(Again, I can't help wondering whether Jacobson was subconsciously nagged by his experience of the years of Malan and Verwoerd, the growth of *onse mense*[6] into the business world, the strong message being conveyed to all *boereseuns*[7] that loyalty to the State equalled patriotism.)

Moreover, instead of dividing his sons and thus ruling them, David shrewdly calls most persistently for their loyalty to one another. He understands that, forced together under the cloak of love for one another and for their father, they will neither achieve the singlehood, each, to challenge him, nor be capable of tolerating any challenge to

143

his power from another.

Jacobson's portrayal of David's character explains the biblically inexplicable reaction on his part to Tamar's rape. In the novel he refuses to subject Amnon to due process of law and he ignores and leaves unpunished Absalom's angry, seditious talk in the throne room the morning after the attack on Tamar. David's passivity makes Absalom's indignation look suspect (as things already stand, Tamar's turning to Absalom for defence has placed her beyond the pale: her action acknowledges power in Absalom). By not punishing Amnon, David reduces that son to a pitiable, guilt-ridden drunkard hardly worth the revenge Absalom takes on him some years later and literally allows Absalom enough rope to hang himself, in due course.

Seeing through Yonadab's eyes, we come to realize that David's rule is based neither on piety nor morality, but that he "rides upon the very crest of that tidal equipoise between the violence of law and the violence of lawlessness. . . ." (124) This very sentence brings to mind the action of the police against Willem of Driehoek in *The Trap*, the routing of a political rally in *The Beginners*, and the tactics of the Compresecor in *The Confessions of Josef Baisz*. David's faith in his own ability to manipulate, his use or non-use of the law according to his whim, his clever employment of subterfuge (more than subterfuge at times as he is capable of believing in all sincerity in his own deceptions) render him unpredictable, wily, protean and, therefore, unfailingly dominant. David responds to each situation unpredictably because each situation is new, unprecedented, and he is in the process of creating himself as king and unifying a contentious people. The reader has to admire David, is certainly fascinated by him, and even at times pities him for the stupidity of his children.

If Jacobson could see similarities to the South Africa he grew up in in David's new nation, then the Sarmeda of *The Confessions of Josef Baisz* is a hideous and blackly comic representation of the country as it is now with intimations of how the violence of governmental lawlessness will become so commonplace as to appear undramatic: in fact, it is possible that the undramatic flatness of too-frequent, too-familiar political harassment and killings is with us already.

In *Josef Baisz* power ploys become the expression of diseased egos jostling for position, and Josef Baisz — mistakenly comparing himself to Judas — betrays everyone he knows, not out of political conviction (which is, arguably, the motive behind David's actions) but out of addiction to the sweet emotion of tenderness he enjoys prior to each act of treachery.

144

In spite of the distaste felt by the reader for the Iago-like Yonadab in *The Rape of Tamar*, he is left with a reluctant acceptance of the idea that, yes, the ends do sometimes justify the means: against a Yonadab there is a David. Yonadab enjoys playing off Amnon against Absalom; he encourages Amnon to rape his sister, then, years later, induces him to meet with Absalom at Boalhazar, knowing that Absalom plans to kill him. Yonadab is by nature a traitor, like Josef Baisz, but his miserable (even if highly complex, twentieth-century) inhumanity is seen against David's presence, his grandeur, his political acumen. In any case, the reader does not have to accept Yonadab as a reliable narrator. (To digress for a moment, I would point to the strong self-reflexive structures of *Tamar*, *The Wonder-Worker* and *Josef Baisz*, a characteristic that undermines very much what I am doing, that is, discussing these novels as if they were works of realism.)

In *Josef Baisz* we are allowed no contrasts between behaviour that is bad but justified and behaviour that is gratuitously and shabbily evil. This later book is infinitely more pessimistic than Jacobson's previous work. In the capital city of Bailaburg, a kind of Pretoria-sur-Volga, each high-placed person spies on the other, and the faceless masses — not to mention the defeated and oppressed Kuni tribesmen — are kept in submission and in entertainment by regular "emergencies" and purges. Children are against parents, brother against sister, husband against wife, and dissidents are sent to Volmaran Island for "rehabilitation". Josef Baisz marries the widow of the man whose suicide he helps bring about, relishing the situation of fear and masochistic attraction that keeps his wife in perpetual polarization against him. The country of Sarmeda is horrible. Its deathly, dreamlike nullity arises out of the destruction of all justice and decency.

A reader might argue that Sarmeda was not intended by the author to represent South Africa. But the names (comically spelt) are all too familiar: Josef grew up in a place called Vliss, people vacation on the Grand Lecke Lake, the Kuni tribesmen drive their herds up the Middelbergen, there is an actress named Dafne Mainckies, and Josef works for a man named Trichardt Serle and sleeps with his wife, a Gita 'S Koudenhoof. The landscapes described in the book are all familiar and there is mention of tension between the older families of the south and the younger breed from the north.

Jacobson's projections for our future are disgusting and yet plausible. If people once believed in the 'Manifest Destiny' of the Afrikaner, it is hard to believe that any still do — except for a few conservative churchmen withdrawn from reality. The very political splintering we witness now is evidence against any such idealism or even laagerism. We've been regaled with Rhoodiegates and Muldergates, and allegations of state presidents salting away funds in Swiss bank accounts, and although our government might not yet be calling itself a "Phalanx of Democratic Control", as in *Josef Baisz*, the presence of military people in political positions and the burgeoning of glamorous uniforms, not to mention the increasing number of military functions (and funerals), seem more than ominous.

Some people say that when South African writers leave, or go into exile (interesting word!) they stop writing because of the distance in time and space between themselves and the source of their imagination. Jacobson's work certainly challenges the value of this warning. As far as I understand, *The Confessions of Josef Baisz* was entirely ignored in this country when it came out; it was hardly reviewed at all. This is a pity. I hope because of what looks like a growing interest on the part of South Africans in their own literature that his future work gets the attention it deserves, and that his acute political insight can jolt us out of familiarity with lies, spies, and treachery.

NOTES

1   This opinion and any others attributed to the author in this paper were related to me during an interview with Jacobson in London in 1980.
2   Jacobson, Dan *The Rape of Tamar* (London: Weidenfeld and Nicholson 1970). All page references are to this edition.
3   In the King James and New English Bibles. In the Rheims-Douay version, Tamar's story comes in 2 Kings 13.
4   Male disgust at female sexuality is an element in Jacobson's work waiting for some feminist critic to explore.
5   Jacobson, Dan *The Confessions of Joseph Baisz* (London: Secker and Warburg 1977).
6   Literally 'our people'; a phrase used to promote Afrikaner nationalism.
7   Equivalent to 'sons of the land'.

146

A Break in the Silence:
The Long Journey of Poppie Nongena

In the introductory essay to her book *Silences* Tillie Olsen writes of

> ... the silences where the lives never came to writing. Among
> these, the mute inglorious Miltons: those whose waking hours
> are all struggle for existence; the barely educated; the illiterate;
> women. Their silence the silence of centuries as to how life was, is
> for most of humanity.[1]

Olsen believes that those who cannot protest against oppression or
make others aware of their suffering will continue to suffer. In particular, she wishes to persuade her readers that the silences of women
conceal vital areas of life. In *The Long Journey of Poppie Nongena*[2]
Elsa Joubert, a professional writer, sympathetic to the plight of a
fellow woman who is black, and moved by her inability to make it
known to the public, has tried to help her break her silence. Joubert
has supplied Poppie with a literary 'voice' which can be heard by the
world, and perhaps especially by speakers of the two official languages
of South Africa. Power to relieve the sufferings of Poppie and of all
other women in her position resides at present with the white speakers
of these groups: society in South Africa is what it is because most
whites remain ignorant of and indifferent to the patterns of black
lives. One of the strongest suggestions implicit in the book is that
it is because women like Poppie cannot speak to the world, indeed,
often cannot plead their cause effectively before the minor officials
who are their immediate oppressors, that they continue to suffer
injustice.[3]

On Boxing Day 1976, when Poppie Nongena, alone and desperate
after the riots and the police repression which followed them, came
to Joubert's house to talk, Joubert realised she had found the woman

147

who could speak for the black women of the Cape, and had begun to understand that her own role would be that of "a tape-recorder, a mouthpiece", as she was later to say.[4]

It may be asked why, in a book committed to telling the lifestory of a black woman in her own words, the most frequently occurring narrative mode is that of an unidentified narrator who is not involved in the action. In their article, "Over de vertel situatie in *Die Swerfjare van Poppie Nongena*",[5] Irene Janssen, Truida Lijphart and Barbara van Ijzeren point out that this unidentified narrator tells most of the story. Poppie frequently takes up the story in her own words, and members of her family, mainly her brother Mosie and her mother, intervene occasionally. Dramatic presentation of episodes, where Poppie, her family and their friends are shown in speech and action, forms an important part of the unidentified narrator's account. The *Standpunte* article draws the reader's attention to the contradictory characteristics of the book's narrative modes: Poppie's and Mosie's narrative is clearly offered to an outsider, since there is much explanation of Xhosa customs as well as of family habits, yet the unidentified narrator uses the same dialect and modes of address (buti Plank, Mama, tata-ka-Bonsile) as Poppie does. Elsa Joubert's explanation of this originally appeared in *Volksblad* of 11 April 1979 and is quoted in the *Standpunte* article: she first tried to make the book entirely from the transcribed recordings of Poppie and her family, but found that these, unedited and unsummarised, were monotonous, and lacked the necessary emphases which would allow the reader to distinguish pattern and development. An omniscient third person narrator's version was even more unsatisfactory, because the effect was of a white person reporting on the life of a black. The third version, which attempted to reproduce the actual situation in which the book had been conceived, had Poppie telling her story and Joubert intervening to supplement and summarise, and was also a failure because Joubert's language and tones were too different from Poppie's. In the final version, the whole narrative was put into Poppie's "key" (*sleutel*), though to avoid the monotony of the first version, the perspective shifted from Poppie's narrative to the unidentified narrator who both summarised and presented incidents dramatically.

Several Afrikaans reviewers have pointed out that the original version of the book, *Die Swerfjare van Poppie Nongena*, is written in an Afrikaans dialect not previously used in literature.[6] There is no doubt that the fact that this dialect remained unrecorded until 1978 meant that the injustices suffered by Poppie and women like her were to a great extent unknown to the rest of the world.

The Long Journey of Poppie Nongena demonstrates another fact, widely recognised yet seldom reflected on in South Africa: it is that the society in which South African urban blacks live is woman-centred. It would be inappropriate here to use the term matriarchal, which would imply a tighter and more uniform kind of family organisation than actually exists; but nevertheless, women, to a far greater degree than men, are the survivors of township life and form the centres of their family groups.[7] Es'kia Mphahlele's narrative of his childhood, *Down Second Avenue*,[8] which deals with township life in the 1930s and with a family group which is fairly recently urbanised, already shows this phenomenon. The narrator is painfully aware of the ways in which males in his family have been inadequate as parents and describes in detail his father's failure to support his wife and children in any sense and his parents' divorce. The pattern, we are told, was repeated in the life of his sister and her husband. Portraits of strong-minded women form some of the liveliest areas in the book.

In *Poppie Nongena* Elsa Joubert is clearly very conscious of the change from patriarchy to woman-centred family life amongst urban blacks: Poppie Nongena's family, as she renders it at the beginning of the novel, is one which is traced through the female line. Her account — and Joubert takes care that we shall recognise that this is Poppie's own perception of her past — reaches back to her great-grandmother, "a rich old woman who grazed her goats on the koppies the other side of Carnarvon." (11) The girl-child of great-grandma Kappie, ouma Hannie, forms the family centre throughout Poppie's childhood. The men of the family, like Jantje, Hannie's brother, who is killed in the Anglo-Boer War, oompie Domani who dies in World War I and Poppie's father who does not return from World War II, are lost or die too early to occupy important places in the family.

The women of the family are forced, even in the late nineteenth and early twentieth centuries, to become family heads as well as sole child-rearers. It is a vital point for the novelist, who will demonstrate that Poppie and women like her are at the very centre of black urban experience, and that the community at large must listen to the narration of a black woman's life or remain out of touch with what desperately needs to be known.

Although women moved to the centre of the family three generations before her birth, their roles at that centre seem to Poppie to have altered with time. Ouma Hannie seems to her to have been the custodian of traditional values. She speaks of her as "very strict with her children.

She wasn't at rest till they were married with lobola money, as well as in church." (12—13) But in fact although Ouma is not what Poppie is forced to become, a black township woman of the late twentieth century, the reader understands that she is far from being a tribal woman in the sense that the women of Poppie's husband's family are shown to be. Ouma's grandson Mosie says "I know I am an Afrikaner" (325) giving the term its traditional meaning of 'speaker of Afrikaans' but also extending it to mean 'citizen' of South Africa, and this sense of himself is inherited from ouma Hannie. Poppie may remember her grandmother as strongly traditional but this is an indicator of Poppie's own remoteness from Xhosa ways: the old woman's strong Christian beliefs and her position in the family, exercising power even over her adult sons, show that patterns are adapting to new circumstances in which men can no longer sustain their old roles. When Hannie expels her favourite son Pengi, her "dry-teat child", from the family because he burnt down the house when he was drunk, we realise that she combines a sense of responsibility to the family as a whole with a perceptive love for each individual:

> The next morning ouma Hannie called the police to take Pengi away.
> He wept and begged ouma: Forgive me, mama. My mama.
> It is too late to weep, Pengi, ouma said to him.
> Ouma went to court when Pengi's case was heard and she watched him being led away to the cells, but he did not turn his head to look at her or at his sisi Hessie.
> Ouma wouldn't leave the courtroom, she stayed sitting on the bench for a long while after all the others, even the policeman, had gone. She prayed to the Lord: Look after Pengi. (47)

Hannie is a decision-maker, in a sense that none of her descendants ever is again, because she, unlike her children and grandchildren, seems to have options. She decides how and whom her daughters will marry, she allows her childless daughter to foster one of Poppie's brothers, she sends Poppie's mother to look after the ailing Hessie. At this stage in the family history it appears that despite the disappearance of patriarchy a new, hybrid culture is growing, part Xhosa and part Christian. The name which Poppie is given at her birth, Ntombizodumo ("girl born from a line of great women"), suggests that her family is conscious of the changes which are taking place in its structure, though her grandmother's name for her, Poppie, meaning Dolly, is sadly prophetic of her helplessness against those who will control her adult life.

Joubert is obviously conscious throughout the novel that her readers must·understand that Poppie, like all other women in her predicament, is a woman who in normal circumstances would be compelled to remain silent partly because she understands only partially and gradually her own experience and rarely if ever relates it to political and social events in the country as a whole. In order to see the meanings of Poppie's limitations, it is useful to place the book by the side of another woman's narrative, *The Diary of Maria Tholo*[9] by Carol Hermer. *Maria Tholo* is a record of the 1976 riots in the black townships of Cape Town, as perceived by a black woman.

The opening section of the book makes it clear that Maria, as a black woman living in Cape Town, is certainly atypical. It identifies her and her husband as members of the numerically small black middle class, who have risen to comparative affluence through their parents' and their own efforts. Her small immediate family is strongly attached to middle class values like education, church attendance and good house-keeping. She and her family are "qualified residents" entitled by law to live in Guguletu. A lifelong series of crises, such as dog the footsteps of the Nongena family and the majority of black families who wish to work in towns, is therefore avoided. Above all, she is highly articulate and is always aware of the relationship between the violence of which she is a witness and the frustration of the black people as a whole. She can respond with understanding to a political orator's description of black consciousness: ". . . sometimes when a cow gets loose, it becomes very violent and starts to take it out even on innocent people . . . ." (7)

Carol Hermer's account of how the book grew reminds us that its main subject is different from that of *Poppie Nongena*. Although the latter has its climax in the 1976 riots, its main theme is Poppie herself, her development and her eventual breakdown, and it is essential to the book that we realise that she is typical as well as individual. The subject of *Maria Tholo* is the riots, and Maria herself is uniquely placed, in that she can perceive and respond as a black woman resident in Guguletu, and at the same time, offer the larger community of her readers an account of what she perceives, one which will relate to what they already know.

Her position is always that of a woman who has much to lose from revolution, but it is also that of a member of an oppressed group who understands why violence has occurred. Some of the pressures under which Poppie Nongena suffers are present for her — fear for the safety of her family and friends, unease at the young people's breach of traditional respect for elders — yet they are present in a very different way. Maria's fear is never stronger than, and seldom as strong as, her excitement and curiosity. Whereas Poppie longs for safety, Maria desires knowledge; Poppie is the victim of the circumstances which Maria observes and records.

There are important similarities between their attitudes which demonstrate their authors' sense of the way in which the 1976 riots voiced sentiments common to all black people. When Maria meets a mob of youths "singing and wielding sticks" she waves her fist and shouts "Power!" (13) Her action is not entirely defensive. When Poppie hears of the riots she is already exhausted by grief and anxiety and it is therefore very significant that she too admits that the rioters are expressing what she feels: "I must be honest. I have my grievances too. If I had the strength I would try to change matters but now I don't have the strength." (318)

Nevertheless it is the differences between the women which are crucial to the books: Maria is in touch with her own community, yet because of her education and comparative financial and social security, on its fringes and able to understand and speak to the outside world, whereas Poppie is at the centre of her family and her community, typical in her sufferings and in the fact that she cannot speak to the world about them. Once we have understood Maria's position in her community we can judge her account fairly simply; Poppie's narrative makes far greater demands on us. She lives her life, even when she becomes an adult, almost entirely without theory.

In the early part of the book, in fact until she leaves the Cape for the Ciskei, Poppie's typical mode is the recall of sensation: she remembers sights and sounds from the past, such as her fear of the water at Doringbaai. (37) Her mode of recall does not change as she becomes an adult: the breakup of her brother Plank's marriage is rendered through the wakeful tension of his brothers and sister who wait for his wife's cry when he beats her. The high sensory content of Poppie's memories lends authenticity to her account; this is a woman who responds very directly to the particular experiences of her own life. And the high sensory content of her memories is matched by their low reflective or analytic content. It is not that she does not learn from her own experience (she almost always responds sympathetically to the experiences of her family and friends) but it is very rare for her to abstract consciously. The result for the novel is that the tone of propaganda is never present: neither Poppie nor the narrator who reports and supplements her words ever asks for reform of the system which oppresses her. The reader however — and it is important to realise that *Poppie Nongena* and *Maria Tholo* are directed at much the same group of readers so far as attitudes and opinions are concerned — must intervene here and fill a silence as important as the one filled by Elsa Joubert's written words. Poppie gives the story of her life, but it is assumed that the reader will be sufficiently well informed to place that story in the context of the legislation which eroded the rights of black people during her lifetime, the alien and often unsympathetic individuals who administer evil laws, and the climate of economic exploitation and social humiliation. Both Maria Tholo and her editor are very aware of all of this larger context, of which they constantly remind the reader. Poppie, however, not only does not relate her experience to the whole social context, but she does not really protest; she cannot, since to do so would be to be possessed of the concepts needed to judge a system which deals unfairly with her. The reader therefore must register that what she suffers is appallingly unjust and must articulate her protest for her.

The patterning of the book, which presents five periods of conflict, helps to guide the reader towards the appropriate responses. In the Anglo-Boer War and in World Wars I and II, the men of Poppie's family have died as brothers-in-arms of the whites. The two major conflicts of Poppie's life, the enforcement of the Pass Laws of the 1960s and the 1976 riots, involved conflict between black and white. These 'wars', more fatal to Poppie's family than the conventional wars of the past, cause suffering for women and children as well as men — indeed, even more than men. They also precipitate the social upheavals which leave Poppie, a woman alone, to speak for her people. In 1960 the systematic humiliation of black men by the police destroys, as Poppie points out, the respect of their children for family heads; the separation of women from their families by the Pass Laws forces mothers of families to act as substitute family heads, as Poppie does as soon as she arrives in Mdantsane in the Ciskei and demands to be given a house on the tarred road.

Without Elsa Joubert's intervention, Poppie is silent: without the reader's intervention, her words are ineffective, but the novel emphasises the fact that she is perceptive, sensitive, loving and strong. The life which she is obliged to lead makes enormous demands on her, only some of which she has been prepared for. Her departure from Lambert's Bay for Cape Town, for example, shows her making an independent decision for the first time. The events of her life up to this point have been largely the result of others' decisions or, like her marriage, almost

153

an inevitable part of maturing. From her arrival in Cape Town, however, it becomes more and more necessary for her to make vital decisions and she has to recognise that her family, though always loving, can help her very little. Traditional wisdom cannot help either, and religion, to ouma Hannie a positive source of joy, seems in the townships to produce nothing better than resigned acceptance of what ought to be intolerable.

Section 42 (178—189) summarises one of the two periods of conflict which occur during Poppie's adult life, her years of struggle to stay in the Cape — the changes in the law which bring about the withdrawal of her work permit, the use of her husband's birthplace as a means of imposing on her the status of an alien, the hours of anxious waiting every week or two, outside the Native Affairs Office to renew her residence permit. The guilt of the white officials at what they are doing is plain to the reader, but their behaviour exhausts Poppie and her husband and reduces them to despair.

What happens to Poppie is that she learns to survive as an isolated individual — isolated in the most literal sense, since her husband dies and she is eventually forced to allow her children to live elsewhere — but she comes to harden herself against experience. Time after time she has suffered what is almost unbearable and the people who control her life have shown themselves completely insensitive, or perhaps uncaring. A small but key example of this occurs when Poppie returns, recently widowed, to Cape Town. She is employed as a maid, and her employer Mrs Swanepoel asks her:

> ... If I go to all the trouble of fixing up your pass and have you registered on my name, you must promise not to get pregnant, hey?
> Poppie did not answer her.
> She only saw the white woman's eyes travelling up and down her body.
> Or are you pregnant already?
> No, Poppie said, I am not pregnant, madam, I'm tied off. (254—5)

Poppie's enforced acceptance of this humiliation secures a pass for her, but this time she does generalise bitterly: "This is the way we know life. We don't mind about justice, about whether a thing is right or not." (255) Elsa Joubert's point concerns the terrible failure in human feeling which allows one woman, herself a wife and a mother, to behave so insensitively to another. Poppie must harden herself to live.

Tolerant affection for her family has always been characteristic of

154

her: she mentions the generosity which prevented her estranged sister-in-law from complaining to her people that her husband beat her; she is always tolerant of her brother's drunkenness; she keeps her love for her sister-in-law Lindiwe over a separation of decades. As her narrative continues, however, even family feeling begins to ebb. When Plank brings his brother's erring wife to her at the end of her own struggle to stay in Cape Town with her husband, she screams "She must go. I don't know what she is looking for here, because my troubles are heavy." (187)

On leaving Cape Town where her husband, mother and brothers will continue to live, she has a more serious failure of feeling: a description of the grief of her family and friends is followed by

> I didn't feel so badly as we pulled out of the station. I must be honest and say: No, I didn't feel badly at all, because I was fed up of the law, I could not stand it any more. (192)

This is a momentary exhaustion but with more suffering will come increasing hardness.

She struggles alone to bring up her children in Mdantsane in the Ciskei, to keep them on the right path, which for her is represented by the school and the church, and away from the murderous bands of skollies, always in the background of her perceptions, who have succumbed to a fate which she dreads for her own children. Tata-ka-Bonsile visits them only once in the four years that Poppie spends in the Ciskei, but she knows of his declining health, though she is power-less to help him. When she returns to Cape Town for his funeral, she learns that even his religious faith failed him. "Because tata-ka-Bonsile of late was no church-goer, mama had explained to Poppie, we could not hold the service in the church. . . ." (233)

The death of tata-ka-Bonsile forces Poppie to seek for work in the Cape. She sends her adolescent daughters, Nomvula and Thandi, to their grandparents in the tribal lands, the fate which she has so long resisted for them, but which is her only alternative to leaving them unprotected in Mdantsane. They are afraid; they weep; but she must harden her heart.

Even in this terrible period, Poppie grows in strength: when Bonsile's illegitimate child is born, she feels sorrow for the girl-mother, whose schooling is now at an end, "but then Poppie made herself strong again. . . . If tata-ka-Bonsile had to return to them in this child, then it was the will of the Lord." (249) She wins a long and painful struggle

155

with herself and her Cape Town family when she agrees to allow her son Bonsile to go to the tribal lands for the circumcision rites. But Vukile, Bonsile's son, is killed on her back by a rioter's stone and her children, from whom she has separated herself in order to keep them safe, are arrested. All these griefs finally force Poppie into insensibility and refusal to act:

> The children will have to look after themselves, Poppie answered. Her voice sounded like her own voice again. But the hardness of heart that had come into her, she knew, would be there for always. I have found my way through everything, she thought, but through this I can find no way. Because this has been taken out of my hands, it has been given over to the hands of the children. It is now my children who will carry on.
>
> Peace will not come, she told Mosie. Even those that wish for peace will be dragged into the troubles. We will have to grow used to that. About that we can't do nothing. (354)

This is no handing over to the new generation; it is simple despair. The miracles of adaptability which Poppie has performed, her courage and resourcefulness all have been destroyed.

What gives the book its poignance is the fact that it is a record of the destruction of enormous human potential. Poppie's acute and sensitive perceptions of the world, her loving, gentle nature, her growth to her full strength in married life, are shown as offering a basis for a new kind of life, related to the old Xhosa values, but also responding to the new circumstances of urban life.

Section 82, the last of the book, ends with Poppie's almost catatonic retreat from the unbearable events which now fill her life. It is easy to believe that the silence which falls at the end is of a completely different nature from the constraints of illiteracy and ignorance which Elsa Joubert and her readers have helped her to break through. Poppie no longer experiences in any active sense, nor does she respond to what she observes. A lifetime of baffling, contradictory pronouncements made to her by the white men who have determined her life, and her own failure to convey any sense of her suffering to them have finally convinced her that no effort of hers can be effective. Her silence from this moment will be that of an individual who has no wish to communicate with the world, who no longer believes that she can do so, rather than that of a woman who lacks information or facility in written language.

Petra Grütter says that Joubert intended the novel to end with

156

Section 81, when Poppie comforts her mother for the loss of Jakkie, who has fled after shooting a policeman. The conclusion of this section is Poppie's statement, ". . . we already know what life is like. We take what comes our way and then we go on. But we don't give up." (346) Grütter claims that after Joubert had ended the book in this way "Life itself wrote the last chapter of the story," a statement which helps the reader to understand one of the puzzles of the book: how can it end with what seems a final lapse into silence by the protagonist when Poppie in fact told her life story to Joubert at some later period? It is not clear from Grütter's article whether Poppie's own children were arrested and Poppie herself became silent after Joubert had provisionally ended the book with Section 81, or whether both Joubert and the black woman (whom she had called Poppie in her book) came to feel that, because of events at this time in South Africa, the book must end in this way. In a sense, it does not matter: the truth, that black women may be driven into an unbreakable silence, is clear.

NOTES

1   Olsen, Tillie *Silences* (London:Virago 1980) p10.
2   Joubert, Elsa *The Long Journey of Poppie Nongena* (Johannesburg: Jonathan Ball in association with Hodder and Stoughton 1980). All page numbers refer to this edition.
3   In his review of the Afrikaans version of the book, *Die Swerfjare van Poppie Nongena* in *Speak* (6) (Autumn 1979) 28—30, Ampie Coetzee makes a number of charges against the book, most of which will be implicitly taken up and, I hope, answered in the course of this essay. Central to my essay, however, is the question which he asks at the end of the review:

> . . . is it possible for the white Afrikaans writer, the member of a privileged ruling class, to write significant revolutionary literature about the struggle of a suppressed people, the black people, whom he doesn't really know?

No South African resident would deny the difficulty of achieving sympathetic understanding of a member of another racial group, but to condemn as presumptuous or useless efforts to do so is a despairing verdict on our predicament. It shows too an excessive preoccupation with race, as if it were the only factor which unites or separates people. Elsa Joubert's response to the black woman's narration of her life is that of a woman and a sister. It is significant, I think, that Coetzee's pronoun "he" ignores the possibility that their shared womanhood could form an important link between the author and her subject.

4   This account of the origins of the book is taken from the review article, "Wie is Poppie?" by Petra Grütter in *Sarie* (November 1978).

5   *Standpunte* (153) (June 1981) 57—66.

6   *The Long Journey of Poppie Nongena* was first written by Elsa Joubert in Afrikaans and published in that language by Tafelberg in Cape Town in 1978. Since the author herself wrote the English version, I have felt entitled to assume throughout this essay that it represents her intentions fully and accurately, though I realise that the English version cannot assert, as the Afrikaans version does, the kinship of Poppie and her like with the other Afrikaans speakers of South Africa. Petra Grütter has commented, in "Wie is Poppie?" on the special dialect in which the book is written, as have André P Brink in "Oor die stil pyn van die ander Afrikaner" in *Rapport* (3 December 1978) and Phil du Plessis in "Die Passie van 'n swart Afrikanervrou" in *Buurman* (December 1978). All three interpret the fact that this form of Afrikaans has been virtually ignored as the will of the majority of white Afrikaans speakers to deny the existence of black Afrikaners.

7   There is no doubt that South African black men have suffered and continue to suffer appalling injustice, and that poverty and low standards of literacy compel the enormous majority of them to suffer in silence. Nevertheless, there are male black South African journalists, essayists, novelists, poets and dramatists; miserable though the chances are for black men to break their silence, they are many times better than those of black women in South Africa.

8   Mphahlele, Es'kia *Down Second Avenue* (London: Faber 1973).

9   Hermer, Carol *The Diary of Maria Tholo* (Johannesburg: Ravan Press 1980). Page numbers refer to this edition.

Burger's Daughter:
A Novel's Reliance on History

M J DAYMOND

Nadine Gordimer has had a long-standing interest in the lives of white South African revolutionaries, particularly in the continuity of ideals across the generations of a family. She speaks of this interest in a recent interview, saying that the socio-political phenomenon of "white hard-core Leftists" presented itself to her imagination as the question of "what it would be like . . . to be the son or daughter of one of those families."[1] When one of South Africa's best known white revolutionaries, Abram Fischer, disappeared while facing charges of treason in January 1965, and was recaptured after ten months underground, she wrote an account of the preliminary enquiry held in the Johannesburg Magistrates' Court which Fischer faced before being committed for trial a second time.[2] Until *Burger's Daughter* appeared in 1979,[3] this article was Gordimer's most direct account of a white South African revolutionary.

Figures of political commitment, white and black, have always been present in Gordimer's fiction, figures such as Max Van Den Sandt, the white South African revolutionary whose suicide is telegraphed to his ex-wife Elizabeth on the day of the action of *The Late Bourgeois World* (1966).[4] But such figures are not located at the centre of the action of Gordimer's earlier novels, whereas the questions that Rosa Burger, the protagonist of *Burger's Daughter*, faces are this novel's key issues. She reassesses her own involvement in her father's cause, discovers her power to choose to take up "the torch"[5] and recognises that since her father's death in prison, the political forces in South Africa have changed, so that revolutionary opposition to the regime can no longer take the form it did in her father's lifetime.

As Gordimer has, by her own testimony, been deeply interested in the lives of revolutionaries for at least thirty years, one question prompted by *Burger's Daughter* is why it has taken so long for her interest to be centrally represented in her fiction. Or, to put the question another way, what has made it possible for Gordimer finally to write *Burger's Daughter*?

It is possible to see in aspects of the novel itself what Gordimer needed for the telling of her story. The first pointer is that it has been conceived of as Rosa's story. Gordimer says in the interview quoted above that the subject of revolutionary lives presented itself primarily as a question of what their progeny would inherit. Figures like Lionel Burger are to be understood by the possibilities for action they give to their offspring and therefore it is Rosa's life that must be the focus of the novel. The central question for her is whether and how she can take up her father's torch but it is one that Rosa does not even recognise until after her father's death. In the same way, her self-questioning is a story that Gordimer could not tell until the epoch represented by Lionel Burger had obviously ended.

It is only when Conrad, Rosa's casual lover, provokes her by asserting the virtues of a self-centred life, that she does question her inheritance. This is because she has been raised in so confident and well-reasoned an ethos that neither personal nor public alternatives have presented themselves to her. Even the pain of being required to pose as Noel de Witt's fiancée, so that she could convey information when visiting him in jail, did not drive her to question her parents' purposes. She is presented as someone for whom the subject of her own life has had to be released before she can reach that questioning self-consciousness that is a child's usual inheritance. A similar sense that history has had to release her subject for exploration is one which seems to have been necessary for Gordimer herself.

When Lionel Burger is jailed, he disappears in a blaze of glory; he and his fellow-revolutionaries remain strong in their vision of radical opposition. But when he dies three years later, his political relevance is almost over, not simply because he is fading from memory, but because a new political factor is emerging. Rosa encounters it on the anniversary of her father's death when Duma Dhladhla asserts that until blacks have liberated themselves, "'We don't accept anything from anybody. We take. D'you understand? We take for ourselves.'" (157) She sees that Lionel's vision, his certainty about solutions and how to achieve them, has been rejected as yet another white recipe for the black people. Rosa's life turns a corner with her father's death, but in order for the question of political forces at a national level to be released for the novelist's treatment, history has had to provide Gordimer with more than the end of an individual life; a new epoch has had to begin. Lionel

Burger's meaning could not be explored until his day had obviously passed. It is the sequence of events now known as Soweto '76 (the bloodshed in Soweto and other centres in June 1976, followed some months later by nationwide bannings and arrests) that Gordimer seems to have felt was the necessary manifestation that South African history had entered a new phase; she has the new factor, Black Consciousness, plus the events which made a whole country recognise its advent, erupt into Rosa's story as forcibly as they did into history.

There are many quiet ironies in *Burger's Daughter* which indicate Gordimer's own recognition that her novel's living off history places it in a somewhat parasitic role. They are particularly strong in Rosa's feeling that she is used by the curious — either purposefully, like the Swedish journalist and later by the biographer, or idly like Conrad. But on the whole, Gordimer's examination of her country's political history through its parallels with her protagonist's life is free from the necessary stasis of the ironic vision. The people of Soweto are shown to be constructively involved in processes which are matched in Rosa's life: they "have begun to see themselves at last as they are; as their children see them", (348) while one of Rosa's recurring questions is "When they saw me outside the prison what did they see?" (13) As well as the thematic parallels built into the book, Gordimer's positive use of history can be seen in her decision to incorporate actual documentation in her fiction. She includes a pamphlet issued by the Soweto Students' Representative Council in June 1977 which, when *Burger's Daughter* was published, had for some time been banned for possession as well as for publication.[6] The organisation which had issued it had also been banned since 19 October 1977. In the fiction, this is the date on which Rosa is detained. Thus Gordimer's act of illegality underlines the link between her fiction and the history which gave it birth. The pamphlet represents the author's selection from within the events of Soweto '76 of the crucial sign that Lionel Burger's era has finally ended, that the burden has passed to the children and that his story can now be told.

By choosing to write about the child of a revolutionary, Gordimer rests understanding and judgement of Lionel Burger on the possibilities for continuity of his vision in a changing world, rather than simply on questions such as the intrinsic value of what he believed in and did. She has coupled her sense that her subject had to be released by history with her wish to judge it from within history. To do this she has allowed the novel's relation to the course of actual events to shape it, especially its ending. Once the question directing the action becomes one of whether Rosa can, in her present world, continue in her father's tradition, Gordimer has to provide recognition of the fact that history has not yet given the full answer to this question. Lionel Burger's epoch can be seen as completed and so depictable in fiction, but Rosa's full story is still in abeyance.

Rosa's imprisonment is in one sense a declaration of uncertainty; she is in the limbo of an unknown future. For this reason the novel's hung ending is unsurprising. The question mark it represents hangs not over the woman herself, but over her place in the world to which she has returned. In this way Gordimer is able to create a very powerful though mixed response to Rosa at the end of the novel. There seem to be three factors in Rosa's imprisonment with which the reader must cope. First, her future cannot yet be known, so the ending is bound to be a suspended one. Secondly, as a known opponent of the South African regime she inevitably runs the risk of imprisonment. Thirdly, the South Africa to which Rosa returns does not afford her the same possibilities of action as her father had, and so she cannot be the same kind of participant as he was. Thus what the novel's ending depicts is the suspension of a woman who has won through to a personal potency of a kind that her world cannot use.

The clumsiness of Rosa's arrest is, on the one hand, a telling reflection of actuality. Countless people were arrested or detained in October 1977 and it was difficult to see a purpose beyond that of general intimidation in their imprisonment. The novel suggests too that when the children of Soweto find a new resolution and "know why they are dying", (349) the authorities can respond to this only through the old concepts of 'trouble-making agitators'. But, on the other hand, while Rosa's inglorious detention reflects actuality, it also gives force to the ironies of her position. She herself has already registered irony when she observes that she is "living like anyone else". (332) Rosa is remembering how Baasie, the black child who was raised as a member of her family until all the children had to be sent away when both her parents were arrested, was never brought back to the Burger household, and is recalling his accusation, made when they met again at the London party, that she had no right to believe that her family "could be different from any other whites". (332) Rosa is registering the ironic truth about her present life contained in Baasie's charge. In her returning to South Africa, she has regained what she calls "the sane habit of our kind" (328) and can aspire to something of her father's "sublime lucidity", (351) but whatever her personal growth, she has returned to a world whose course has, for the time being at least, passed her by.

Our response to Rosa's return is not held by these ironies, for it rests on the recognition that in her return she has made a gesture of personal and public loyalty which sets her apart from what Baasie means by 'her kind'. Rosa herself gives her sense of her return with her customary reserve; perhaps her most poignant utterance lies in her wondering how her father would have responded to the prospect of children, perhaps his own children, "hand-in-hand, approaching guns". (349) She is confident that he foresaw this new source of "revolutionary initiative" (348) and that he would have known from within himself what was happening to these people, but still she fears that even her father might have been excluded from it: "It's something peculiarly their own?" (349) Under such questions, Rosa's brief, muted reflections join with the other narrating voice's indifferent rendering to give what Rowland Smith has called, perhaps misleadingly, a "neutrally" presented account of the novel's closing events.[7] It is true that the novel does not give extensive explicit expression to the intense, complex feelings involved in Rosa's return and imprisonment, but they are powerfully present and have been made so through the structural properties of the work.

There are many structural features of *Burger's Daughter* which indicate Gordimer's awareness of the questions involved in writing fiction within an unfolding history and of balancing a recognition of that history's course against her protagonist's claims on the reader's responses. The first-person narration and the novel's three-part structure are both very clear indications of the care and intensity with which Gordimer has constructed her picture of an epoch and its heritage, and in them she allows her consciousness of the needs and nature of her art to show itself to a degree that is unusual in her work. Rosa's first-person narration accompanies that of another, unidentified voice which recounts with a flat coldness the events on which she subsequently meditates. Her monologues are addressed in turn to three different confidants: to Conrad, to Katya (the first wife who defected), and to Lionel Burger himself. In each case she addresses an absent figure, for, as she says to Conrad, "If you knew I was talking to you I wouldn't be able to talk." (17) She is not engaged in self-communing but is speaking to another person through whom she can at that moment best perceive and understand her own reality.

In most modern novels, first-person narration is a signal to readers that they will encounter a consciousness which cannot be relied on to give either an accurate or a complete picture of events and feelings. The narrative mode indicates that a subjective view of matters can be only a

163

partial one and that in the act of recall, of reconstruction of the past, remembered events are coloured by the motives or needs of the present. Rosa's narration is given in three discrete stages, at three different times, so that it is notable that when she is speaking to Conrad, she speaks without knowledge of what is to happen to her during her visit to Katya, and similarly when she speaks to Katya, she has no foresight of the confrontation she will have with Baasie and of her return to South Africa. As Rosa does not narrate her story from a single point in time and is only briefly shown, in part three, in complete possession of her life, she is a narrator without the certainties that Dickens gave the adult Pip or even those of Ellison's voluntarily suspended Invisible Man. In this respect Gordimer might seem to be allying her protagonist with the narrator-protagonists used by a novelist like J M Coetzee in his explorations of the violent ambiguities of knowing and yet not knowing. But this is a dimension of first-person narration that Gordimer has not chosen to use in *Burger's Daughter* and it can be supposed that the clarity and honesty of the will to know that is displayed by Rosa at each stage of her narration is the novelist's tribute to what Rosa calls "the sane habit of our kind". (328) It is made clear in her daily encounters that Rosa is a guarded woman. She has learned the necessity of self-reliance and silence, just as she has learned to record nothing but the mundane in her diary, so that as a person she is one who gives nothing away while as a narrator she is one on whom nothing is lost. After her active reserve, the fullness with which Rosa speaks to her absent confidants is, in the first place, touching.

It also creates great confidence in Rosa as an interpreter as well as a narrator of events. This confidence is further built up through the interactions between her monologues and the sequences given by the other narrating voice. This other voice is that of disembodied power, expressive of the world Rosa was born to oppose:

> She tramped slowly across the tarmac, disappeared in the shadow of the plane's wing and — there she was — appeared again in the sun. She climbed the metal stairway to the darker shadow of the door, not turning to look back. Surveillance watched her go in. (191)

It is the voice of Surveillance surveyed. The menace in its meticulous, inflexible observation is what serves to give definition to the value of Rosa's steady, personal gaze.

The interaction of the voices is one which is also used to prevent

164

Rosa's retrospection from pushing the whole fiction into a comforting past. The novel opens with a brief, impersonal picture of the fourteen-year-old Rosa outside the prison waiting to send a hot-water bottle to her mother. Then, after the question "When they saw me . . . what did they see?" identifies Rosa's awakening concern with self, the narration shifts to her reconstructions of her childhood. Prompted by Conrad's curiosity and assertions that self-gratification is what matters, Rosa is recognising that she has never known the pain and luxury of choice, and that she now has to reconstruct her past life so as to identify the processes by which a life dedicated to others was the choice made for her. As Rosa reflects on the disparate traditions which claim her through her full name (she is named for Rosa Luxemburg and for her Afrikaans grandmother, Marie), her narration ceases to grapple with memories alone and she catches up with events in her current life. With this shift, the narration takes on a new rhythm of fairly regular alternations between the alien narrator's account of an event and Rosa's reflections on it. Thus, although Rosa's narrative is divided into three acts of narration, separated in time, the effect is not simply that of three blocks of retrospective reflection. Within the narrative's three parts, the surveillance voice is generally used to recount actions sequentially, moving through time in the way of traditional narration so that the reader has a sense of events actually unfolding. What is pictured in this way is immediately followed by Rosa's interpretation of its significance. This is the pattern of the treatment of the death of the tramp at lunchtime in a Johannesburg park; of the visit to Lionel's old colleagues, Dick and Ivy Terblanche, and their daughter Clare's request for help; and of the visit to the apparently enlightened man with good government connections, Brandt Vermeulen. The meeting with Marisa Kgosana and the party at Fats's place are different — Rosa alone recounts these. The scene of the donkey being thrashed is also given only by Rosa, but as it comes after the reader has seen her departure through surveillance narration, and as it constitutes her explanation of why she left, it too has the effect of being reflections on a known event.

Rosa's view is always made to be the illuminating one and so the reader comes to feel and to rely on its humanity. This is not to deny that Rosa finds herself mistaken from time to time; she does, but the recognition of a mistake is given to Rosa herself. The reader has, for example, no prior knowledge of what Baasie's attack will suddenly reveal to Rosa, and her decisive response to it serves to confirm her ability to hold her world in her grasp.

Rosa's monologues in the novel's second and third parts actually occupy a smaller part of the narration than in the first, but by this stage the power of her presence is such that her mediating responses are what the reader remembers, and relies on. It is this undiminished grasp of her world which is Rosa's conscious achievement at the end of the novel, for she returns to South Africa in order to regain the capacity to understand that she has inherited from Lionel. It is in part because her imprisonment cuts off the reader's access to her grasp of her world that the open end of her story has the power to disturb that it does.

In placing all the novel's demonstrated expansion of understanding within Rosa's grasp, Gordimer gives her sense of the calibre of her protagonist. Against this tribute, it may be said that the novel's three-part structure has been used to recognise the place of such a person in South Africa's history. A different sense of un-used possibilities operates in the structuring of Rosa's story. Its three parts are clearly in dialectical relation to each other, but any expectation that the final stage will represent a synthesis, a new Rosa emerging from the processes of the two previous stages, is not altogether fulfilled. Rosa is left on the side-lines of her world, and in prison, and whatever personal development may have occurred in her is denied expression in action. The force of this denial is one which Gordimer leads her reader to feel through the form of *Burger's Daughter*, for it emerges from the assent won for the necessity and appropriateness of Rosa's previous actions. The chief of these is her journey to France which she undertakes because she is impelled to test, through her own actions, her changing sense of her life's meaning. Her return to South Africa is a similar act of recognition and exploration; this pattern means that her being jailed is felt as an unwarranted halt to the process. In formal terms, the dialectic cannot follow its expected pattern, and because this pattern exerts a claim of naturalness on the modern consciousness akin to the feeling that night must follow day, Rosa's being prevented from expressing the meaning of her return seems to violate natural law.

The events which drive Rosa out of South Africa, which impel her into action, are very carefully constructed to demonstrate that she needs to know more about the world beyond the one she has inherited. In the immediate political context she finds that her parents' vision is being discounted by Duma Dhladhla's generation, and in a related but much wider sense, she finds through an encounter with death that the superbly reasoned quality of her parents' vision has not prepared her for all the dimensions of life. She remembers her brother's death, but

166

it is not until she witnesses the tramp's death (it is the antithesis of Lionel's: an anonymous, silent death; one for which no obvious social cause can be seen; one which makes comment, explanation, attribution of reason or responsibility impossible; which makes objection seem irrelevant) that Rosa realises that her parents' selfless courage when her brother drowned actually denied her something important. Her first reaction when she sees that her inheritance does not prepare her for as much as she had believed, is to feel cheated. It is this feeling which impels her on her betrayal of her father: her visits to Brandt Vermeulen.

After this step, Rosa remains for some time undecided about using the passport she has acquired. And then the scene with the donkey forces her out. Rosa's narration of it draws attention to her own efforts to present the scale of her reaction, "I'm making my own metaphors for suffering".(196) Her self-awareness comes from her knowledge that when she sees the man, his family and the donkey he is thrashing, all convulsed in a single agony, it is as though she is seeing for the first time her country's suffering. As though she had not known it before, as though she knows it now in a way that Lionel's sacrifice itself could not give her, and she flees.

She flees instinctively to Katya, the other woman who has defected in the belief that Lionel's way of life, in demanding too much, leaves too much out of account. The personal imperatives and the note of self-criticism in Rosa's choice of Katya are clear and convincing. She seeks a life of private, sensual pleasure such as she has never known before. That she should go to a "lotus land"[8] is also expressive of general political realities in South Africa. Her choice is a demonstration that for active white opponents to oppression, polarisation is complete, compromise is impossible and there can be no middle ground in South African life. Rosa's kind know only The Future and the world they oppose. There are no degrees of opposition; the choice is clear cut and complete.

For a time it seems that life in France and Chabalier's love will supply what Rosa feels herself to have been denied, and that it will be enough. Explicit statement is not what Gordimer uses to indicate that this is an illusion which cannot be sustained; it is the patterned form which shows that Rosa is bound to recognise her illusion. She will again encounter scenes which match, though in less dramatic form, those which confronted her in South Africa with suffering and death. When, for example, she finds the poor woman who has "slipped her moorings" (300) she begins to understand that "no one can defect". (332) Didier demonstrates to her the illusions of freedom entertained by one who is kept, and it is at his mistress Donna's party that Rosa sees that she is amongst people who have long forgotten the claims to which her father's life was dedicated, who have forgotten that in some countries people die for "ordinary civil rights". (296)

That Rosa is unlikely to find a satisfying place among the Left-wing of Europe is being strongly suggested, but she is not yet ready to see it. She is still held in her belief that she can have both the intensely personal fulfilment of being Chabalier's mistress and an involvement in the daily realities of life by taking a role in the French branch of the anti-apartheid movement. Then, when she meets Baasie at the party in London, she encounters two debilitating possibilities which await exiles in Europe: that of resting on past heroism (her father's in this case) and that of being occupied by the resentments and hatreds which imprison Baasie. It is here that she sees fully her mistakes and that she must return to South Africa to regain what makes her most herself: the dispassionate, selflessly analytical power she has inherited from her father. She sees that she cannot be other than a creature of her time and her place. The world at large must contain what Chabalier's love has introduced her to: ladies and unicorns, olive groves filled with the nightingale's song and art galleries with Bonnards. But if her own world is on a course which allows no place for such things, then she cannot, alone, hope to attain them for herself. She cannot be other than Lionel's child.

In reporting Rosa's imprisonment, the closing pages of the novel reflect history by denying the story resolution. But, they carry in this denial a strong emotional charge which distinguishes Gordimer's novel from the emptiness of the endings used in many contemporary novels which choose uncertainty as the true reflection of man's lot. Unlike Beckett, for example, Gordimer is able to give the reader an insight into how things might be different. This sets *Burger's Daughter* apart from her earlier work which dealt with revolutionaries in South Africa. *The Late Bourgeois World* was, like the later work, published just after a shameful event in South Africa's history: the shooting in Sharpeville in 1960 of a group of people who were protesting against the country's pass laws. In both novels Gordimer undertakes an account of the role of radical white opponents of the regime, but the later novel, while it is set in a period in which things have worsened, conveys a picture of revolutionaries in which their actions, feelings and prospects matter very much more than do those of similar people in *The Late Bourgeois World*. When its protagonist-narrator, Elizabeth, wakes in the middle of the night knowing that she will use her grandmother's bank account in the way that Luke has asked, to launder funds for the revolutionary cause, she asks herself why she is agreeing to be used in this way. She concludes finally that, "You can't do more than give what you have."[9] Of all the claims she has encountered that day, Elizabeth rates her own lowest of all, and with this, her ability to give. In a curious way, her own rather sardonic grasp of her married life and political involvement leads her to discount herself. She is fully aware of what Max could not accept: the limitations of her possibilities in her time and place. It is a factor on which the conclusion of *Burger's Daughter* also rests, and yet, while its placing in Elizabeth's consciousness leads the reader to share her own rather diminished feelings for herself, Rosa's similarly limited political prospects have a different effect. This is because much of Elizabeth's judgement of her present role is based on what she has seen in Max. His political allegiances were emotionally based, for his choice of radical activity was one of defiance against his neglectful, smugly rich parents rather than one of considered conviction. As such it forms a pitiful cry for attention and Elizabeth's focus in her reflections is on the revealed weakness at the core of his actions. The needs of self are what moved Max Van Den Sandt, and he stands in sharp contrast to the selfless dedication of which Lionel Burger is capable. He is a hero who gives his life to the needs of others whereas Max takes his life in a last despairing gesture of need. Although Elizabeth sets herself apart from her ex-husband, she does take the measure of her own political potential from him. This estimate is confirmed for her by Luke's request and so the novel's final picture of involvement is of a wryly passive woman agreeing to be used because she can find no argument against it.

Rosa, on the other hand, has Lionel Burger behind her. And it is his standing behind Gordimer's later novel that makes it possible for a work written at a time of greater despair to carry a portrait of greater hope. This hope rests in the complex meaning that the reader recognises in Rosa's imprisonment: in returning to South Africa, Rosa does not necessarily seek to pursue her father's course exactly, yet she has demonstrated a potential for heroism which cannot be given expression in the world to which she now belongs. Then she is imprisoned by the powers to which she is opposed. Yet for all this, the reader is left, like Rosa, "somehow livelier" (360) at the end of her story. So much promise in Rosa, so much denied for the time being; the passive acquiescence of an Elizabeth cannot be the direction Rosa's story will take.[10]

NOTES

1   Gardner, Susan "'A Story for this Place and Time': An Interview with Nadine Gordimer about *Burger's Daughter*" *Kunapipi* 3 (1) (1981) 99—113.

2   Gordimer, Nadine "The Fischer Case" *London Magazine* 5 (12) (1966) 21—30.

3   Gordimer, Nadine *Burger's Daughter* (London: Cape 1979 and Harmondsworth: Penguin 1980). Page references appear in brackets in the text. The pagination of both editions of the novel is the same.

4   Gordimer, Nadine *The Late Bourgeois World* (London: Cape 1966).

5   Gardner p100.

6   Gordimer, Nadine et al *What Happened to Burger's Daughter or How South African Censorship Works* (Johannesburg: Taurus 1980); and Roberts, Sheila "South African Censorship and the Case of *Burger's Daughter*" *World Literature Written in English* 20 (1981) 41—48.

7   Smith, Rowland "Living for the Future: Nadine Gordimer's *Burger's Daughter*" *World Literature Written in English* 19 (1980) 163—173; p172.

8   Smith p166.

9   *The Late Bourgeois World* p160.

10   Since this article was written, Nadine Gordimer has published an essay, based on a lecture given at the New York Institute for the Humanities in October 1982, in which she examines the position of white South Africans who want to see change in their country. She uses herself as representative of the "segment" of the white population who are preoccupied with the question of *how* to offer themselves to a future South Africa. She quotes Bishop Desmond Tutu and Mongane Serote, saying that blacks must learn to lead and whites to follow, blacks to talk and whites to listen, and she delineates the inevitably confused actions of South Africans living out "the interregnum" while seeking to discern their way to a future. The picture is more explicitly optimistic than the conclusion of *Burger's Daughter* in that Gordimer feels able to record a black friend's encouraging comment, "whites must learn to struggle". To her it conveys a faint hope that whites will be able to "look for some effective way, in the living of their own personal lives, to join the struggle for liberation from racism".
Gordimer, Nadine "Living in the Interregnum" *The New York Review of Books* 29 (21 & 22) (Jan 20, 1983) 21—29.

Mongane Serote:
Humanist and Revolutionary

DORIAN BARBOURE

On 16 June 1976, twenty thousand Soweto schoolchildren marched in protest against the proposed introduction of Afrikaans as a medium of instruction in secondary schools.[1] Although the students intended to demonstrate peacefully, police at some point opened fire on the crowds, and a number of pupils were shot dead. This sparked off a wave of violence, rioting and destruction throughout the country and within the first week alone there were at least one hundred and seventy-six deaths.[2] Soweto, however, remained the centre of revolt, and like Sharpeville before it, 'Soweto 1976' has become a symbol of resistance and oppression. Furthermore, in Soweto, the 'disturbances' were not limited to rioting. Pupils organised school boycotts as well as work boycotts in August and September; a protest was organized against new rent increases, the Soweto Urban Bantu Council[3] was discredited for its role in the increases, and a more representative interim committee, the Committee of Ten, was established in its place. Police reaction to the disturbances was severe. Although police action has been officially exonerated, there have been many claims that teargas was used, that crowds were baton-charged, that demonstrators were shot at and killed, that police opened fire at funerals, and that there were systematic raids and arrests in Soweto.[4] Government reaction was also severe: detentions without trial were sanctioned,[5] Black Consciousness organizations were banned, and the popular black newspaper, *The World*, was closed down. One response has been an increase in acts of sabotage, an indication that many people in the black community have begun to feel that only violent resistance will bring about change.[6]

On the literary scene, a number of black writers have attempted to chart the significance of the Soweto era, popularly referred to as the period of Power. Among the novels that emerged from this period, Miriam Tlali's *Amandla* (1980)[7] and Mbulelo Mzamane's *The Children of Soweto* (1982)[8] present more or less factual accounts of the activities of the high-school pupils who attempted to sustain resistance to the system. Sipho Sepamla's very different *A Ride on the Whirlwind* (1981)[9] makes popular fiction out of student and guerilla co-operation in acts of revolutionary retribution. But the most powerful and penetrating exploration of the Power period, which also situates it historically and psychologically, is Mongane Serote's *To Every Birth Its Blood* (1981).[10] Significant from a literary point of view as well, it is one of the most important South African novels to have emerged recently. It is this novel that I choose to discuss.

The origins of 'Soweto' as John Kane-Berman and others have shown, are to be found in the early 1970s. Serote's output spans this crucial decade, his first volume of poetry, *Yakhal'inkomo*, appearing in 1972. From the outset it was a decade of increasing political ferment during which the rise and establishment of Black Consciousness organizations was probably most crucial.[11] Rejecting what were seen as liberal compromise solutions, these organizations both reasserted the value of a specifically black identity and openly challenged the apartheid state. Although the emphasis on racial oppression rather than politico-economic factors has been challenged, Black Consciousness attitudes have widely permeated black popular consciousness, and have certainly influenced Serote's work. For this reason it seems important to trace his literary development.

* * * * *

The most obvious problem that faces the reader in *To Every Birth Its Blood* is the relation between the two parts of the novel. The second part's sudden shift from first-person narration to third-person narration, the time shift, and the shift of focus to a set of characters referred to but never central in the first part, are initially disconcerting and bewildering. But gradually, on closer examination, significant patterns begin to emerge.

In relation to the second part, the first part of the novel reveals itself as the story of defeat and despair. This section is seen through the eyes of ex-journalist and unsuccessful actor,[12] Tsi Molope. Personally defeated, Tsi registers the world as defeated too. For example, the members of his immediate family (the Molopes), are broken or damaged: one brother, Fix, has been detained; another brother, Ndo, is irrationally violent and constantly abuses his wife; his parents are old, empty and silenced, having fought to make a future for their children, and failed; and his sister Mary, initially bewildered by a frightening world and misguided by trashy escape fantasies, falls pregnant and is rejected by her parents.

More generally, the bitter realities of black experience in an apartheid society are felt with painful intensity. His home, Alexandra, is itself seen as a symbol of the defeat of the black man: it is the "Dark City", the polar opposite of the "Golden City"[13] which is the symbol of the white man's success; and the two are understood as integrally related. There are the degrading incidents, too, which spell defeat: the permit raid, the humiliating visit to the police station to obtain a new permit, the insults of the lift-man in Tsi's newspaper building — all the "shit" the black man resents, but has to put up with.[14]

In the same way — as Jane Glegg notes in her review of *To Every Birth Its Blood*[15] — the first section is pervaded by the uncertainties and fears surrounding Fix's detention, as well as the activity-in-exile of Tsi's friends, Anka, Boykie, Themba and Tuki. Furthermore, the arbitrariness with which state power is employed is underlined by the central incident which dominates the first half of the novel. Responding to the news of further detentions, and reflecting on the way he could no longer bring himself to observe the "tumour" and "rot" of apartheid society as a reporter, Tsi thinks back to the experience of naked police intimidation and brutality that has fundamentally changed his life. This incident is related as a flashback, a point which tends to be missed in the complex interweavings of Tsi's thought processes. He recalls how, on the way back from a newspaper assignment in the Transkei, he and his photographer friend Boykie were stopped by police, physically assaulted, and held in solitary confinement for a week. According to Boykie, who had been driving, the ostensible reason for this police action was that there had been a dead body lying in the road. This incident galvanizes Boykie into furious hatred and opposition to the system, but Tsi's response is to feel undermined and emasculated: for him the incident serves to focus the black person's vulnerability and impotence. This is underscored by the response of Tsi's white-run newspaper. The incident is immediately made into a "story" — an insignificant story, moreover, "in some corner, on page two" in which Tsi is also racially categorized as a "black reporter". (124) This is the point from which it becomes impossible for Tsi to report the "terrible township images", (135) and from which his sense of defeat and despair takes over. It is thus inaccurate to respond to Tsi as simply a "feckless drunkard",[16] as reviewers have tended to do. Rather, one should see that this series of traumatic events has wrenched him out of a relatively comfortable and stable position of social adjustment, and precipitated his severe state of psychological weariness and *anomie*.

Part One of the novel presents, through Tsi, an anatomy of a people's defeat. This defeat involves a world of experience which separates people from each other in their individual suffering, and is thus accurately portrayed through an isolated individual consciousness. From an epistemological viewpoint, what is captured here is the psychological response to a battering external world: it is the way in which the environment acts upon and damages individuals that is explored. And it is precisely this subject-object relationship which is to be reversed in the second part of the novel. But before I go on to explore this claim, it is necessary to refer to the McLean's College episode. As head of the research unit for the correspondence school, Tsi experiences a period of both material success and psychological health. Interestingly, his commitment to the school and its educational aim (that of supplementing the inadequate official state education) takes place after the beginning of the Power era in the early 1970s, the point from which Serote traces the new mood of black assertiveness and resistance to the State.[17] This mood naturally involves the waning of previous feelings of inadequacy or impotence, but Tsi's choice of commitment is shown to represent a false alternative, and what is significant is the disillusionment that the disengagement ultimately brings. As Marius Schoon notes in his review of the novel, Part One ends with the failure of a liberal approach to change.[18] However, it is not only that the irrelevance of liberal institutions is established: in relation to Part Two, the crucial contribution of Part One is that the impotence of the isolated individual is graphically presented.

*   *   *   *   *

If Part One sensitively records the anguish of the individual brutalized by a harsh world, Part Two presents the engagement of a growing number of people in an organized struggle to overthrow the system. The focus shifts from an individual consciousness to a group of people who will become comrades; first-person narration is abandoned for a more objective third-person narrative mode, and the emphasis on subjective feelings and suffering increasingly gives way to action as The

Movement grows in strength.

As I have indicated, the action of the end of Part One is affected by the first manifestations of Power. In a sense this can be seen as a transitional phase,[19] marked in the novel by the metamorphosis of Tsi's parents. No longer withdrawn and silent, they begin to talk about Fix and attend both his trial and the first freedom funerals. Thus the pre-conditions for the rapid growth of commitment to The Movement are established here. Although Power dominates Part Two from the outset, Serote does not immediately present a miraculously transformed community. Instead, Part Two opens with the desolation of Tsi's friend John following the police shooting of his wife Nolizwe, and relationships and friendships are initially as unsatisfactory as they were in the first part of the novel. But even here there is a different note: John may be emotionally deadened, but this means that his heart "has frozen to steel", "that he was a deadly man". (168) And with Nolizwe's friend Onalenna, a very different, firm and forward-looking discourse begins to emerge: in answer to John's anxiety about the future, Onalenna is insistent that their task is to consider ways of determining that future. (180)

Then, too, the family on which the narration focuses in this section is very different from the Molope family. This is the strong Ramono family. Ramono himself has been engaged in underground political activity, and his wife Grace has both the faith in her husband and the psychological strength necessary to endure his period of imprisonment. The relationship between Ramono and his daughter, Dikeledi, is also constructive. It is subtly indicated that with the defeat of the old-guard leadership of the resistance, a new guard emerges to take its place, and there is also the suggestion that links between the two generations are highly valuable — the older generation having a political wisdom acquired through long years of experience. Significantly, it is Ramono who warns of the dangers of too heavy an emphasis on race. In a discussion with Dikeledi he questions an exclusively Black Consciousness perspective. For Ramono, as for Serote, the struggle should not be defined in racial terms, but should rather be seen as the struggle against a determinate social and economic system.

It is not, however, Ramono who draws Dikeledi into The Movement. The catalyst for the new generation of dissidents is Oupa, Tsi's nephew, the illegitimate son of Tsi's sister Mary. Thus Mary's disgrace and expulsion from the family in the previous generation is followed, in the very different mood of the later seventies, by her son's determination and political dedication. It is Oupa who convinces Dikeledi and John that they should join The Movement after Ramono has been sentenced to fifteen years' imprisonment. This in itself marks the transformation taking place in black society. From here, until we return to Tsi at the end of the novel, the growing momentum of The Movement is captured through the widening of focus to incorporate an increasing number of individuals. The focus is also upon action — guerilla activity and sabotage — which rapidly escalates.

Of course, it is those individuals who are strengthened through dedication to a group, and ultimately to the masses, who are enabled to act: it is in this way that the impotence, debilitation and alienation of the isolated subject is overcome. Thus one could perhaps say that it is The Movement that is the central protagonist of Part Two. This is most dramatically suggested by the lyrical descriptions of The Movement which establish an emotional undertone or counterpoint to the action. The Movement is symbolically presented in terms of spreading roots, (326)   the sea, and the wind, (359)   descriptions which are particularly striking in contrast to the harsh and angry description of Alexandra in Part One. But while one is in no doubt that commitment to The Movement is supported by Serote, the dangers of revolutionary activity are not shirked. Oupa is captured, tortured and killed after the Blue Granada operation and Mandla, too, is killed. Nor does Serote present revolutionary engagement as resolving private difficulties. Onalenna's relationship with the confused Yao remains fraught with difficulty even after his return from the United States. Themba's and Granny's relationship breaks down, the destruction of the relationship showing inevitable private-public conflicts which are almost impossible to resolve. Even the strong Ramono family have one failure: their son Morolong, named after a prominent political leader, is ironically not able to cope with the pressures of succeeding, and becomes a street-youth dropout.

On the whole — the exception being Mandla — the revolutionaries are not portrayed as faceless political machines: they are human individuals who have responsibly chosen to commit their lives to political struggle. This is in marked contrast to Sepamla's very disturbing presentation of the stupidly aggressive and automaton-like guerilla Mzi in *A Ride on the Whirlwind*. Nor are they glowingly portrayed as national heroes and heroines, as Miriam Tlali in *Amandla* and Mbulelo Mzamane in *The Children of Soweto* tend to present their characters. And Serote does not romanticise violence itself. Once again Sepamla's novel offers an instructive comparison: his choice of the political-thriller form in *A Ride on the Whirlwind* can be seen as presenting guerilla activity as a source of glamour and excitement. Finally, the struggle for freedom is not presented as inevitably victorious. The immense difficulty of such a struggle is underscored by the projection of total war at the end of the novel, and there is no outright prediction of which side will ultimately win. One is left with the agonizedly uncertain thoughts of Tsi in exile (jolted by Oupa's death, but still drinking and still confused) standing in a bread-queue, with South African Defence Force bombers flying overhead. However, one is also left with the birth of a baby: the hope, which also stands as inspiration, that the bloodshed and violence will lead to a liberated South Africa.

$$* \quad * \quad * \quad * \quad *$$

My central argument is that the two sections of the novel are balanced against each other, Part One exploring suffering, despair, and the helplessness of the individual, Part Two offering the hope of a different future through concerted political activity. Turning to Serote's poetry, one realizes that these two poles form the primary themes or motifs of his work. In his earliest volumes of poetry, *Yakhal'inkomo* (1972) and *Tsetlo* (1974),[20] a significant proportion of the poetry captures the harshness of black experience through a rendering of the poet-protagonist's anguish, despair and weariness, and painfully records the destruction of individuals in a ghetto society. On the other hand, the inevitability of change is captured in the images of dawn following darkness, in the change of the seasons, and in the symbols of birth and the river — all of which Serote is to use again and again.

In his next two works, the long epic poems *No Baby Must Weep* (1975)[21] and *Behold Mama, Flowers* (1978),[22] Serote begins to explore the relationship between the individual who has suffered and the collective activity required to end that suffering — between "memory",[23] on the one hand, and the future on the other. Both poems offer a representation of the narrator's psychological-emotional state, the "intricate canopy of nightmares"[24] which in many ways parallels Tsi's suffering consciousness. In *No Baby Must Weep* the violent experiences of the black child's growing up are captured: here the street is both crucial educator and destroyer, and it symbolizes the black man's dead-end journey. *Behold Mama, Flowers* again expresses the anguish of oppression, but this time it is not charted in individual developmental terms, but rather in socio-historical ones: memory is the record of the oppression of black people through history.

Black individual and communal experience is always imaged retrospectively in terms of pain. But in *No Baby Must Weep* there is also the river, the deep, "dark" stream of black history into which the individual merges. Ultimately this river is destined for the sea, which is yearningly envisioned as "blue", "free", "vast" and healing. (51) And the river symbol is accompanied by an image of an experienced "tearing", the earth "spreading" — the intimations of some kind of new birth. (21) However, the conclusion here is ultimately bleak: although the only hope of liberation lies with the "river", the narrator feels trapped by this necessity, and the future is presented in terms of a weeping sky and a flower without petals. (61) In this poem it seems that Serote conceives the individual-collective relationship in terms of an *opposition*, and is hesitant about the inevitable loss of individual autonomy in a collectivity. In *Behold Mama, Flowers* this opposition disappears, and Serote is concerned to chart the necessary journey towards commitment. It is both the necessity of such a commitment, and also the difficulties which beset it, that are explored: the poem can be seen as the enactment of an increasing understanding which leads up to the conviction that the black individual's place is *rightfully* in communal struggle.

In *No Baby Must Weep* the river symbol is recurrent but ultimately not fully endorsed, for the river is seen as the historically conditioned *fate* of the individual, rather than his salvation. In *Behold Mama, Flowers* on the other hand, a number of symbols are used to capture intimations of a different, a liberated future; but the symbols are not as insistent as in *No Baby Must Weep*, and are also always placed in dialectical relation to the struggle necessary to attain freedom. Early in *Behold Mama, Flowers* for example, it is stressed that before "the sun shines on our heads" there will have to be destruction of the "walls" which stand. (14) Later, when the poet reflects on freedom, the striking image used to capture political activity is the "agile tiger", "in love with life". (48) And near the end of the poem an affirmation of the inevitable progress towards freedom is made in terms of the progress of time and the seasons, although the narrator foresees that he is likely to "fall" as others have fallen. (58) But, and this is crucial, their "word" will remain as inspiration, and the final note is affirmative: "behold the flowers, they begin to bloom". (61) The flowers without petals of *No Baby Must Weep* have become the blooming flowers of the later poem.

* * * * *

Looking back over the whole *oeuvre* there are two basic developments that are immediately striking. The first is the increasing complexity of Serote's work. *No Baby Must Weep* is the pivotal work. In this poem, instead of simply exploring experience thematically as he does in the two earlier volumes, Serote attempts to express a more consistently articulated political vision. The central aspects of his political understanding are integrated into a meaningful whole: the themes of the painful past and an anticipated future become the two halves of a perceived politico-historical relationship, in which the drive towards freedom is seen to be based upon memory. It was in order to present this understanding, and to explore all the difficulties encountered — both psychological and actual — that Serote felt the need to express himself in bigger, more continuous works. The novel can be seen as a culmination of this process.

Secondly, Serote's work becomes increasingly radical or committed. Even in his early work, a development can be traced: in *Yakhal'inkomo* a number of the poems are clearly addressed to a white audience, and the message is perhaps above all:

> White people are white people
> They must learn to listen.
> Black people are black people,
> They must learn to talk.[25]

Tsetlo, on the other hand, is harsher and more uncompromising. There is the recognition of the inevitability of violence on both sides, and the message here is rather that "black child's laughter will ring in the dark sky". That violence will be necessary, is also found tragic: "only/ I wonder where I'll cleanse my hands".[26] This is ultimately the conclusion of Serote's next work, *No Baby Must Weep*, too, but by *Behold Mama, Flowers* the revolutionary struggle is more firmly endorsed, and once again *To Every Birth Its Blood* represents a culmination. What is new in this work is the amount of attention — half of the novel — paid to revolutionary activity; and commitment is presented far more concretely. In other words, what has been offered as a generalized imperative in the poetry, becomes in Part Two of the novel an actual organization, The Movement. In presenting commitment and struggle so explicitly and tangibly, the novel renders the message far more pointedly since it is openly linked to a particular grouping. The imperative becomes a clearly defined, and socially available, dedication to a specific course of political action.

179

This granted, there is one criticism I would like to make of Part Two. As I have shown, Serote suggests that the isolated individual may overcome his defeat through dedication to the political struggle. The formal structuring of the novel implies that it is commitment to a group, and ultimately the community, that is decisive. However, while it could be argued that The Movement sets out to act for the benefit of the whole community, the group is actually comprised of intellectuals who are totally isolated from communal organizations. Unlike the situation in Sembene Ousmane's *God's Bits of Wood*, the struggle for the community is not undertaken *by* the community: hence the undue emphasis on destructive rather than constructive political activity.

There is also one constant positive feature of Serote's work which merits attention. This is his humanism, which involves a deep-rooted concern for individual happiness and wholeness. From *Yakhal'inkomo* through to *To Every Birth Its Blood* there is the characteristic concern for children, old people and the family that Nadine Gordimer has noted,[27] as well as the vision of an alternative form of life which underlies his rejection of present reality.

Above all, the way in which present political conditions serve to destroy the black individual is explored in all of Serote's work. Given this, he increasingly comes to believe that for the sake of future wholeness, armed struggle is the socio-historically necessary course of action. Central to his vision is the way in which the conclusion is always presented in relation to the determinants, action in relation to memory, objective necessity in relation to individual suffering, The Movement in relation to the story of defeat. As opposed to perspectives which emphasize hate, blood-lust or revenge, which see revolution *in itself* as the goal, or which set out to polarize issues in terms of racial categories, Serote's is a truly positive contribution to South African literary and political life.

NOTES

1   My account of the Soweto disturbances is heavily indebted to John Kane-Berman's book *Soweto: Black Revolt, White Reaction* (Johannesburg: Ravan 1981). A second book consulted is Gerhart, Gail M *Black Power in South Africa: The Evolution of an Ideology* Perspectives on Southern Africa 19 (Berkeley: University of California Press 1978).

2   Kane-Berman p1.

3   The only officially recognised civic body in Soweto. Kane-Berman p4.

4   Kane-Berman chapter 3.

5   The Committee of Ten members were detained; but the most important detention, and subsequent death, was that of Steve Biko — now, like Nelson Mandela and Robert Sobukwe, established as a national hero.

6   Kane-Berman p10.

7   Tlali, Miriam *Amandla* (Johannesburg: Ravan 1980).

8   Mzamane, Mbulelo *The Children of Soweto* (Johannesburg: Ravan 1982).

9   Sepamla, Sipho *A Ride on the Whirlwind* (Johannesburg: Ad Donker 1981).

10   Serote, Mongane *To Every Birth Its Blood* (Johannesburg: Ravan 1981). All bracketed page references are to this edition.

11   SASO (South African Students' Organization) and BPC (Black People's Convention) were the two most significant Black Consciousness organizations.

12   Tsi had felt "naked" acting, and could not continue in the consciousness-raising Takalana Theatre project.

13   Johannesburg is popularly referred to among blacks as *Egoli* — gold.

14   Serote has described this "shit" in his early poem "What's in this Black 'Shit'"; see Serote, Mongane *Yakhal'inkomo* (Johannesburg: Renoster Books/ Bateleur Press 1972) p8.

15   Glegg, Jane *Staffrider* 5 (1) (1982) p34.

16   Glegg p34. For a more glaring example of this attitude, see Achmat Dangor's review in the same issue of *Staffrider*.

17   Serote traces the new mood from the era of campus revolts, when "universities, black universities, were going on strike". (139) The first student uprisings began in 1972 at the University of the North after student leader A D R Tiro was expelled from that University. In 1974 mass rallies organised in support of FRELIMO were cancelled, causing further campus unrest.

18   Schoon, Marius *"To Every Birth Its Blood*, Mongane Serote" *MEDU Art Ensemble Newsletter* 4 (1) 35—38.

19   Historically, the period 1972—1976.

20   Serote, Mongane *Yakhal'inkomo* (Johannesburg: Renoster Books/Bateleur Press 1972) and *Tsetlo* (Johannesburg: Ad Donker 1974). Bracketed page references are to these editions.

21   Serote, Mongane *No Baby Must Weep* (Johannesburg: Ad Donker 1975). Page references to the poem are to this edition.

22   Serote, Mongane *Behold Mama, Flowers* (Johannesburg: Ad Donker 1978). Page references are to this edition.

23   *Behold Mama, Flowers* p12, p37 and "Notes for a Fighter" p84.

24   *No Baby Must Weep* p44.

25   "Ofay-Watcher, Throbs Phase" *Yakhal'inkomo* p50.

26   "Sunset" *Tsetlo* p62.

27   Gordimer, Nadine *The Black Interpreters* (Johannesburg : SPROCAS Ravan 1973).

Sheila Roberts's Concern with Stereotypes in her Short Stories

J A KEARNEY

Although Sheila Roberts's collection of short stories, *Outside Life's Feast*,[1] won the Olive Schreiner Award in 1976,[2] it does not seem to have earned any critical attention apart from the original reviews. One of my motives in writing this article is to show how undeserved this neglect is. Apart from the stories in *Outside Life's Feast*, Roberts has written at least nine others. Since interesting relationships seem to me present, not only amongst the collected stories but also between these and the others, I have decided to work on a selection from the total set of short stories so far as it is known to me. I hope that by the time my comments appear, Roberts's new collection of stories, entitled *This Time of Year*,[3] will have been published.

I shall not attempt to compare Roberts's short stories with those of either Nadine Gordimer or Doris Lessing, her two eminent predecessors and peers in the field, because much spadework analysis of Roberts's stories needs to be undertaken first. One general conclusion is, nevertheless, relevant here. Roberts has, I think, been determined to avoid the central racial emphasis of many of the Gordimer or earlier Lessing stories. Her purpose has been to explore predicaments in which the racial factor, while significant, is not necessarily the focal or overriding one.

A consistently significant aspect of such predicaments in Roberts's stories is the way in which certain stereotypes held by characters limit or damage their relationships. That the characters themselves hold such stereotypes, distinguishes them from the writer's own use of one-dimensional characters, necessary to some extent in all fiction, but particularly so in the brief confines of a short story. For my purposes then, a stereotype may be most simply defined as a fixed mental perception or image in the mind of a character. Chief amongst the stereotypes which recur in Roberts's short stories are those which involve the perceptions men and women have of each other and of themselves in relation to each other, and the perceptions that members of a family have of each other's roles within the family. My purpose is to show the variety of ways in which Roberts makes the reader freshly aware of the functioning of such stereotypes in everyday South African life, and the kind of ironic realism she brings to bear on possible interactions between them. Most prominent is her interest in the operation of the passive female stereotype. Employing a range of tones from the poignant to the comic, Roberts impresses one by the degree of her compassionate insight into these operations, as well as their apparent inevitability and self-perpetuation. Whether a stereotype is voluntarily adopted or is imposed, her concern is with those who suffer as a result. In placing racist stereotypes in a complex perspective of other interrelating mental fixities, she has a unique contribution to make to South African literature. If she too has occasional, unwitting recourse to stereotypes, this serves to remind one of the difficulty of her task, and to emphasise her more characteristic control.

Since it's impossible to group and comment on all of Roberts's stories without repetitive discussion, I have chosen to concentrate on seven of her stories with some glances at others to demonstrate my claims. In order to give some emphasis to the development of Roberts's interest in stereotypes, I shall consider these stories in chronological order of publication. This sequence should also help to reveal Roberts's keenness to experiment with form and narrative point of view, adapting for her own needs the techniques of earlier twentieth-century writers such as Joyce and Faulkner.

Next Time

In this story Roberts reveals the plight of Mikey, only son of an alcoholic ex-miner: desperately exhausted as a result of his father's night-long clamouring, and sickened by his obscene behaviour, Mikey decides to force him into quietness with a blow from a stick. The power of the story is derived from the absence of any conventional filial feeling in the son, despite his mother's agonised wishes. Hatred and loathing and a sense of shame give him one obsessive wish: to rid himself "next time" of the father's presence. No thought of what lies beyond fulfilment of this wish can gain entry to his tormented consciousness. He fears that his mother (epitome of the passive female stereotype) "will never stand up to him but only sink down more and more and smoke and smoke until the tiredness finishes her." (27) She has no way of dealing with his outraged feelings against his father except to appeal to the commandment "Honour thy father". Such an appeal has the force of stereotype morality only, with no relevance to the child's existential situation: "I hate him he's your father Mikey I said honour thy so he asked me so do you expect me to love a pig like him he's not my father." (27—8) In her passivity, the mother attempts to excuse and defend the father though the son's vehement dismissal of her argument suggests that her indulgent tendency may very well have aggravated the father's loss of self-control and self-respect.

Roberts invites one to enter with full sympathy into the agony of Mikey's mother, trapped by stereotypes of role and morality and so prevented from finding a solution to her husband's disintegration and her son's hatred. Moreover the mother's descriptions of the father, both before and after the blow, while conveying the son's revulsion, also evoke the reader's pity for the father. But the insistent call of the story is on our sympathy for Mikey, his own possibilities for life gravely reduced because of parents who have both collapsed into stereotyped roles: the mother who "must maar keep the peace" (28), and the father who has persuaded himself that he is a victim of fate.

Wretched self-consciousness as a result of his home life makes Mikey appreciate school uniformity. At the same time he is anxious to assert his Englishness as if he must cling to some conception of superiority amidst his general sense of the family's degradation. This urge is all the more compelling because the other boys' teasing comments seem to trace evidence of his sickening home conditions: "I couldn't care that the ous call me rooinek and sometimes white rat because of my hair and face. At least I am not a hairyback I tell them . . . ." (27) It is through this psychological defence mechanism that Mikey becomes able to build up the image of himself as a figure with authority and power who alone can be the redeemer of his mother and himself. Unfortunately this image has in it too much of brute masculine dominance for it to have any positive redemptive value: "I have got a week to find myself a strong kierie so that next time I can hit him. Just on the side of his head. Not too hard." (25)

Ironically, the doctor who attends the (presumably half-dead) father makes implicit use of the filial stereotype to offer Mikey an escape route from blame: no-one could imagine that the boy might be responsible for the father's injury. Mikey is thus saved, at least in an external social sense, by the same conception of son-father relationships which he has been driven to defy. In the final passage, however, his fantasy of being deaf and blind disturbingly echoes his father's solipsistic drunken states. His brief attainment of that ardently wished for state of quiet involves a heightened sense of pathos, with its powerful but illusory evocation of a new world and new Adam. Saddest of all the implications of Mikey's fantasy of Paradise is that it apparently has no place for his ineffectual mother: possibly because her "bawling" after the assault on the father has brought a new threat to his peace of mind.

Roberts's first two stories both involve first-person narrators. In the first, *The Touch of Your Hand*, the rather self-conscious, quasi-poetic diction in parts of the story make one begin to feel that there's an inappropriate posing on the narrator's part, or to suspect that authorial detachment has not been fully achieved. In the case of *Next Time* however, Roberts succeeds in sustaining the impression of a fifteen-year-old boy's consciousness. Continual Afrikaans-isms cast gently humorous irony on Mikey's anxiety to be regarded as English, while the diction in general remains credibly within the range of his age and social group. It is Roberts's use of schoolboy slang as vehicle for rendering Mikey's deep inner anguish that is perhaps the most remarkable feature of this story. Even the poignant lyricism of the final passage remains firmly Mikey's, not his author's.

Cleft Stick

This story opens with a young policeman as first-person narrator. His sexist and racist assumptions, particularly his conviction that Ty, the dissolute miner, was hardly to blame for attempting to have sex with his servant because his wife was "mad in the head" (85), are the veil beyond which the story probes. Although only four paragraphs are needed to reveal the policeman's state of confusion and prejudice, his admission "man sometimes you feel sorry" (85), provides an ironic keynote to the story. He's sorry *only* for the husband, of course, and then for the wrong reason, whereas Roberts succeeds ultimately in eliciting compassion for wife, servant *and* husband — indeed, even her rendering of the policeman's consciousness, while involving sardonic humour, is not unsympathetic.

Central in establishing the perspective of the entire story, is Alida's view from her lounge window. She could see that

... the recreation hall was almost in the centre of the township, the houses of the personnel being in a geometric arrangement round it. Probably the ground-plan of the township formed a very pleasing, orderly design when seen from the air. The houses themselves were evidence that a mind of passionate orderliness had achieved satisfaction, for each street was restrained to only two variations of the basic design; one variation on this side and one on that. (87)

This "mind of passionate orderliness", a South African representation of puritan consciousness, is the only one to receive satisfaction in the story, and its satisfaction becomes the fundamental cause of the lack of satisfaction for any of the protagonists. The immediate effect of the "geometric arrangement" is that the characters cannot see each other except in stereotyped fashion; more drastically still, the image that husband and wife employ of themselves is not the one held by their spouse or by the policeman. Alida wants to be regarded by the police, and presumably by Ty too, as a "poor, but hardworking woman" (86); by Ty, however, she is regarded persistently as an "aasvoël",[4] or otherwise as "dry and stiff", "dried out" (89); by the policeman as "mad in the head". What Alida actually reveals is an alternative version of the passive female stereotype, one which requires minimal shifting from its customary form: the practice of passive resistance, especially in sexual relations. Alida's single moment of active intervention in her circumstances, her attempted suicide after the police have taken Maatjie away, seems to be required of her mainly because Ty has stepped beyond the bounds of *his* stereotyped role: perpetual drunkenness is socially tolerable, attempted sex with the servant is not.

Ty ranges through a whole series of images of himself, each in some way self-excusing or self-pitying. Only one, "I'm a pig" (89), coincides in category but not in force, with Alida's vehemently bitter "'Bladdy vark! ... Rubbish, that's what you are!'" (88) Ty's vision of a sexless, unresponsive wife is no more to be considered reliable than is his sense of himself, nor does he at any point begin to contemplate his share of responsibility for their plight. Yet his intense sense of frustration and his conflicting responses towards Maatjie, make him a pitiful, rather than a corrupt or amoral figure. We're made to feel that the surrounding rigid geometry is largely responsible for prompting the kind of responses husband and wife have been led to make. Sympathy for Ty is further created by the self-righteous relish of watchful neighbours who alert the police and are clearly excited at this opportunity for applying the stereotyped judgment of total reprehensibility. But then, Roberts induces one to ask, what else is there to provide relief for them either?

Our pity for Ty is, however, qualified by two factors: first by his readiness (admittedly, only out of desperate cunning) to lay a charge against Maatjie for leading him astray, and secondly by the far graver state of Alida's despair — she is found "trying without courage to saw through the skin of her left wrist." (92) The neat line, the result of her sawing, is shown as the pitifully tragic outcome of the surrounding deathlike geometry. Final and utter contempt for her husband, freeing her from the last vestiges of her passive resistance, frees her simultaneously from the wish to retain *any* form of identity.

Alida's viewpoint is conveyed impersonally while that of Ty is conveyed through a combination of first-person and impersonal narration. This inevitably creates a sense of some underlying difference in their status. Is it that Roberts feels she has a more intricate task in rendering the offender's consciousness because he has broken one of the most sacred of South African white taboos? One is inclined towards this answer rather than to suppose that Roberts would find Alida's shifts of consciousness less interesting to unravel than her husband's.

For No Reason[5]

The action of this story involves no immediate violent crisis as in *Next Time* or *Cleft Stick*: a family group consisting of two sisters, Ann and Denise, their two brothers, Ann's child and her boyfriend, Koen (not the child's father evidently), visit a nearby farm. Denise seems to be driven by a vision of machismo, of a man who is tough, daring, fearless and successful; since Ann's boyfriend seems to fit this image, she provokes him to reveal how closely he does in fact match it. There is a deliberately willed quality in her attention, and although Koen shows no overt desire to flirt with her, he seems to find it hard to resist her challenge. She dares him to go riding bareback with her. Her return first, on her own, suggests either that he has found the experience far more uncomfortable than he expected, or that he has the capacity, in the long run, to detach himself from pursuit of a stereotyped idea of masculinity.

The image of herself which Denise tries to project for most of the story, is that of independence and spontaneity, a readiness to spurn anything as mundanely restrictive as previous family arrangements.

187

Ann's comparative reticence, together with the fear expressed by her little boy and by the owl they watch, suggests a significant and in a way necessary fear of life from which Denise is trying to escape. For Denise, fear has no place in her perception of what life should be like. Her indignant rejection of Ann's reminder about the need to get home to their mother's lunch, and the special relationship with Koen that she tries to demand for herself, extend our impressions to cover the factor of sensitivity in general: Denise has, or will allow herself, little concern for the feelings and needs of others.

Denise's chief means of trying to remain aloof from emotional difficulties and others' needs seems to be her arousal of the heroic male stereotype. Koen's lack of interest, followed by the reminder soon afterwards of Karel's suicide, seems to undermine her pose, and she sobs all the way back, ostensibly over Karel's gassing himself "for no reason at all." (62) Mrs Nel's earlier comment that "it's too much city life that turns them into moffies and queers . . ." (60) is possibly meant to suggest a reason for the young man's suicide. But if the title does suggest that no one reason would adequately account for Karel's action, his fear of life nevertheless remains the crucial motif of the story. Denise's own sobbing, however exaggerated or exhibitionistic, is an implicit admission that her stereotype of masculinity and her brash challenge to female passivity provide no lasting solution. Had she been more rigidly bound to her desired impression of men or of herself, she would probably have scoffed at Karel's fear of life.

The poignant, ironic close to the story reveals how Ann's reticence and insecurity, as well as the nervousness of her child, make a strong, dependable male presence a necessary one for her. Her compliment to Koen as she enters her mother's securely bourgeois home shows how, in having to make sure of him after her sister's manoeuvres, she seems compelled to do so in the very terms chosen by Denise. What makes the story one of Roberts's finest achievements is her detached sympathy: no animus towards Denise emerges, while the restrained, conventional elements of Ann's personality win sympathy, but prevent her from being the focus of the writer's or reader's rapt admiration. The sombre undertones of the story leave two painful realisations: the limitations of the passive female and heroic male stereotypes, and simultaneously, the way in which the pressures of life seem to make their predominance inevitable.

. In this second study of the effects on a family of an alcoholic father, Roberts elaborates the correlation between a sense of failure and a stereotype-ridden consciousness. The father is prejudiced not only against "kaffirs", but against all other nationalities, including the English if they're not from South Africa — excepting, of course, the King and Queen. Towards Afrikaners he displays markedly contradictory attitudes: on the one hand he's glad to be working for the Nats (from desperate relief that he has any job at all); on the other hand, he can afford to regard Afrikaners in general as "low people". At first we're almost deliberately misled by Roberts's comically satirical presentation of his views into supposing that they merely provide useful material for character assessment. But the full implications of his prejudices become clear when his wife has to go to hospital for her latest delivery and the girls' parent-inspired terror of "kaffirs" is shown to be misplaced indeed: it's their own father of whom they can be more justly terrified.

This father thoroughly exploits the notions of filial obedience and maternal submissiveness. The daughters provide a convenient audience for his lengthy self-commiserations; he has so little awareness of their ordinary needs, that Bevvy, the youngest, is forced to remain seated even when it's clear that she cannot control her bladder any longer. Desperately insecure and vengeful because of his own childhood suffering, he seems blindly determined to use the girls as scapegoats to enact his mental retribution on a harsh society. It's presumably because the girls are so conditioned by the model of passivity offered by their mother, that no thought of desperate violence occurs to them as it does to Mikey in *Next Time*. Their remedy lies in fantasies of escape. Even Bevvy, in the final line of the story, proclaims her impulse to "'ride away . . . and never come back.'" (22—23) Yet the effect on her of their neighbour's dog — her pathetic shaking and teeth-grinding — is a reminder that one cannot simply ride away: the marks are too deeply burnt in. The pathos of the children's helplessness is made more acute by the fact that they *can* appease the vicious dog by throwing it food; for their father, however, they can do nothing. Their wish for a romantic, bicycle-borne freedom is a moving aspect of the story, revealing signs of a vitality which is continually thwarted but must have spontaneous expression. It also has wry overtones: Roberts prompts us to ask whether these girls, in their blind urge to escape an oppressive, wretched home, will not rush into marriage, deceived by vague and romantic promises? And might not they, in their turn, demand recompense from *their* offspring for *their* suffering?

Roberts's sardonic irony and sense of pathos are forcefully blended in the drivelling climax of the father's tirade "'. . . I'm going . . . to buy a pay . . . per . . . doll . . . . That I can ca . . . all my . . . ee . . . own . . . .'" (21—22) Here is the passive, male-gratifying, female stereotype in its plainest and crudest terms. The use of a widely known golden oldie reinforces Roberts's perception of the way emotional immaturity, with a long history of social conditioning, coincides with this infantile wish for possession and control of a totally yielding female.

Granny Kersting[6]

In relation to the stories analysed so far, *Granny Kersting* provides strong evidence of the flexibility and broadness of Roberts's concern with stereotypes. Joey, the grown-up orphan who has been brought up by Granny Kersting, has to learn how little her Gran is compatible with a vision of grandmothers as kindly, protective creatures. Humour, playing on a range of domestic and maternal possibilities within the stereotype, temporarily obscures the frightening revelation contained in the dénouement.

In a retrospectively effective ironic opening, Granny Kersting herself invites Joey to observe how little she fits the stereotype of Grannies. The old woman's own concern is simply with her physical shape so that humour is sustained throughout Joey's surprise at what appears to be an unusual degree of individuality and forthrightness in her guardian. Then Grandad's funeral service offers a significant, though hidden, warning of what is to come: Joey would like real feeling to have been shown; instead she is left with a packaged, sterile substitute — so too, the feeling she thought her Gran possessed turns out to be an empty illusion. Granny Kersting's treatment of her new husband, Major Horace Pound-Jenkins (whose very name suggests a preposterously conventional military figure), leads to Joey's stunned discovery that her grandmother deserves no devotion or affection. The two syllables of her name are aptly combined and provide a probable Afrikaans pun on 'Christian'. Moreover her callous exploitation of the senile Major shifts his status dramatically from cardboard stooge to touchstone of humanity.

Granny Kersting does not conform to the passive female stereotype. But that leads one to ask whether it is not possible that the story

190

involves an attempt to portray, with some sympathy, the alternative patterns of behaviour that may develop when a woman has sufficient strength of will to resist passivity. Two glimpses of Granny's past indeed seem intended as partial explanations for her hardness and self-seeking: first Grandad's early affairs, and secondly Gran's confession to a family friend that "although she had had ten babies in her time, she never knew what 'nature' was." (100)   But Granny Kersting's lack of "nature" doesn't seem attributable entirely to suffering at the hands of a male chauvinist. It may be that a more fundamental lack of "nature" has been present all along, one that might help to explain Grandad's interest in other relationships.

Coming In[7]

Coming In seems distinct in tone and treatment of character from any of Roberts's previous stories. Here one finds compassion combined for the first time with a gentle, unsardonic humour as she engages us with the perplexing and disillusioning experiences of a French immigrant family from Algeria. What comes as a relief in the opus so far is the ordinariness and likeableness of the family, as well as their unstrained relationships with each other. One is inclined to feel that the shift to non-South African protagonists is a significant one for Roberts. Of course the family's likeableness is a feature of the overall irony: their prejudices, of which they're unaware, make them not so different after all from their new South African compatriots.

Luc, on his first night in a Johannesburg hotel, persuades himself ruefully that he hadn't expected a Promised Land. Yet he has to acknowledge to himself also that he did expect *something*, and that his anticipation was bound up with a sense of white South Africans as wealthy. That consideration has now to be replaced by the thought that the family may have come among barbarians. With delicate irony Roberts offers Luc's sense of what is civilised, as derived from his upbringing in Algeria: the images reflect an affluent, sensuous, materially refined existence — clearly Luc had hoped that South Africa would surpass these attractions. Then, in Luc's memory of the family's train trip, Roberts juxtaposes very unobtrusively the mother's use of the train handbasin as a toilet because of her fear of public facilities, with the parents' horror at the sight of thronging blacks on the platform. Without making the new immigrants objects of ridicule, Roberts amusingly induces one to register what is contradictory in their outlook. Luc advises his parents, saying " 'Do you want to polish and scrub floors at your age? And do washing and ironing? So . . . wait . . . don't be prejudiced.' " They respond with " '*Tous ces noirs*,' murmured Papa. 'I shall have to pray God,' decided Maman.'' (140) These are wonderfully comic moments in the story, exposing a complacent sense of superiority, while preserving sympathy for the tense, nervous, and so very naive arrivals.

The hotel receptionist, once she has been reassured that Algerians count as whites, alters her attitudes and, without the slightest sense of incongruity, switches to a soothingly hospitable role, inviting "Maman" to accept the conventional white view of South Africa as the "finest [country] in the world". (142) The climax takes the receptionist's unease a stage further by way of hilarious counterpoint. One of the typists at the office where Luc finds employment, fits him, as soon as she hears that he's French, into the potential role of Latin lover, while the other asks to have him moved away from her because he's Portuguese and "if her father sees her talking to a Portuguese boy or a Jew boy, he'll break her neck." (144) Not surprisingly, Luc is shown turning mentally to his own stereotype of the "good place": "He wondered suddenly how Oncle Henri was getting on." (145)

Roberts invites us to sympathise with, even as we laugh gently at, her characters' predicament. Stereotypes seem inescapable for Algerians and South Africans alike, but Roberts persuades us here to face this aspect of reality with detached irony and amusement, rather than with obsessive bitterness.

*   *   *   *   *

Two of the stories which seem to have been written specially for the book *Outside Life's Feast, All That Jazz* and *The Boss*, bring together stereotypes of race and sex, while the latter, like *Coming In*, includes stereotypes of nationality also. Unfortunately, Roberts's zeal in *All That Jazz* to attain a genuine, no-nonsense liberalism, seems to make it necessary for her to rely in her turn on stereotypes. Bill's negrophilia is no mere comic touch as in the case of the secretaries' neatly contrasting biases in *Coming In*, but the cause of a serious crisis for the female protagonist. Although Bill's black friends' offensive behaviour is meant to reflect unfavourably on him, it seems contrived for the sake of justifying his girlfriend's misery. Their sordid vulgarity may too easily be taken to endorse the view that black sophistication is inevitably superficial. It's true that the story is narrated largely through the conversation of the protagonist and her friend, but this doesn't offer sufficient counterbalancing irony. Bill may be a very particular kind of white, but the blacks can scarcely be prevented from acquiring representative status in the absence of more congenial black characters.

Like *Granny Kersting*, *The Boss* treats ordinary disappointment and irritation humorously, revealing a frightening kind of callous deceit. There's much well-observed and engaging comedy in the 'kugel' and 'bagel' couple's sharp, sarcastic rejoinders to each other. Lilly, in her anxiety to retain her husband's interest, reveals her stereotyped ideas of what men like. What is specially interesting about the characterisation is that Lilly's banal revelations about models from her glossy magazine, involve, in a comic and superficial way, the impulse to dispel false notions and assumptions, whereas it's precisely the stereotyped idea of woman as passive sex object which gives rise to such a magazine in the first place, thereby permitting social tolerance of the type of exploitation that the story is to reveal in Vicki, the helpless young coloured woman. She is simply a means of ensuring a good time for the hotel boss at the gambling table and in bed; her feelings, even her overt public protest at his manipulation, are ignored. What serves to highlight the egoistic holiday gratification of the Boss, is Selwyn's and Lilly's chagrin, and desire for compensation, because their expectations of a 'perfect' holiday have failed. A further ironic connection between the two couples is that Selwyn is surprised to detect in himself, as a South African male, real feelings of protectiveness and tenderness towards Vicki. One blemish in the story is Selwyn's stereotyping of the Assistant Manager. His explicit surprise at finding himself thinking "You bastard of a Jew-burning Nazi" (75), convincing and natural as it may be in a young Jew, can't quite undo the force of repeated reference in the narration to the Boss as "The German". The Manager's race *does* seem, apart from Selwyn's feelings, to be a significant factor in the treatment of Vicki.

Mbiti Herself[8]

This is perhaps the most unusual of all Roberts's stories so far and Mbiti is the most memorable of Roberts's female characters except for Granny Kersting. Much risk has been taken in this portrayal, since Mbiti turns out to be very close to one of the well-worn white stereotypes of black women — likely to be lascivious, with an unquenchable sexual appetite. Bartho, the young white South African artist who has been married for four years in Botswana to Mbiti, whom he first met as a prostitute, is one of the more admirable of Roberts's male characters: our sympathy for him is not just a response to pathos, as in the case of Ty in *Cleft Stick*, and the reason for the failure of his relationship with Mbiti is not because he has sought to model himself on some version of the heroic male stereotype.

Happiest with Mbiti when she fitted into the role of "decent Tswana matron", Bartho wonders whether she might not re-adopt tribal customs if he were to leave her. Part of the attraction for Bartho of the Tswana matron's style lies in its quaintness, a reminder of powerful colonial influence:

> He loved the long skirts . . . . He made many sketches of her in those dresses and she had encouraged in him this period of his calmest and most painterly art. Her walk had been stately and her dignity flawless. (13)

While this passage does not mock Bartho, the implication is that his interest in Mbiti is dependent on a stereotyped notion of her as tribeswoman, a notion which, in its stress upon stateliness and dignity, leaves out of account the energy and uniqueness in Mbiti "herself".

Furthermore, Bartho's initial interest in Mbiti was directly due to his wish, revealed late in the story, to find through a black woman what he feels he can't achieve with a white woman: "He would never have been able to lose himself in them, he knew, which was what he wanted most: to lose himself utterly and all his consciousness of being a white South African." (15) The inference, once again, is that such a wish involves too little awareness of Mbiti herself: any willing, sexually appealing black woman would have served his purpose as effectively. It's plausible, because of this special need, and his general ineffectuality, that Bartho is unable to convince Mbiti that a stable marriage is better than her former way of life. Her harping on his whiteness seems to be the result of her intuitive realisation that his own racial identity is actually uppermost in his desire for her, a way of keeping herself free from his unwitting exploitation.

Bartho's suffering, revealed especially through the tormented sexual imagery of his woodcuts, draws him strongly into our sympathy, sustaining the effect of his gentle concern for the sleeping children. Yet the fascinating, unique qualities of Mbiti's brief speeches, above all her contemptuous dismissal of Bartho's suggestion that she works for money, "Munnee-munnee-munnee . . ." (12), win similar favour for her. The ending, Bartho's decision to leave Mbiti and return to South Africa because of her persistence in reverting to the lifestyle of a casual bar prostitute, invites no simple moral disapproval of either character. Pathos is the dominant feeling as Bartho drives away from the house where the children still lie sleeping, desperately trying to escape the sound of Mbiti's harsh, mocking laughter. Roberts succeeds here in taking the subject of inter-racial marriage, about which South Africans are all too ready to form stereotyped judgments, and offering a study that has some points in common with such judgments, but serves to confirm none as a whole. The poignant, disturbing irony of the story lies in the way Roberts's narrative focus engages us with Mbiti and Bartho as particular individuals, in a way that they seem unable to do for themselves.

* * * * *

Roberts's most recent stories, *The Works* and *My Turn to Go* sustain her compassionate, detachedly humorous stance. In *The Works*, however, the analogy between the protagonist's lost car and her threatened hysterectomy seems rather contrived, largely because rediscovery of the vehicle allows her to attain a new sense of herself, a fragile spirit of optimism and freedom. Possibly Roberts has been unwise here in giving realism too broad a symbolic scope — details such as the vicious dog in *And Never Come Back Again*, or the owl in *For No Reason*, seem to suit her purposes better. While one therefore appreciates Roberts's attempt to suggest a woman's potential emergence from her passivity, one feels that the writer is too close at this point to deliberate feminist didacticism. *My Turn to Go*, which deals specifically with a Centre for Battered Wives (my formulation), seems more promising. The female first-person narrator, who is a nervous, but intelligent, long-standing inmate, is skilfully used to recount the action of the story: the arrival of 'Baby' Williams with her child, and her husband's attempt to reclaim her. Roberts's own realism, wry humour and compassion find an effective focus in the similar qualities of the woman who runs the Centre. Attie Williams is no caricature of a wife-basher; his wretched, anxious condition is rendered with pathos rather than anger, and in a fine stroke Roberts makes him experience, with the narrator, the effect of a brick hurled by another husband who elides male brutality into mean, vicious cowardice. The narrator's frail hovering between the desire to return to the world and a relish of the security and solidarity of the Centre provides a movingly imagined, non-doctrinaire entry into a predicament that is only very gradually becoming part of everyday civilised concerns.

Sheila Roberts's independent pursuits as a short story writer have permitted her a wide-ranging concern with the functioning of stereo-typed roles and images in South African life. Race plays a part, though not invariable or dominating, in this process. This achievement is best represented, in recent years, by stories such as *Mbiti Herself* and *My Turn to Go* in which compassion and narrative poise go hand in hand. Others, such as *The Lie of the Land* and *Knobs and Nikes*, reveal attention to a more restricted set of stereotypes, in particular, a dominating concern with female passivity, or with reaction against it, and a corresponding loss of compassion and poise. One hopes this latter tendency will not prevail since, while avoiding *racial* stereotypes, it gives disproportionate emphasis to others. My guess is that the publication of *This Time of Year* will offer yet more surprising revelations of Roberts's enterprising individuality, and no excuse for further neglect of her work.

NOTES

1   Roberts, Sheila *Outside Life's Feast* (Johannesburg: Ad Donker 1975). Bracketed page references in the article are to this edition.
2   See *The English Academy Review* (Nov 1982) p105.
3   Since this article was written, *This Time of Year* has in fact been published (Johannesburg: Ad Donker 1983).
4   "vulture".
5   Jean Marquard's comments on this story in the introduction to her anthology *A Century of South African Short Stories* (Johannesburg: Ad Donker 1978) are helpful and perceptive.
6   *Granny Kersting* has recently been republished in the anthology *Under the Southern Cross: Short Stories from South Africa*, edited and introduced by David Adey (Johannesburg: Ad Donker 1982) 240—250. The page references are to *Outside Life's Feast*.
7   *Coming In* was not included in *Outside Life's Feast* but was published in *On the Edge of the World* (Southern African Stories of the Seventies) edited by Stephen Gray (Johannesburg: Ad Donker 1974) 134—145. It appears again in Gray's updated version of this anthology, entitled *Modern South African*

Stories (Johannesburg: Ad Donker 1980). *IZWI*, in which the story first appeared (as also *We're Just One Big Family*, the other story of the pre-1975 era which was not included in *Outside Life's Feast*), was a journal of South African fiction, poetry and art. Crown Mines, Johannesburg, was responsible for its publication, under varied editorship, from 1971 to 1974. The page references are to *On the Edge of the World*.

8   *Mbiti Herself* appeared in *Contrast* 46, 12 (2) (Dec 1978) 9—17. Page references are to this publication.

Fugard's Confessional Analysis: *'MASTER HAROLD'* . . . *and the boys*

ROB AMATO

On Monday they say they've banned *'MASTER HAROLD'* . . . *and the boys*. On Tuesday there's this wonderful headline:

CENSORS UNAWARE OF FUGARD

The censors' readers didn't know it was his play. A system, perhaps? Like examination numbers to avoid prejudice? But they were given the play with the *title* attached, surely? But then, perhaps, they need to take the long view and avoid the ephemera of current theatre. The South African press has followed the play from New Haven to New York, quoted passionately favourable reviews, reported Tony Awards. Surely somebody, somewhere along the line . . .?

The play is banned as an 'undesirable' publication. The censors state that this is because it contains obscene language and not because of its political content. Professor A Coetzee, Director of the Publications Control Board (an artistic version of the Oilseed Control Board and the Meat Control Board), "declined to say how a copy of the play, which is not yet generally available in South Africa, had come to the Board."[1]

These two statements are good to read between. *Undesirable* is a good word for censors to use, for they do in fact deal with the deep desires of complainants who swing them into action. Some South African abroad was perhaps so galvanized by the experience of the play that he ferreted out a text (through what stratagem?) and caused it to "come to the Board". The censors, like any policing force, must preserve the anonymity of their informants. He won't be known unless some day he runs, naked, down Eloff Street, proclaiming his guilt. And those who agree (also anonymously) to read for the censors use obscenity of language as cover for their act of suppression, which is of course intensely political.

The play is subsequently unbanned with various critical bulls emanating from Pretoria about literary merit justifying the use of four-letter words. Those who would administer our psychic lives make another tactical move. In the new, relaxed, sophisticated dispensation, room can be made for works of this sort.

Discussion of the implications of the banning can only proceed by surmise because there was no public hearing. My surmise is that the play was seen, from a right-wing perspective, as too pessimistic a view of the possibility of good race relations in South Africa. The play delineates, with great accuracy and emotional impact, the cruel, sado-masochistic hegemony which controls the consciousness of whites and blacks and warps their psyches. It hurt, so they banned it. Its warmth and comedy don't come easily off the page to offset its gloom. Presumably they thought some depressed playwright had offered an unbearably bleak vision, as obscene as its language. Undesirable.

The play offers no surface pointers to ways to transcend the horrors of the South African situation. It shows a really painful and perhaps irremediable breakdown of love between a black man and a white boy whose closeness has been profound. Its climax hinges on the boy, bitter and furious, insisting that the man call him master — "Master Harold".

Hally: ... Think of it as a little lesson in respect Sam that's long overdue and I hope you remember it as well as you do your geography. I can tell you now that somebody who will be glad to hear I've finally given it to you, will be my Dad. Yes! He agrees with my Mom. He's always going on about it as well. 'You must teach the boys to show you more respect my son.'

Sam: So now you can stop complaining about going home. Everybody is going to be happy tonight.

Hally: That's perfectly correct. You see you mustn't get the wrong idea about me and my Dad Sam. We also have our good times together. Some bloody good laughs. He's got a marvellous sense of humour. Want to know what our favourite joke is? He gives out a big groan, you see, and says: It's not fair is it Hally? Then I have to ask: What Chum? And then he says A Kaffir's Arse ... and we both have a good laugh. (*The men stare at him with disbelief*)
What's the matter Willie? Don't you catch the joke?

You were always a bit slow on the up-take. It's what is
called a pun. You see fair means both light in colour
and to be just and decent. (*He turns to Sam*)
I thought you would catch it Sam.

Sam: Oh ja, I catch it alright.[2]

In bald and reduced terms Sam's response is to present his backside
for Hally's inspection and to start to walk out. Hally quietly calls him
back. He stops and looks expectantly at the boy, who spits in his face.
Sam contains his desire to hit Hally ("I don't want to help! I want to
hurt him.") and then proceeds to reveal the boy to himself. This
revelation works both as an indictment of one particular psyche and as
an analysis of a widespread and tragic process which has brought the
man and the boy to this pass. The play's final and perhaps most dominant
image is of the two black men remaining in the tearoom to dance out
one Lena Horne number on the jukebox (Willie will walk home because
he uses his busfare to pay for this complex catharsis) while the boy goes
off, broken and in deep shame.

The poor readers who decided to ban the play had one massive
disadvantage too many. They did not know that the person represented
by that broken boy would exit from that terrible impasse to write the
Fugard canon, and that, at fifty, he would present a play showing that
his boyhood mind was as trapped as theirs have remained. If you don't
know that *'MASTER HAROLD'... and the boys* is in one of its most
important aspects a portrait of the artist as a young man, you cannot
perceive its depth of analysis and its humanity.

Various points in the "Chronology" of Fugard published (also in
Fugard's fiftieth year) by Stephen Gray tally with the play.[3] Fugard's
father was crippled, as is Hally's in the play. Fugard's boyhood name
was Hallie and his mother ran the St George's Park Tearoom, where the
action is set. Fugard has himself described the play as

very painful. In a certain sense it is autobiographical — I was like
that, frustrated, intellectually arrogant, cruel to those who offered
me the most.[4]

If you argue, as I do, that Fugard's dramatic method has involved
allowing his imagination full rein on descents that he might have made,
cliffs that the observing writer has looked down but somehow moved
away from, then you are bound to allow your own imagination some
rein on the autobiographical elements of the works, even if this involves

some indelicacy. The indelicacy is no greater than would be that of perceiving the deep personal revelations that an actress like Yvonne Bryceland sees it as her duty to make through her art. Fugard writes like a Grotowski actor acts.

Johnnie in *Hello and Goodbye* is a portrait of what Fugard might have become, an immobilized wreck crippled by devotion to his father. Seen in this way it becomes a companion piece to *'MASTER HAROLD'* in which an attempted rejection of his father leads Hally into his guilty fury at the blacks. Don, in *People Are Living There* is Fugard as what Don Maclennan has called a 'brain-tweaker', an impotent existentialist and would-be writer, unsaved by energy or discipline from his 'Despair'.[5] Dimetos is Fugard but with 'Single Vision' and in 'Newton's Sleep' (see the Blake epigraph to the piece), a social engineer who despairs of his effectiveness, Fugard as craftsman at war with Fugard as truly humane story-teller (Dimetos tells Lydia that he is "an artisan, not an artist.") Boesman is often seen (especially by black critics) as Fugard-but-black and many see him as Fugard become unaccommodated man. Piet Bezuidenhout in *A Lesson from Aloes* is an isolated Afrikaner whose passion is English poetry and who is married to an English South African. He is very conscious of being an Afrikaner and of what this role implies in the world's eyes, which is the main burden of Fugard's comments about himself in the film *Fugard's People*.[6]

In *'MASTER HAROLD'* we are, for the first time, invited to contemplate a character avowedly 'like' Fugard. The formula, if the complex processes involved in the plays cited above can be reduced to a formula, therefore changes. Hally is not Fugard unrescued by understanding or unpossessed of some quality of strength or circumstance which Fugard is blessed enough to have. Hally is Hallie, but in a permutation worked on for dramatic analysis, and, since we know so much of Fugard from the canon and his role in our culture, in a permutation which in some measure imports non-textual information for its full effect.

Three months before his fiftieth birthday on 11 June 1982, Fugard opened a production of a play set in 1950, when he would have been seventeen or eighteen. Hally is seventeen in the play. If the end of the play is bleak and the young white boy is shown as grossly and apparently incurably unable to transcend his emotional paralysis and his racism — his hegemonically controlled consciousness — then it must be recognized that the whole body of plays on the subject of life in South Africa is there as part of the equation too. Fail to see the play in the light of the canon and in a sense you fail to see the play.

And in the canon are also the collaborative plays which are an extension of the phenomenon we observe in progress in 'MASTER HAROLD' — the collaboration of minds coming from different educations and manifesting different world-views, experiencing great intimacy and joy but sharing a common hegemonic influence on their consciousness and contemplating a common tragic experience. Winston Ntshona and John Kani have made, with Fugard, a theatre different in certain central aspects from his non-collaborative work. Broadly speaking the difference lies in the degree of optimism the plays 'allow' their audiences. Russell Vandenbroucke has pointed to this:

> Fugard admits that collaboration does not always allow the opportunity to aver the personal statement he wants to make. "Yes, there is some difference between what I want to say and what we have said." *Sizwe Bansi* and *The Island* are more optimistic and hopeful than Fugard's own vision.[7]

A crucial image in 'MASTER HAROLD' is that of ballroom dancing. Sam, without ever descending into a comfortable or saccharine version of his faith, is concerned to prove to Hally that life has aspects which can be dealt with using the same kinds of learned skills and innate abilities that ballroom dancers use. He is on the verge of getting Hally to write his school essay on 'A world without collisions' — using ballroom dancing as a political metaphor — when Hally is confronted with the fact that his father has come home from the hospital. Hally's attempt to deal with his love and loathing of his father in a telephone conver-sation with him is watched by the two men in the tearoom. Hally cannot bear his situation of enforced bad faith (he lies to his father and flatters him) and launches into the temper tantrum/release which precipitates the terrible collision which ends the play. Collaboration between the essentially optimistic Sam and the determinedly depressive Hally is shattered. Sam is a witty and wise tutor but he fails, in his own estimation, to teach the boy how to redeem himself from his self-punishing hatreds. This 'failure' is the subject of analysis by the now-mature and experienced Fugard, who is still testing the optimisms of South Africans and whose 'pessimism' is, in turn, being questioned by them. Whether 'Sam' in fact failed to save Hallie in the long run is a question raised by the play.

A paper entitled "Art and Revolution in South Africa: The Theatre of Athol Fugard" was distributed at the Conference on *Culture and Resistance* in South Africa held in Gaborone in July 1982. It argues that although Fugard is hailed by liberal critics as a lonely St George emerging from a theatrical vacuum to attack the apartheid dragon, he is in fact insufficiently allied to the struggle that is being fought here and is not enough involved in the reality of South African majority theatre, which is anything but a vacuum. He cannot actually transcend his class position as a white South African artist paid by local and overseas liberal theatres and their audiences. He cannot understand the true nature of the experience, or the struggle, of the majority in South Africa and has, in his plays of sole authorship, presented black characters as capable only of stoical perseverance.

The paper sets out some South African applications of Gramsci's 'rule' and 'hegemony'. Although there are differences between Gramsci's Italy and South Africa, what Steven Biko called the Anglo-Boer culture of South Africa has become the common cultural weapon of the white group. *Cultural* control has become vital in the retention of power. That intellectual independence can be illusory and that intellectuals, like artists and scholars, can play a crucial role in the cultural hegemony has been shown by Gramsci. Because

> the black proletariat and peasantry are able to produce the basis for a genuine alternative hegemony and a non-exploitative society . . . Fugard's work must . . . be re-examined as it relates to the interests, cultural, political and economic, of these classes, henceforth referred to as the majority.[8]

The article concludes that Fugard's effective resistance to hegemonic control is limited, on the grounds that:

> there is no depiction in these plays [the non-collaborative] of other, more fundamentally oppressive aspects of the apartheid system. For instance, the inability of a few white and black individuals to love each other and marry, though deplorable, cannot be compared in terms of human loss and misery with the dumping of reservoirs of cheap black labour in the undeveloped and unsustaining veld. The latter is absolutely central to the lives of the majority of South Africans, the former on their fringes. In these plays, Fugard's opposition to apartheid confines itself to an indictment of racialism but not of the exploitative and destructive nature of capitalism as it operates in South Africa. The effect of emphasizing the former is to obscure the latter, which is especially regrettable when a playwright's work can command an audience in . . . capitalist countries . . . .[9]

This charge demands some answering. The early novel *Tsotsi* (1958/9) and the plays and films *No Good Friday* (1959), *The Bloodknot* (1961), *Boesman and Lena* (1969), *A Lesson from Aloes* (1978) and *Marigolds in August* (1979) are all non-collaborative works and all deal very explicitly with the problems of migrant labourers or unemployed, rejected people, urban and rural, and with the psychic and bodily destruction which the policy of labour reservoirs causes. That the writer finds himself able to minimize this powerful and over-arching element in Fugard is symptomatic of a failure to see Fugard in his most important role, that of a questioner of life and theories, writing in the tragic mode and taking cognisance of the complexity and subtlety of the oppressive structures of the country. It is perfectly true that capitalism is not *named*, so far as I know, in the entire canon, as the original sinner, the fount and origin of the migratory labour monstrosity. It is this, I infer, and not the thematic content of the plays that really offends the paper's author.

This inference may not be justified but it raises a question. Does Fugard share the assumption that capitalism is the fount and origin of our evils? The answer is a refusal of the question. He has said that the moment he starts to function on the level of political analysis "I think flatly, I think superficially — the magic goes out."[10] At no point in the canon is the playwright's voice heard directly and this means that a convention frees his mind, the actor's mind, our minds from the intrusion of prior judgements. We are invited to empathise with character as much as we are invited to contemplate the South African experience. And if, as I argue, a major theme in Fugard is the varying permutations of hegemonic control of consciousness — usually unconscious processes — conscious delineation of this theme on the part of characters would be both analytically and dramatically invalid.

As the plays stand and in view of Fugard's reticence on the question of Marxism, it is possible to read him as a Marxian portraitist *and* it is possible to read him as a traditional liberal or even conservative analyst arguing for a deep decency and perceiving the economic structure of the country and its class relations as central but not exclusive elements in the making of its pain. Everyone, then, can come to the plays with his political universe intact, as it were. All might find, however, that the experience of the plays knocks whatever hopes they might have had of their particular philosophy-applied-as-cure rather hard. The pessimism question.

The Gaborone paper finds Fugard guilty not only of failing to provide any encouragement but of perceiving blacks as incapable of changing their situation or even affecting it:

But South Africa testifies to the daily struggles of the oppressed majority. There have been and still are strikes, boycotts, uprisings, sabotage, urban guerilla actions, passive resistance, stonings, killings, creativity, music, dance, protest literature and journalism, political parties and associations — all manner of struggle. Yet where in Fugard's work is any of this? Compare for instance the battle of the people of Crossroads to resist removal with the behaviour of Boesman and Lena. Again, therefore, Fugard's portrayal of 'the human condition' in South Africa is partial — in both senses.[11]

The moving rhetoric, and it *is* moving, of this passage has a kernel of truth about Fugard which gets crushed under the advancing forces. The kernel of truth is that Fugard does not concern himself with people whose effectiveness is manifest. There are political activists in Fugard but they are either frauds (as the article points out Watson is in *No Good Friday*) or burnt-out cases, like Piet and Steven in *A Lesson from Aloes*. But burnt-out cases are in a sense purged and Fugard's interest is in the purity and energy for good and evil of the ostensibly defeated, in the residual strengths that they manifest. He is a specialist in damaged psyches, a portraitist of individual, valuable people damaged by a cruel society and made cruel by it. This is social analysis in the tragic mode. To call such writing "partial in both senses" is to call in question the political legitimacy of tragedy.

* * * * *

The act of playmaking, it is no stunning revelation to point out, involves empathy with character. This element is modified or eliminated in highly stylized theatre or very abstract theatre but it is there, in increasing intensity, in farce, melodrama, comedy and tragedy, forms which have been determinedly mixed since the Renaissance. The empathy of the playwright with his characters involves his own emotions as well as those of his audience. Fugard has a basic emotional method whose workings may be divined from the texts. I call it, for the purposes of analysis, his binary emotional imagination. He does not, as it might be fair to say Shaw does, clothe arguments in characters as a primary process. His primary process is intense empathy.

Fugard has given many accounts of the emotional voyages that have been formative in his art. One report is especially striking. In the

"Introduction" to *Three Port Elizabeth Plays* he reports his comment (to Don Maclennan) on the imperatives he felt as they watched a real Lena on the banks of the Swartkops River:

> ...just a sense of the possibility of the sacrilegious and the sacred, of a demand that the truth be told, that I must not bear false witness.[12]

Within the context of this sacred respect there is a process which must be set against his 'feeling-with' character. Although ostensibly fighting with other characters, each Fugard character is patently involved in a great judging-against himself. When this is achieved with great intensity, a modern psychological tragedy arises. *And when the character's judging-against himself is the result of unavoidable social pressures, of the hegemonic control of his psyche by an entrenched, distorting power structure, this modern psychological tragic form also acquires the function of social analysis.* The play as a whole becomes a clear statement of deep anger and regret even though the playwright's voice is not heard, not even through a privileged character.

The plays present evidence of a process, hegemonic control of consciousness, that we should become aware of, not by theory but by empathic analysis. They have the distinct social function of presenting powerfully moving case histories which we may take into account (if that describes the process) in our own struggles to resist and survive. Piet Bezuidenhout is speaking both of rule and hegemony when he says:

> an evil system isn't a natural disaster. There's nothing you can do to stop a drought, but bad laws and social injustice are man-made and can be unmade by men. It's as simple as that. We can make this a better world to live in.

He notices that Gladys has been watching him and listening very carefully and adds, deprecatingly:

> | | ... You've been very patient with me. |
> | Gladys: | It wasn't difficult. I saw the man I first met very clearly again. It's been a hard time for you, hasn't it? |
> | Piet: | No more so than for everybody else, and certainly less than for Steve.[13] |

Even though we are moved by Piet's calling up of his old optimism we know that he has deep doubts. His judgement-against himself is that he is a dreamer, and this judgement is only momentarily suppressed. The point is that this is precisely the judgement that the establishment he has tried to attack makes of him. He has internalized this judgement and so, with great bitterness at her sense of her betrayal of him and of herself, has Gladys. And Steve's mind, the mind of the former black activist and bus-boycott orator, is also influenced, as is evidenced by his preparedness to believe Piet to be a traitor, by his hegemonically-enforced sense that dreamers are unstable, that they lose out and become desperate.

Gladys's decision to return to the mental hospital at Fort England, to the probability of shock therapy, is also a function of the state's, the system's, the culture's control of her consciousness. The isolation of the couple from social life starts with the brutal invasion of her private life by the Special Branch (they look at her personal diary) and ends with her elevation, with no further interference from the Branch, of their action into psychic rape. She has completed their work for them.

The most terrifying and pessimistic aspect of the play is that Fugard clearly does not regard *understanding* of the process of hegemonic control of consciousness as necessarily effective proof or help against its devastations. Gladys is capable of expressing her understanding of the process with incredible force and a declared sense of irony, and yet knows that she is trapped:

> *Gladys:* You're a good man, Peter, and that has become a terrible provocation. I want to destroy that goodness. Ironic, isn't it! That which I most hate and fear about this country is all I seem to have learned. (78)

Gladys sees the whole country as "turgid with violence", like Piet's poor innocent aloes appear to her to be. Fugard's characters are generally both as vulnerable and as turgid with violence as are those aloes. Those who have judged against themselves, who have internalized the adverse stereotypical image of themselves that the hegemony uses to suppress them, are always close to violence as a release, and since the point of that violence is to provide at least the illusion of superiority over others, it has strong sexual and economic elements. The plays are full of studies of sadomasochism, and in the manipulations which the characters practise upon one another, sexual and economic leverages alternate and blend.

207

It may be that what I have called the binary emotional imagination of Fugard involves a kind of authorial sadomasochism. When the character has been reduced to the pit of despair, Fugard's own ability to love him is released and, with the benefit of great performance, so is ours. By virtue of the thoroughness of his self-exposure, the baseness of his sadomasochism, there is a complex purification. It is not a redemption that is aimed at, at least not within the character's experience, but a respect for his own rigour. The playwright's cruelty is a testing analysis, but it is transmuted into the cruelty of character.

* * * * *

Fugard has often revealed his indebtedness, his passionate response to Albert Camus. The "Lecture Given in Athens on the Future of Tragedy" which Camus presented in 1955 seems to me to describe, in very useful terms, some of the processes we witness in *Boesman and Lena*. Camus makes a start on a theory of tragedy by asking in what way it differs from other forms of theatre:

> ...the forces confronting each other in tragedy are equally legitimate, equally justified. In melodramas or dramas, on the other hand, only one force is legitimate. In other words tragedy is ambiguous and drama simple-minded. In the former each force is at one and the same time good and bad. In the latter one is good and the other bad (which is why, in our day and age, propaganda plays are nothing but the resurrection of melodrama).[14]

Camus's contempt for modern "propaganda plays" spills over somewhat in his denial of ambiguity to what he calls drama. Good propagandists in the theatre know about ambiguity too, and about the ambiguity of their own roles in the world. But Camus's value here is not in his treatment of drama and propaganda but of tragedy:

> The ideal tragedy, on the other hand, and especially Greek Tragedy, is first and foremost tension, since it is the conflict, in a frenzied immobility, between two powers, each of which wears the double mask of good and evil.[15]

It is important to consider the degree to which this approach to tragedy might pull the playwright away from a socially forceful type of theatre. At first thought it would seem that Camus's theory makes tragedy apolitical. The anonymous critic from Gaborone and the Pretoria censors both want melodrama, or drama, in Camus's terms, and Fugard, if we apply and accept these terms, writes tragedy. But it is not apolitical tragedy. When one seeks to apply the theory to *Boesman and Lena* it emerges that Fugard has both applied and extended the theory so that while he has set up a balance of equally legitimate forces, "each wearing the double mask of good and evil" he has *also* made a powerful political critique of a great evil force. The play can be seen both as an analysis of a couple reduced to the lowest rung on the ladder of abuse and exploitation that is capitalist South Africa — "white man's rubbish" — *and* as an allegorical (though realistic) treatment of the sadomasochistic elements immanent in any coupling, heightened in these characters because they are so exposed and deprived. *Boesman and Lena* is both a model-in-little of the specific relationships of modern South African racist and sexist capitalism *and* it is *Every-couple*. The strange thing is that while both readings may be taken, for critical purposes, through to their separate conclusions, both are valid. What the play is *not*, is one which fails to reflect the effects of capitalism.

But what, if Camus's theory is applied to the play, are the two powers, or forces, each of which is both right and wrong, good and evil? They are not the forces of the state set against the individual spirits of Boesman and Lena. The state is, as it were, one more of the elements which batter the two people. It is to them an unremittingly evil force that may smile fleetingly, grotesquely.

The two people themselves embody the two forces, not separately, but in a fugue. In this fugue the two characters alternately take on the dominant and submissive roles. They are engaged in a sadomasochistic playing-out of the tensions they feel as they struggle to adjust to the terrible denial-of-self that their hegemonically-imposed value structures seem to demand. For example, Boesman brings Lena to the point where she may have to ask him who she is. She parries his cruelty with her own threat, used throughout the play, to leave him, and with her own questioning of *his* identity. He threatens her with "a bloody *good* hiding".

> Lena: *Aikona!* I'll go to the police.
> Boesman: You tried that one before and what happened? 'She's my woman, *baas. Net 'n bietjie warm gemaak.*' 'Take her' . . . finish *en klaar.* They know the way it is with our sort.[16]

He has established that the system is as indifferent to her as are the elements, and, most importantly, that the system's value structure dovetails with his perfectly. The way *it* is with their sort is perfectly understandable to the police. They are beyond decency. And in this argument his sadism finds its logic:

> Lena: Not this time. My name is Mary, remember. 'Don't
>   know this man, *baas.*' So where's your proof?
> Boesman: (*Holding up a clenched fist*) Here!   (181)

This, the saddest and most devastating of the plays, is also the most elating in its catharsis. This elation is very complex but one of its chief elements is that the play does in fact answer the implications of hegemonic racism with a vengeance, through the power of the tragic stature it gives to the characters.

Boesman thinks of himself as a male member of a defeated people and his pain is because he still has pride, is a man, a member of a certain race, trying to survive. In his perception, another race proves to him, in destroying the pathetic rubbish he has been using to fight the elements, that his race is defeated. He is right. It is. 'Bushmen' and 'early men' as races, as cultures, as societies, what you will, are being destroyed. But it is only a part of him that accepts that this is his fault, and that the white man's assessment of him is accurate. And Lena knows that their humanity is actually indestructible, and their race still present and holy to them, even if they have no war-dances. She frightens Boesman out of his hegemonically induced self-contempt by the threat of death. A flash of terror and horror is brought on to Boesman by Outa's death and by Lena's threat that the other race, again, will hang him for killing Outa. He is punch drunk enough to believe her improbable prediction. All those deaths, of infants taken silent from Lena's *moer* and buried by Boesman, now come into this moment of confluence. The terror is great enough. He may or may not perceive that it is control by others of the means of production that has put him where he is, but he *knows* that he is a man, at the end of the play, that he is coupled with a woman and that they will continue together or apart till they die a terribly foreseeable death. He *feels himself*, as Fugard's stage direction says of Lena, when she says "*Haai, Yessus!* Look at it. *Pap ou borste, ribbetjies.*" (209) "*Die vrot mense*" (182) experience a catharsis.

Those who object that Boesman and Lena are not conscientized into action have to recognize that Fugard is like Bacon said Machiavelli was: he writes about what is, not what ought to be. The majority of the

210

vast numbers of people that continue to be 'removed' are closer to Boesman and Lena than are the Crossroads people who fought and won a very limited battle — (one that is being refought in another Cape Town ghetto, Guguletu, as I write). The reason we want to be exposed to Fugard's vision is that it is truthful as well as cathartic. The millions of Jews who could not resist are redeemed not only by the actions in the Warsaw Ghetto and its parallels. They are also redeemed in the truth of their tragedy of failure, a failure which has the unbearably paradoxical elation of tragedy in so much of the writing devoted to the subject.

It has been suggested to me that Lena's bread and water with Outa constitute a eucharist.[17] She 'pays' for it by giving up her wine to Boesman. Perhaps her wanting to be Mary is linked to this. There is a sense in which she perceives her ritual as a failure; many of the plays involve rituals which are perceived by the characters as failures. Millie's party,[18] Piet Bezuidenhout's reunion with Steven, Dimetos's hopes in the lemon grove for Lydia and Danilo, Hester's search for the past (a ritual disguised on the conscious level as a search for money), Queenie's search for dignity (the table cloths and curtains). These characters perceive their rituals as failures.

But the *plays*, in full and successful performance and with audiences prepared to, able to, open themselves to the catharses, constitute in-themselves-successful *rites*. This is an answer to the charge of pessimism that is laid at Fugard's door.

* * * * *

The climax of '*MASTER HAROLD*' is Sam's revelation to Hally of the true nature of the kite-flying episode which the boy has, through an unconscious process, filtered and distorted to satisfy the demands which the hegemonic influences have made upon his psyche. He remembers the kite-flying as an entertainment devised by Sam to fill an otherwise boring afternoon. What he has suppressed is the fact that Sam made the kite and flew it with the boy to re-establish his ability to live after a very South African boyhood trauma, that of having to recover his drunken father from the pub with Sam's help.

211

Sam:	Then I loaded him onto my back like a baby and carried him back to the boarding house with you following behind carrying his crutches. (*Shaking his head as he remembers*) A crowded Main Street with all the people watching a little white boy following his drunk father on a Kaffir's back! I felt for that little boy, Master Harold. I felt for him. After that we still had to clean him up, remember. He'd messed in his trousers so we had to clean him up and get him into bed. (91)

There is a striking parallel with *Oedipus Rex*. Just as Sophocles withholds from his hero the 'other' story of his childhood until Oedipus's defensive cruelty and presumptuous underestimation of Tyresias are at their highest pitch, so Fugard brings Hally to his most desperately assertive point — spitting in Sam's face — before the traumatic memory is resurrected for him by Sam. It seems to me that Hally cannot stay in the world of the tearoom, has lost that magic afternoon world, cannot accept Sam's several attempts after the spitting to save the situation, because the resurrection of the trauma makes him, again, at seventeen, perceive of himself as guilty of the one crime which South Africans who are white simply can't commit. The central commandment of the hegemony of apartheid may be 'Show not thy weakness to thy neighbour race, to the helots'.

For Hally the weakness that has been shown is that of his father and that weakness is physically grotesque. The exposure is past, incurable and therefore ever-present. His father's continuing failure to deal with his body waste has been stressed often in the play. The shame is intolerable.

Whenever he has faced the prospect of losing authority in the tearoom Hally has, jokingly or in earnest, invoked his powers as white person, as teacher and transmitter of information, as employer with a massive economic leverage over his two friends/elders/servants/peers/pupils/teachers/employees. He has pontificated on great men, congratulated himself and his people on freeing Sam's ancestors from slavery, he has boxed and packaged religion, Shakespeare and Napoleon. He has wielded a ruler on Willie's backside and as a stage direction puts it, he "struts around like a little Hitler, ruler in hand, giving vent to his frustration". (60)[19]

But now, at the end of the play, once the trauma has been resurrected, he cannot invoke the hegemonic value structure because the trauma itself embodies his massive debt of love for Sam, and his undeniable love for his father ("I love him Sam").

Sam is also trapped. He can no longer call in question his own manhood by forgiving the boy for the baseness of his racism, as expressed in his desperate hubris. Sam has suffered and accepted Hally's hegemonically induced bullying as a way of building the boy's self-respect. He must now stop this process to save his own self-respect:

I mean, how do I wash off you and your father's filth? (91)[20]

The conflict has now been purified into a manifestation of Camus's vision of tragedy. "All can be justified. None is just." The two forces, each having in this case a fundamentally different world view *at this stage of their development* face each other in a frenzied immobility till they break apart. Hally and Sam are like Boesman and Lena, in conflict under the apparently elemental influence of hegemonic control of consciousness. Is it likely that they will be able to meet again? I think that the answer is no, but the implications of this answer are changed when one considers that the canon of plays has been Hallie Fugard's life work, and the fact that this play is a loving apology to the real man who was Sam, made thirty-two years later, and pondered, certainly, throughout that time.

NOTES

1   References in these two paragraphs are to a report in the *Cape Times* 7 December 1982.
2   Fugard, Athol *'MASTER HAROLD'... and the boys* typed playtext, 1982, p82. Since this article was written, the play has been published by Oxford University Press (Oxford: 1983) but quotations from the typed playtext have been retained in preference to the published edition. Bracketed page references in the text are to the typescript. In this passage and throughout the play, the OUP edition substitutes "A nigger ..." for the South African "A Kaffir ..." The latter was used in Fugard's Market Theatre production in 1982.
3   Gray, Stephen "Chronology" in *Athol Fugard* (Southern African Literature Series 1) edited by Stephen Gray (Johannesburg: McGraw Hill 1982) 3—16.
4   *Cape Times* 6 December 1982, under the headline "'MASTER HAROLD' Ban Flabbergasts Fugard."
5   Maclennan, Don "The Palimpsest: Some Observations on Fugard's Plays"

The Bloody Horse 1(3) (Jan—Feb 1981). Re-published in *Athol Fugard*, p219.

6   *Fugard's People*, film directed by Helen Nogueira, 1982.
7   Vandenbroucke, Russell "Robert Zwelinzima is Alive" *Yale Theatre* 7(1) (Fall 1975). Re-published in *Athol Fugard* p197.
8   "Art and Revolution in South Africa: The Theatre of Athol Fugard." Anonymous article distributed at Gaborone, Botswana, on the occasion of the Conference on *Culture and Resistance* in South Africa, 1982; p1.
9   "Art and Revolution in South Africa" p5.
10 Hodgins, Robert "Interview with Athol Fugard" *News/check* (Johannesburg) 27 July 1967, p27. Quoted by Don Maclennan in *Athol Fugard* p222.
11 "Art and Revolution in South Africa" p5.
12 Fugard, Athol "Introduction" to *Three Port Elizabeth Plays* (London: Oxford University Press 1974) p*xxi.*
13 Fugard, Athol *A Lesson from Aloes* (Oxford: Oxford University Press 1981) p35. Bracketed page references in the text are to this edition of the play.
14 Camus, Albert "Lecture Given in Athens on The Future of Tragedy" in *Selected Essays and Notebooks* edited and translated by Philip Thody (Harmondsworth: Penguin 1970) 192—203; p196.
15 Camus, p197.
16 Fugard, Athol *Boesman and Lena* in *Three Port Elizabeth Plays* (London: Oxford University Press 1974) p181. Bracketed page references in the text are to this edition of the play.
17 By a colleague, Jenny de Reuck.
18 Don Maclennan refers to this as a "maimed rite" in *Athol Fugard* p222.
19 The OUP edition (p89) substitutes "despot" for "Hitler".
20 The OUP edition (p57) reads "I mean, how do I wash off yours and your father's filth". This alteration (which *was* followed in the Market Theatre production) may not be an emendation at all; the typescript might have been in error. If it is an alteration, what was an idiomatically accurate line has become a bad one.

Alternative Politics, Alternative Performance: 1976 and Black South African Theatre

IAN STEADMAN

> It is not the duty of black theatre to conscientize the white man. . . . Right now black consciousness must take up all the room and refuse to be prostituted. . . . We say that if the white man wants to see what is going on in our world let him do the impossible, get a permit and come into our township. . . . To perform before whites in their plush places serves to preserve the status quo. . . .
>
> Mango Tshabangu, 1975

The established theatre in South Africa by the beginning of the 1970s, according to history as interpreted by the dominant group, was 'white'. Landmarks in this history were the founding in 1938 of the Federation of Amateur Theatrical Societies of South Africa, the creation in 1947 of the National Theatre Organisation, the formation in 1956 of the South African Association of Theatrical Managements, and the establishment in 1963 of the government-subsidised Performing Arts Councils. Less well known is the alternative history of South African theatre: the work of Herbert Dhlomo and the Bantu Dramatic Society in the 1930s, of Union Artists in the 1950s, of popular entertainers in the townships in the 1960s, and the gradual evolution of alternative forms of theatre based on an emerging radical political consciousness in the 1970s.

The 1970s saw the end of attempts by liberal whites and educated blacks to present a united front against the status quo. With the emergence of a greater militancy in the 1970s, organisations such as the Black People's Convention and the South African Students' Organisation began to posit a radical independence from white influence. Black Consciousness turned its back on white liberalism and turned towards radical politics. Black theatre went the same way: turning its back on

215

the dominant tradition, it created alternative directions in South African theatre. These alternative directions attracted attention when the political events of 1976 brought them to prominence. Why was this alternative theatre not recognised before 1976? What new directions has it taken since 1976?

Towards a cultural study: the discovery and criticism of performance

Two related problems confront the researcher in a study of South African performance. On the one hand, this performance must be discovered: it has not always enjoyed the privilege of being 'archaeologically' excavated, recorded, documented and published. On the other hand, the tools of discovery must be sharpened: the researcher brings to any enquiry critical attitudes which must themselves be subjected to critical analysis. South African performance has too often resisted discovery for the same reasons that it has resisted rigorous critical assessment: work in both areas, in discovery and criticism, has been bound by conscious or sub-conscious preconceptions about the function, nature and significance of cultural artefacts.

An 'archaeology of theatre' allows the researcher to treat performance as extra-textual and to use research methods from ethnography, oral history and cultural anthropology. The scholar has to excavate the record of *performance*, of which the text is merely a blueprint — when there *is* a text (popular entertainments are seldom recorded in print). Archaeology, redefined, attempts to excavate the complex factors involved in performance. As one commentator suggests, the distinctive claim of an archaeology of theatre is to show the vast chasm that separates text from spectacle by studying *process and transformation* rather than *product and continuity*.[1] The textual product of theatre is, after all, merely an edited version of the creative processes which went into the performance. In the established history of South African theatre, selective studies of textual products have created a continuity of *dominant* tendencies. An archaeological excavation of *alternative* tendencies will create a more complete history. In order to discover these alternatives it will be necessary to dispense with traditional preconceptions which have favoured the dominant forms of South African theatre. The search for alternative theatre, that is to say, necessitates a search for alternative critical attitudes. Instead of 'reading' theatre in order to unpack a parcel of meanings, criticism must reveal theatre to be a symptomatic manifestation of inter-related

216

textual, contextual and ideological factors.

The notion of an appropriate critical attitude has been frequently raised in studies of African literature. It has become necessary, in order to study African cultural artefacts, to make visible the hidden structures and relations which affect the received 'meaning' of those artefacts. In the case of alternative theatre in South Africa, this means situating theatre within a pattern of culturally mediated social relations. The relationship of forms of theatre to notions of cultural change and continuity must be elaborated. This in turn necessitates a description of the concept of culture in so far as it affects this study. Three major factors have to be considered here. First, it is incorrect to speak of 'Culture' without specifying its plurality as a dialectic between different cultures. There exist tensions, conflicts and contradictions both *between* and *within* cultures. We cannot, therefore, speak of the evolution of *a* way of life or *a* cultural tradition in South Africa. Instead, we have to consider the dialectical development of *ways* of life and of the forms of cultural expression which emerge in this process. Secondly, one should not define culture by reference to sets of texts. The very *selection* of those texts is significant. Concrete social habits and practices determine the arrangement and selection of preferred texts in terms of the cultural tendencies and norms of those who do the arrangement and selection. A knowledge of how certain texts come to be considered exemplary or desirable explains how a *dominant* cultural tendency becomes established. By studying these processes critically, we will understand not only the way cultural norms are established, but also the social relations and interests which these norms express. Thirdly, when a cultural tendency becomes dominant, there are always alternatives which are being suppressed and subordinated to the dominant order, especially when their themes and techniques are predicated upon *resistance* and *struggle* against dominant tendencies. These three factors are indispensable to the major objective of this paper which is to make visible the invisible: to demystify cultural determinants and mediating elements in the received images of alternative South African theatre.

Alternative performance in South Africa until 1976

1976 was a watershed year. On the surface, the role of black theatre in South African cultural and political history might seem to be of minor interest. A closer study, however, reveals that black theatre is an index of social consciousness. During the early 1970s various organisations devoted to the principles of Black Consciousness espoused the belief that the way to political nationalism was through cultural nationalism. Black theatre practitioners sought an identity for black theatre which would be commensurate with the political ideals of Black Consciousness. As these political ideals, in the face of intransigence by political authority, became increasingly radical, so too did the themes and techniques of black theatre. When evaluated within a broad cultural context this theatre attains significance as a radical counter-cultural theatre.

Like its counterpart in the United States of America during the 1960s,[2] black theatre in South Africa during the 1970s evolved from a consciousness born of social and political pressures. 'Blackness' came to be defined in positive terms as an assertion of pride-in-being-black, an assertion which was intended as a conscious rejection of canonized white norms and standards. While there exists a certain idiosyncratic factor in the description of any theatre in terms of colour or race, the creators of Black Consciousness theatre prior to 1976 were dedicated to exactly this cause. In fact, earlier work by black theatre practitioners can be distinguished from work by practitioners of Black Consciousness theatre by reference to the differences between the concepts 'theatre for blacks' and 'black theatre'. The former merely involves black people as participants or spectators, while the latter makes a forceful and assertive *statement* about black pride, dignity and aspiration. This statement was militant and didactic, and necessarily so: the theatre of protest pulls no punches.

It is impossible to provide here more than a brief outline of activity in black theatre during the last few decades. Nevertheless, in the fifty-year period from the formation of the Bantu Dramatic Society in Johannesburg to the present day, it is possible to discern significant landmarks in black theatre. In 1933 Herbert Dhlomo founded the Bantu Dramatic Society, which began its activities with a production of *She Stoops to Conquer* and moved thence into production of African plays, amongst them one by Dhlomo himself entitled *The Girl Who Killed to Save: Nongqwase the Liberator*. This was the first play published in English by a South African black writer. Dhlomo's vast contribution to black South African writing in general has only recently been appreciated,[3] and his important position in the history of South African theatre still awaits proper recognition. Sporadic attempts were made during the 1940s to introduce dramatic performances into the curricula of high schools in the Transvaal, and by 1948 black drama

218

on radio was in evidence. Because of the idiosyncratic socio-political structures of South Africa, however, black theatre was not given the means or the recognition it needed to develop alongside the established white forms of performance. It is not surprising, therefore, that black performance was soon to turn its back on attempts to emulate white traditions, and discover its own forms. Thus it was that in 1959 the white establishment was taken somewhat by surprise with the emergence of a unique brand of musical theatre: *King Kong*. While this musical provided a platform for the careers of a number of its performers, and indicated new directions for black theatre practitioners, its real significance lay elsewhere: from the proceeds of its phenomenal success, Union Artists, the producing company, was able to form the African Music and Drama Association in 1959. Black theatre was provided with the means, a venue and a school to train a new generation. One of the products was Gibson Kente.

Gibson Kente is largely unknown to the white theatre-going population of South Africa. This is despite the fact that he is arguably the most popular playwright-director in South African theatre history. Having served an apprenticeship in the shadow of Union Artists, Kente embarked in the late 1960s upon a career of popular township musical dramas that include *Manana, The Jazz Prophet, Sikhalo, Lifa, Zwi, I Believe, How Long, Can You Take It, School Girl, Mama and the Load, Lobola, Too Late, Hard Road* and, at the present date, another production that is in preparation. These are all highly successful musical entertainments built upon simple plots which, however, allow Kente to create images of township poverty and destitution, hope and aspiration. While he has been criticised by more radical Black Consciousness proponents for being a-political, Kente's theatre succeeds in creating social comment and criticism — sometimes by implication, at other times by direct proselytism.

Kente's work is testimony to the vast popularity enjoyed by the township musical. Following his example, many playwrights created popular forms of theatre which have enjoyed considerable financial and artistic success. Sam Mhangwane's *The Unfaithful Woman*, in the same mould as Kente's musical dramas, has been periodically revived over a period which now exceeds twelve years — each time to popular acclaim.

It should be apparent from this brief account that the still unwritten history of black South African theatre is a significant history, and that black theatre in South Africa is an important cultural index. It is not surprising, therefore, that with the emergence of a radical political consciousness, many black leaders would advocate using theatre as a means of conscientization:

> One of the basic tenets of Black Consciousness is totality of involvement — no fragmentation or distraction — unite ourselves and respond as a cohesive group .... The term Black Culture above all implies the freedom by us to innovate without recourse to white values ... whatever we do adds to the richness of our cultural heritage. The adoption of Black Theatre and drama is one such important innovation which we need to encourage and to develop .... [4]

Political authorities soon perceived the significance of black theatre as a cultural and nationalistic institution. Under the terms of the old Urban Areas Act of 1945, officials of the West Rand Administration Board were given power to demand private viewings of performances in order to assess their suitability for public viewing. Furthermore, playwrights were compelled to submit scripts to the West Rand Administration Board officials before permission could be granted for performances in Sowetan community halls. During 1975 there were numerous confrontations between West Rand Administration Board officials and Sowetan playwrights.[5] Clearly, black theatre in Soweto prior to 1976 was not ignored by the authorities. The closeness of its ties to aspirant black nationalism was, however, only fully realised once the full force of that nationalism emerged in 1976.

The very nature of theatre as a dynamic means of communication made it, during the period preceding the student demonstrations of 1976, an ideal vehicle for the popularisation of the political aspirations associated with Black Consciousness. A communally shared discourse in an environment of political unrest contributed to the growth of a politically motivated theatre. This theatre often became didactic 'agit-prop' theatre of the kind advocated by Erwin Piscator and Brecht in the years following World War I in Germany: uninterested in finding an élitist audience, this theatre searched for theatrical images rather than literary complexities, and resorted to slogans and proselytism rather than philosophical and rational debate. In short, aesthetic considerations, at least as they were defined by white standards in literature and theatre, were subordinated to political considerations. This theatre searched for theatrical images of socio-political import. Its themes and techniques cannot be divorced from its function.

Shanti, an example of this form of theatre, has only recently been published — outside of South Africa.[6] Its banning by the authorities and the circumstances of its author's death have made this play representative of the theatre of Black Consciousness.[7] The People's Experimental Theatre, formed in the Indian township of Lenasia, and the African Sowetan group called Shiqomo joined forces in 1973 to produce the play. It is a simple story about the love between an Indian girl and an African man who is committed to the cause of liberation in South Africa. The play is a simple polemic, with the characters speaking at times directly to the audience about their aspirations to political freedom. In performance, this enjoyed responses in the form of salutes, exclamations and cheers. On the page, such audience response is not apparent, and the dialogue may seem to consist of little more than slogans and empty proselytizing. Within the context of performance, however, the play attains significance as an important *performance event*: a communal discussion of political frustration. The play *Shanti* was considered significant enough to be used as one of the major documentary exhibits in the so-called 'Treason Trial' of 1975. The People's Experimental Theatre was listed as a subversive organisation, the leading practitioners of that theatre group were charged under the Terrorism Act, and one of the charges stated that the accused conspired "... to make, produce, publish, or distribute subversive and anti-white utterances, writings, plays, and dramas. ..."[8]

'Soweto 1976' has become a catch-phrase. The events precipitated by the youth of Soweto which occurred across the country in June 1976 were a symbolic rejection of white authority: the new generation of black South Africans would *force* the change that had for so long been delayed. They would do this in the cultural sphere by asserting conscious alternatives to the dominant culture. Black theatre would be in the forefront of this process as a conscious signifying practice. 1976, that is to say, crystallized the dialectic between black theatre and South Africa's idiosyncratic political structures.

Critical preconceptions: the response to Black Consciousness theatre

Why were the alternative forms of South African theatre largely ignored until the radical events of 1976 forced them upon the attention of the general white establishment? The answer to this question becomes an illustration of the necessity for broad cultural perspectives in criticism of theatre.

Clearly, associated with hegemonic control, the dominant cultural norms and tendencies in South Africa have been 'white'. Even as recently as 1977, a government commission of enquiry into the performing arts could state:

> In a personal interview, the Chairman of the Commission was told by the Secretary for Bantu Administration and Development that the Government Department assumed full responsibility for any matter in connection with the performing arts, so far as black people were affected. He had been asked about this in the interests of those black inhabitants who are living in the country's White residential areas. Having been given the assurance that any needs which might exist or arise received or would receive the direct attention of that Department, the Commission devoted no further attention to this population group in its inquiry. . . .[9]

Thus did a government commission of enquiry, barely one year after the events of 1976 (the report was being compiled during the course of those events) relegate out of contention the theatre of the majority of the population.

Preconceptions about the function, nature and significance of theatre have been instrumental in the creation of a dominant tradition which excludes from consideration any of the alternative forms. The first of three major preconceptions, based on dominant cultural tendencies, relates to ideas about the *function* of theatre. The growth and development of western theatre is related to social and ideological contexts, and ideas about the function of that theatre are therefore products of that relationship. The notion of theatre as a mode of 'art' which should satisfy certain canonized standards of taste is the prime manifestation of these ideas. The theatre of Black Consciousness in South Africa, concerned as it was with unique social and ideological contexts, rejected these standards which were born in alien contexts. This theatre saw its function in terms of an active political role and evolved aesthetic considerations as a product of that function. Protest theatre demands change. In doing this it radicalizes both form and content. Just as Black Consciousness committed itself to a counter-ideology, so did Black Consciousness theatre commit itself to counter-cultural alternatives in performance.

Attitudes about the *nature* of theatre explain a second major preconception: the preferred forms of theatre of the dominant group in South Africa exhibit formal and generic qualities based largely upon western European literary standards. Obviously the theatre of Black

Consciousness would not exhibit these qualities. Many of the plays, though their creators were speakers of African vernaculars, were performed in a slang idiom which was necessitated by the cosmopolitan structure of township audiences. 'Tsotsitaal', an idiomatic slang composed of indigenous vernaculars including Afrikaans, with only occasional expressions in English, became a popular comic device in the township musical dramas of Gibson Kente, and similar deliberate distortions of language 'purity' occurred in the radical plays. Critics searching for conventional English literary qualities would not find them in these plays. Nevertheless, one critic writing in a Johannesburg newspaper could still claim that, "If performers cannot master basics like understandable pronunciation and clear diction there is really no point in getting as far as opening night. . . ."[10] The need for an "understandable pronunciation and clear diction" is here being asserted from a Western European literary point of view. These demands were not shared by the largely black audiences who interrupted the performances with spontaneous cheers, agreements and exclamations, whenever poetic images of political liberation were spoken on stage. These expectations about the nature of theatre are subsumed under what may be called "the aesthetic response".[11] The theatre of Black Consciousness, rejecting literary qualities based on the aesthetic response, evolved its own distinctive qualities. These were based primarily on theatrical *images* rather than literary sophistication: on action and slogans presented in didactic ways. Form and technique in this theatre were products of its function.

The third major preconception which is attributable to a dominant cultural perspective, is that of the *significance* of theatre. The significance of the theatre of Black Consciousness in 1976 is that it was symptomatic of a new direction in radical black politics. The failure of the status quo to take cognisance of black political frustration in Soweto in 1976 is matched by its failure to recognise the potential for theatre to work in ways perceived by Piscator and Brecht. The communal code of discourse, established by a militant didactic theatre in the context of political anger and frustration, ensured that theatre practitioners were in the forefront of political activity. No longer merely writers and performers, they were active leaders: actors in the political scene. Of the thirteen defendants brought to court under the Terrorism Act in March 1975, five were prominent theatre practitioners: Saths Cooper, Strini Moodley, Lingam Moodley, Sadecque Variava and Solly Ismail. Commitment in the theatre of Black Consciousness had come to mean a commitment to demystifying social, political and ideological facades and demanding change. The commitment of these practitioners of theatre must, then, form the basis for an analysis of the efficacy of their work.

In Althusserian terms these three major preconceptions — about the function, nature and significance of theatre — were the ideological apparatus which served to perpetuate the dominant tradition and to exclude from consideration the alternatives to that tradition. They therefore served to create a sense of continuity in South African theatre history: a false continuity which ignored alternatives. Raymond Williams elaborates:

> What has then to be said about any tradition is that it is in this sense an aspect of *contemporary* social and cultural organisation, in the interests of the dominance of a specific class. It is a version of the past which is intended to connect with and ratify the present. What it offers in practice is a sense of *pre-disposed continuity*.[12]

The task of criticism within a wider cultural context should be to demystify such preconceptions, showing them to be social practices which affect the received 'meaning' of theatre in South Africa.

Alternative performance since 1976

Historical hindsight is an easy game. A vision of the significance underlying contemporary events is much more difficult. The theatre of Black Consciousness can be seen to have significantly affected theatre during the period up to 1976. What can be said of black theatre after that date? Clearly, black theatre is no longer a phenomenon which exists outside the cultural awareness of the dominant group. It has become part of the multi-cultural complexity of the South African identity, but it would be too easy to claim a niche for it beside 'white English theatre' and 'white Afrikaans theatre'. Black theatre has taken many diverse paths since 1976, and while the theatre of Black Consciousness could boast a label which identified its themes, methods and intentions, black theatre after 1976 cannot boast a common identity. An interview with leading personalities from black theatre in a local newspaper contains contradictory opinions in this regard.[13] Fats Dibeco and Ken Gampu, two highly successful and acclaimed actors, reject the notion of a black theatre and claim that "there is only theatre", while Maishe Maponya maintains that "as long as blacks do not have equal rights, there'll always be black theatre." Maponya's comment is apt. If the concept "black theatre" is to be used at all, it cannot refer merely to the colour of its practitioners: *Sizwe Bansi is Dead*, devised by one white man and two black men, would pose a definitional problem. In using the concept after 1976, Maponya is referring to any theatre in South Africa where the subject matter has to do with *identification with a set of values*. These values may be more or less synonymous with Black Consciousness, but they refer to the same principles. Nevertheless, as with the critical perspective necessary in an analysis of Black Consciousness theatre, black theatre after 1976 requires a broad cultural perspective.

Writing in 1981, one playwright could urge these principles:

> As dramatists writing for the stage, we should master our art in relation to our African cultural values and our ghetto lives. Situate our spirit of resistance within the context of our historical past. Avoid being either American, European or English. Be African. . . .[14]

If there is a major distinctive feature in theatre created after 1976, it is in the movement towards Africanism. Blacks and whites have striven to create theatre that would be rooted in the lives of its audience. Institutions such as the Market Theatre and the People's Space, and smaller performing groups around the country, have begun breaking down the barriers of segregation. Legislation preventing racial mixing in theatres was finally dropped in 1977, and many plays were created which involved 'mixed' casts. Fugard's success prompted similar attempts to create plays about South Africa's unique social problems. The artistic and commercial success of plays such as Barney Simon's *Cincinnati* (1979) and *Woza Albert* (1981) and Paul Slabolepszy's *Saturday Night at the Palace* (1982) have created the impression that South African theatre, having eradicated previously imposed race barriers, is on the threshhold of a distinctive identity. The dominant traditional tendencies are no longer hermetically sealed from alternative developments: preconceptions have been undermined, and the theatre has been able to create forms and themes pertinent to South Africa's unique problems.

If Black Consciousness theatre is a phenomenon of the past, and if the dominant tradition has been assimilated with alternative traditions, what are the new alternatives? What directions have been taken since 1976 by black theatre?

While institutions such as the Market Theatre and the People's

Space can legitimately claim a multi-racial identity, the political economy of South African theatre necessitates a closer investigation of the implications underlying this claim. The statement by Tshabangu which prefaces this paper is as pertinent after 1976 as it was before.[15] The white theatre-going public in Johannesburg may well believe that black theatre is what they see performed at the Market Theatre. That theatre, however, is selected for performance by a management which makes its own decisions regarding suitability and possible financial success. Meanwhile, without a theatre in Soweto, many groups create performances in garages, cellars, community halls and churches. Reminiscent of the off-off-Broadway movement of the 1960s, this activity may be regarded as the new alternative in South African black theatre. Occasionally, of course, a few of these performances are recognised and invited to the established venues. In many cases, however, black theatre remains isolated in the townships. On rare occasions, as happened with Maishe Maponya's *The Hungry Earth* in 1981 and Matsemela Manaka's *Vuka* in 1982, these performances are invited to other countries by parties interested in the other face of South African theatre. In short, while the radical politics of Black Consciousness gave recognition to alternative forms of theatre before 1976, the contemporary absence of radicalism disguises the fact that alternative forms still exist.

Matsemela Manaka's work for the theatre in South Africa first became prominent with the banning of his first published play in 1980: *Egoli* (City of Gold). In this work about the conditions of working-class life in the gold mines of South Africa, Manaka presents a theatrical metaphor for the unique conditions in South African social and economic life. The two characters, who take the names of the original actors, John and Hamilton, are like Beckett's Vladimir and Estragon. They are inextricably trapped in a relationship where neither can do without the other. They work in a mining compound, they share reminiscences about life on the mines of South Africa, and they recall, in a dream sequence, a period of forced labour when they were chained together. In performance, the chain becomes a powerful metaphor: the condition of black workers in South Africa is tantamount to slave labour, the chain signifies the inextricable partnership of all blacks against the forces of oppression, and the breaking of the chain is the goal of all workers. In the central climactic scene of the play, when the chain is broken to the accompanying rhythms of a popular freedom song, Manaka's theatre succeeds in evoking from black members of the audience participatory exclamations and salutes of recognition. In this young playwright, alternative black theatre promises new directions. He

226

is by no means alone in this, but his work exhibits representative characteristics. Manaka's SOYIKWA performance group was founded in 1980 for the creation of his second play *Imbumba* (The United). The original cast members, Danny Moitse, Ronnie Mkhwanazi, Makarious Sebe and David Sebe, have worked closely with the author in his development as a director and playwright. Manaka is not a writer of plays so much as a *maker* of plays. Workshops, rehearsals, rescripting and improvisation are basic ingredients in the theatre of SOYIKWA. The group does not cling to any notions of purity of style or form. Their idea of theatre is eclectic, borrowing from numerous sources in accordance with what is theatrically viable. Manaka believes in a theatre of images, not of words. The image in theatre is a device manifested in both physical and symbolic terms: in Manaka's theatre it becomes the central dynamic thrust of the plays. *Imbumba* is based on such an image. The original poster design for the production of the play represented in graphic outline the picture of a trident stabbed through a human hand which bled at the points of incision: unity will exist, even through pain and sacrifice. Set in a labour compound, the characters in the play suffer the indignities of oppressive working conditions under the arrogant control of a foreman, a black Nduna. In remarkable physical detail, the audience is witness to scenes of hard labour, destitution and physical deprivation. This is all presented through mime and the visualisation of the actors — elements that cannot accurately be communicated textually. When three actors mime the transport of large boulders, sweating and straining for minutes on end, exclamations from the audience at the sight of rivulets of perspiration created by this *mimed* activity, at the simulation of street sounds through the human *voice*, and at the sight of realistic beatings and assaults on stage, are testimony to the efficacy of Manaka's work in performance.

Manaka's group created, during 1982, a new work entitled *Pula* (Rain). The present writer witnessed the work in four different venues. The differences between them were a demonstration that the very meaning and significance of theatre is transformed by its conditions of performance. When a performance deals with prostitution and destitution, and is interrupted by a cacophony of sounds and screaming from offstage — a *real* prostitute who has been cheated of her earnings just outside the church hall which houses the performance — then theatre attains a significance unmatched by the "plush places" referred to by Tshabangu in the preface to this paper. Manaka's *Pula* was first performed for an audience of two in a garage measuring fifteen square metres. It was then performed in the Blackchain Hall, a stark, bare

227

room in Soweto, to a full house which interacted without inhibition when the actors, in character, engaged them in conversation, offered them drinks and, in one case, invited a young girl to dance — the scene being a shebeen in Soweto. The play was then presented in the Nunnery Theatre on the campus of the University of the Witwatersrand in Johannesburg, and then in the Market Theatre. The metamorphosis of the production as it was presented to different audiences and in different venues, was an aspect of its very meaning in each case. The text of the play, as yet unpublished, remains merely a scenario of the action and meaning. An archaeology of such theatre is necessary in order fully to appreciate its many implications.

Towards a South African theatre: the multiplicity of performance

Scholars of South African theatre are plagued by definitional problems. The diversity of theatrical forms in this heterogeneous society has prompted diverse critical attitudes to these forms. The terms 'white theatre in English', 'white theatre in Afrikaans', 'black theatre in English', 'black theatre in the vernacular', and many others, are symptomatic of the self-consciousness created in cultural discourse in South Africa. What has become apparent as a result of this self-consciousness, is the need for a new definition of theatrical discourse. Throughout history there have been numerous examples of innovative cultural forms which have provided active critiques of the status quo. Only rarely does it occur, however, that a work manages to transcend the conditions of functioning which are themselves the object of its critique. The theatre of Black Consciousness refused to operate within the aesthetic and political framework dictated by dominant cultural preconceptions. It was dedicated to *change* and could not thus operate from a platform of values built out of the very system under attack. Instead of operating within the existing institutional framework of theatre to launch a critique, the theatre of Black Consciousness created a conscious counter-cultural platform. As a result, dominant tendencies in South African theatre have begun to be measured against alternatives. More significantly, as a result of these developments, critical attitudes and responses have had to be re-assessed. Alternative theatre has necessitated alternative critical language.

Out of the amorphous conglomerate of South African theatre types, modes and styles, it is possible to trace, since 1976, the beginnings of a growth of an indigenous theatrical tradition defined not in terms of

228

linguistic or ethnic factors, but in terms of the role and function of theatre. This theatre creates its own forms and techniques independently of any received tradition. It draws its inspiration from complex and idiosyncratic structures. Its audiences are elements in those structures. South African theatre is beginning to emerge as a conscious signifier of South African culture.

NOTES

1   Clark, Ve Ve A "The Archaeology of Black Theatre" *The Black Scholar* 10(10) (1979) 43—56.
2   See Williams, Mance *The Colour of Black Theatre: A Critical Analysis of the Black Theatre Movement of the 1960's and 1970's.* Ph D dissertation (University of Missouri-Columbia 1980).
3   Through the editorial work of Visser and Couzens in various issues of *English in Africa.*
4   Biko, S "Black Consciousness and the Quest for a True Humanity" in *Essays on Black Theology* edited by Mokgethi Motlhabi (Johannesburg: Christian Movement 1972).
5   See *Rand Daily Mail*, May to July 1975 for various reports.
6   Shezi, Mthuli *Shanti* in *South African People's Plays* African Writers Series No 224 (London: Heinemann 1981).
7   Mthuli Shezi had been vice-chairman of the Black People's Convention in 1972, and died after he was allegedly pushed under the wheels of an oncoming train during an argument with a white railways official.
8   Attorney-General's report and charge sheets, 1975. The documentary exhibits are housed in the archives of the National English Literary Museum in Grahamstown.
9   *The Report of the Commission of Enquiry into the Performing Arts* August 1977, Paragraph 425 (Pretoria Government Printer 1977).
10 Steyl, Inez, in a review of *The Sun Will Rise, The Star* 2 April 1980.
11 ". . . it is on the delineation of 'aesthetics' that we have first to fix our attention. From the description of a theory of perception aesthetics became, in the eighteenth century, a new specializing form of description of the response to 'art' . . . as 'aesthetics' and 'the aesthetic response'. All problems of the multiplicities of intention and performance could then be undercut, or by-passed, by the transfer of energy to this other pole . . . its aesthetic properties." Williams, Raymond *Marxism and Literature* (Oxford: Oxford University Press 1977) pp149—150.

12 Williams p 116.
13 *Sunday Post* 4 July 1980.
14 Matsix "The Babalaz People" *Staffrider* 4(3) (November 1981) 32—4.
15 Tshabangu, M *S'ketsh'* (Soweto: New Classic Publications) (Summer 1974—5) p 19.

APPENDIX

A representative selection of alternative theatre from 1971 to 1982

Published Plays

Dike, Fatima *The Sacrifice of Kreli* (Johannesburg: Ad Donker 1978) and *The First South African* (Johannesburg: Ravan Press 1979).

Govender, Ronnie *The Lahnee's Pleasure* (Johannesburg: Ravan Press 1981).

Kente, Gibson *Too Late* African Writers Series No 224 (London: Heinemann 1981).

Leshoai, B L *Lines Draw Monsters* (Johannesburg: Ravan Press 1977).

Manaka, Matsemela *Egoli* (Johannesburg: Ravan Press 1980).

Mda, Zakes *Dead End, Dark Voices Ring* and *We Shall Sing For The Fatherland* in *Three Plays* (Johannesburg: Ravan Press 1981).

Mekgoe, Shimane *Lindiwe* (Johannesburg: Ravan Press 1978).

Mtsaka, Makwedini J *Not His Pride* (Johannesburg: Ravan Press 1978).

Mutwa, Credo V *uNosilimela* African Writers Series No 224 (London: Heinemann 1981).

Shezi, Mthuli *Shanti* African Writers Series No 224 (London: Heinemann 1981).

Workshop '71 Company *Survival* African Writers Series No 224 (London: Heinemann 1981).

Unpublished plays
(dates of first performances are indicated)

Bacchi, G	*The Deviant* 1975	
Bantseke, K T	*Cry, Black Woman* 1973	
Dibakwane, W	*The Marriage* 1973	
Gumbi, N	*Zwelibanzi* 1973	
Gwebu, A	*Curse of the Blue Blood* 1973	

230

Johnson, K	*Revenge* 1975
Kente, G	*How Long* 1973
	I Believe 1974
	Beyond a Song 1975
Khanyile, D	*Name It* 1975
Khorombi, Daisy	*Wild Fire* 1972
Khuvango Society	*Isandlwana* 1980
Lebelo, M	*Shivering Shock* 1973
	uMlungu 1974
	Keep Your Promise 1974
	Are you Serious? 1974
	Power Drunk 1974
Macu, Ridgeway	*Matter of Convenience* 1975
Magagula, C	*Just Because* 1976
Malunga, C	*Respect Yourself* 1976
Manaka, Matsemela	*Imbumba* 1979
	Pula 1982
	Vuka 1982
Makhene, B	*Zimbi* 1974
Maphisa, P	*Hope* 1975
Maponya, Maishe	*The Hungry Earth* 1979
Maqina, Rev. M	*Give Us This Day* 1975
Maredi, D	*Prisoner of Rome* 1971
	Strive to Lose 1975
Matitse and Mshengu	*The Frame* 1975
Mohlamme, Boikie	*Mahlomola* 1972
	Amen 1980
Mofokeng, Z	*The Train* 1976
Mokae, Z	*Come a Home, Chile* 1973
Montsho, Alfred	*The Secret* 1971
Matlhabane, Israel	*Love and Hate* 1972
	Why Naked 1974
	Confession 1975
Mqayisa, K	*Confused Mhlaba* 1974
Mtembu, M	*Shame* 1972
Mthoba J & Mshengu	*Uhlanga* 1975
Msiza, S	*Soweto* 1976
Nchapi, F	*Be Careful of Her* 1976
Ngale, N	*Never Despair* 1974
Ngema, Percy	*Save the Children* 1980
Nomoyi, B	*Why?* 1973
	Born to Lose 1974
Oliphant, O	*Vendetta* 1976
Rachilo, Sol	*The Township Wife* 1972

Raletebele, G	*Adultery* 1974
Ray, Dan	*Nyatsi* 1971
Samenza, A	*Repent* 1976
Sepamla, S	*Cry Yesterday's Fall* 1972
Setuke, P	*The Butterfly* 1974
Sibanda, M	*Deaf 3* 1974
Sinxo, G B	*Cruel Love* 1975
Sithole, B	*At Long Last* 1976
Skosane, A	*Ekhaya* 1976
Sojane, A	*Until When?* 1975
Thabethe, P	*Uphi Umthakathi* 1976
Tsambo, Elizabeth	*Blessings* 1972
	Where Lies the Future 1972
	uMendo 1973
Williams, Sam	*The Question* 1971
Workshop '71	*Crossroads* 1972
	Zzzip! 1973
	Small Boy 1976
	Survival 1976

Giovanni Jacopo, Adamastor, and Livingstone: Voices in Altercation

AUDREY FAWCETT CAHILL

Douglas Livingstone has often spoken and written of his childhood experience as a refugee from the Japanese invasion of Malaya, and something of the lens of the survivor still affects his vision today, and refracts into complexity his view of the world around him: what is most precious to him presents itself as that which is most hardly won and precariously held.

His recent volume of poetry, *The Anvil's Undertone*,¹ gives a good indication of the range and intricacy of his concerns, and of the control required to hold the different aspects of his personality in balance. As in his earlier works, he appears as an animal lover, with a healthy respect for the instinctual life and for the natural economy (*Bataleur* and *A Piece of Earth*); also as a profoundly compassionate person, who wants healing and wholeness for all (*A Natural History of the Negatio Bacillus*), even while as a realist he sees the impossibility of such a result (*First Seed: First Blood*). The scientist in him knows how necessary science is even to the most isolated and primitive regions of the modern world (*August Zulu*), yet the poet sees that science addresses itself only to a part of the human condition (*Reciprocals*). Even the poet in him is divided, for he is in some respects a Romantic, seriously committed to many values no longer quite fashionable in literature, and at the same time a thoroughly modern thinker, who is fully aware of the climate in which he works. He is, in addition, a wry humorist, constantly turning his dry wit upon his own seriousness, and preserving it from solemnity.

It is this opalescent complexity which sometimes baffles the reader with sudden shifts of tone and undermining twists of action. While such shifts are almost always successful where they occur in the shorter poems, in the longer ones they are often difficult to relate, resulting in what Michael Chapman has described, in the case of *August Zulu*, as "mere random collocations", so that "it is difficult to discern a controlling purpose in Livingstone's approach to his material".[2]

What is felt as a problem by the reader implies, I think, a corresponding problem for the writer. The task of subordinating disparate views to a single unifying principle is clearly one of the greatest technical challenges for a poet, and it naturally increases with the length of the poem and the disparity of attitudes which present themselves. It is this aspect of one of his longest and most recent poems which I wish to examine. The poem is entitled *GIOVANNI JACOPO MEDITATES (On An Alabaster Adamastor)*, and appears on pp 62—8 of this book; it is Livingstone's response to the request for a statement on his own position as a poet in South Africa at the present time. Characteristically, he refuses a simple answer, but he seems now to have found a more satisfactory way of dealing with his need to speak in several voices.

His method is to bring into confrontation two personae who have featured in his earlier poems. One is the mythical Adamastor created by Camoens, and recreated both by Roy Campbell and by Livingstone himself; and the other is the Giovanni Jacopo who has featured in some of his earlier poems — first and most frequently in *A Rosary of Bone* (1975), and once again at the end of *The Anvil's Undertone* (1978). There are still many difficulties for the reader, especially the reader who is not familiar with Livingstone's earlier work; but they no longer derive from reversals of attitude in a single speaker, and they no longer appear as disruptions in the unity of the poem. In this case, the conflicting attitudes are simplified, exaggerated, and polarized, being given to two warring speakers. The main problem for the reader now becomes the problem of any drama or dramatic poem: the location of the voice of the poet among or beyond those of his personae.

In the earlier poems entitled *Giovanni Jacopo Meditates*, the voice of Giovanni Jacopo seems to be close to the voice of Livingstone himself. It is, however, a simplified voice, and the first of the series, subtitled *(On Aspects of Art & Love)*, gives a clue to the relationship:

GIOVANNI JACOPO MEDITATES
(On Aspects of Art & Love)

The Poet's or Playwright's Function
Is to embark physically

Upon the Consciousness of his Generation;
Not merely as the Conscience

Of his Time; nor solely to reflect
Disintegration, if Disintegration

Is the Shaker of his Time's stormy Seas.
But to anchor a Present,

Nail to its Mast
One Vision, one Integrity

In a Manner so memorable
It fills Part of a Past.

A Poet's or Playwright's Enthusiasms,
These. The proper Pursuit

For a Gentleman remains to master
The Art of delaying his Orgasms.[3]

The thought expressed in the first fourteen lines is serious and intelligent, similar in content to the thought expressed in many of Livingstone's lyrical poems which employ a single, serious voice. One of the most significant differences however, is that Giovanni Jacopo's voice is not modern: the archaic "&" and the capitalization of the nouns draw attention to the archaic imagery, in this, as in others of the group, to do with sailing ships and navigation by the stars rather than with space craft and computerised navigation. The wit belongs somewhere around the seventeenth century, a time when the conjunction of 'modern' science with traditional philosophy and theology made paradox a common mode of thought, and when contraries were habitually yoked together in harmony. The fine statement of the first two sentences is not negated by the humorous twist at the end; instead, the amorist's joke reinforces the impression of an integrated personality, for whom both poetry and love-making are necessary and serious aspects of a whole and harmonious life, and fit to be joked about because they are serious.

This personal integration is the second characteristic which distinguishes the voice of Giovanni Jacopo from the voice of the modern poet. The created character seems to represent the harmonious person that the poet would like to be, and that perhaps he is at times;[4] Giovanni Jacopo does not experience the alienation of which Livingstone sometimes writes, and which he diagnoses so brilliantly (and clinically) in *A Natural History of the Negatio Bacillus.* Even the meditation (*On Drifting*),[5] which is about the disorientation following upon abandonment by a loved one, gives a powerful impression of a life unified and controlled by the force of love. Indeed, Giovanni Jacopo's integrity as a person seems to be linked to his role as a lover. If half the truth is that "Love makes fools of us all, doesn't it?"[6] the other half, affirmed in this group of poems, is that, however transiently, love makes whole and healthy people of us all.

From the poems published so far, it would seem that Giovanni Jacopo speaks for the romantic, poetic, heroic side of the poet's personality. If some of his attitudes are not quite modern, it does not matter, for he is set a few centuries back in literary history at a time when he can reasonably hope to be a well-rounded gentleman, and to see his life as a unity. The limitations of his vision become technical advantages for the poems in which he features, for all that he meditates on is held together by his unifying vision.

In his meditation (*On an Alabaster Adamastor*) Giovanni Jacopo is not the main speaker, but he is important because his introduction and conclusion frame and judge Adamastor's tirade. His plight is significant:

> As in a Daze, I heard, aghast
> The harshest Tones that ever rasped Man's Ears.
> (The Accents haunt me still).   He glared, & I
> Was torn between the Poker & my Pen.

Although he is in a dilemma, it is practical rather than emotional: horror and rage characterise his response, and continue to do so consistently, both as he records the words of the figure, and as he takes up the poker and smashes its head. His speeches are short, but he is given the first and the last word, and his final *coup de grâce*, for all its comic absurdity, is a kind of vindication of what he stands for.

The six sections spoken by Adamastor are the most difficult to place in relation to the implicit voice of the poet; but, as with Giovanni Jacopo, a knowledge of Adamastor's literary history helps to determine his status. In Camoens's *The Lusiads*,[7] he is the spirit of the Cape of Storms who prophesies "shipwreck and catastrophe" to the sailors who dare its hostile waters, and death and destruction to those who attempt to colonize the land. Originally one of the Titans who rebelled against the Gods, Adamastor is betrayed by his love for Thetis, and at the moment of embracing her is turned, in Camoens's version, into the rocky Cape Peninsula, and, in Livingstone's play, into the whole continent of

236

Africa. Livingstone adds an element of violence to the story:

> Herakles counting corpses, near forgot,
> But searching, found and pulped the Giant's head
> As he lay dying, half-submerged by tides,
> This Giant, born with travail for his lot,
> Divided, doomed, was in confusion led.
> Around his shores my lovely Thetis rides
> With thorn and grassy plain his form is draped.
> The continent of Africa is shaped.[8]

In *Adamastor Resuscitated*, published as a separate poem in *Sjambok*,[9] but also part of the play, the fallen giant stirs briefly, but subsides, leaving twentieth-century suburbia drinking sundowners in a parody of the celebration prepared by Venus for the returning mariners. In both versions of the myth, Adamastor is silenced, but remains a threatening presence:

> The ended day.
> Does the day exist?
> The earth, the sky, the ocean, when man no longer remains?
> Brave little fellow
> Cavorting out of the darkness; capering and somersaulting
> Across the pages of history.
> Wrestling with continents as gigantic as giants and always winning:
> Postponing the enormity with electricity and drains . . .
> Except one giant,
> One hulking solemn mass of scrub, forest, desert and rock —
> The Adamastor of this story.
> Here there can be no victor.
> By their struggle each will survive.
> Elsewhere the winners will be too choked to live.
> Here, but here, the maniacs are manacled together in hate
> Until the end of it.[10]

Adamastor's prophecies are not altogether fulfilled, because of the heroism and persistence of man, the "brave little fellow"; but they are not altogether empty, either. Like the dangerous Cape itself they remain as a perpetual possibility, and a lurking threat.[11]

Something of the same ambiguity attaches to the words of the Alabaster Adamastor. In relation to him, Giovanni Jacopo is the "brave

237

little fellow" who, like Herakles, once more pulps his head. He dissociates himself from what Adamastor says, but he takes it seriously enough to record it. His horror surely arises from the element of truth in the attack: it is a real threat because it is full of the most damaging kind of falsehood, the truth distorted. Adamastor's criticism is indeed a criticism that can be levelled against the worst South African writing, but he makes no exceptions, and draws no distinctions. Much of it can also be read as an analysis of the seductions which tempt even the best writers, and which Livingstone himself must have felt:

> Earning Bread
> From expiating ancient Faults chalks Scores
> For stints of Sanitation, rinsed in Print.
>
> The Occident by Accident displaced
> Due South looks longingly at West & North
> Or East.   Receded Tides of Empire left
> A Wake: a Conscience-struck, bereft, pale-faced
> Parched Populace who ache to hold their Own.

Likewise there is the temptation to retreat:

> Some leave, of course, take Refuge in Disdain;

and the more general temptation which technical facility holds:

> Quick Fix of Ink;
> In lieu of Guts: brief dangled Novelties.

Livingstone, in his own person, has said rather similar things — not indeed of anyone else, but of his own decisions and attitudes. In the early 1960s, in response to a questionnaire sent to a number of poets, he claimed that for him it would be "too facile to 'escape' or join emotionally-fixed ranks of *blancophobes* and *negriphiles* (sic)";[12] and in 1976, asked whether he believed in inspiration, he answered:

> I do believe in inspiration but I think that the poem is a product of perspiration . . . I think I only have one published poem without any corrections. But sixty drafts is commonplace.[13]

It would seem, then, that in spite of the horrified response of

Giovanni Jacopo, the poet himself assents in some measure to the criticisms voiced by Adamastor, and they are not to be dismissed quite as summarily as Giovanni Jacopo's action suggests. There is, however, an important difference: Adamastor's accusations are made with the intention of asserting the worthlessness of the writer's enterprise, and of persuading him to stop trying. It is this implication that Giovanni Jacopo resists, and answers by taking up his poker.

In the central sections of the poem, Adamastor distorts and derides most of the choices open to South African writers: there are those who withdraw from the world about them and find refuge in a Nirvana of private experience, and there are those who write or praise protest verse because that is what is fashionable. Behind these two attacks is the implication, Adamastor's but not Livingstone's, that genuine art is not possible in South Africa at the present time.

This view is made explicit in Section IV, in which political rather than literary factors are cited as reasons for giving up. Because

> The expected Cataclysms stultify,

and because

> Religion here is Property & Sport,
> . . . .
> So you make Artefacts instead of Art.

If the voice of Adamastor coincides with the voice of Livingstone anywhere in the poem, it is surely in the grudging admiration given in these lines:

> Some doughty Souls portray the secret Norms
> Of private Life, while hoping to impose
> These on the Body Public.

In "An Interview with Livingstone" the poet says:

> There are a great many explicit recipes for being human: great works of philosophy, religion, et cetera. I think a great poem is an implicit recipe, no matter what its subject . . . .[14]

Both Adamastor and Livingstone see dedicated poets as "doughty Souls"; the difference is that Adamastor dismisses them as "Purblind

Dolts".

At this point it becomes clear that Adamastor is playing the role of Tempter, tempting the poet with his own doubts; and the greatest temptation is not any of the more obvious evasions or compromises suggested in the first three sections, but the temptation to give up altogether.

Having begun by denouncing practices that Livingstone has always done his best to eschew, Adamastor's diatribe narrows through a piece of invective against the isolationism and 'Englishness' of Natal to a personal attack, in Section VI, against the poet himself. Though the words of this section are still addressed to Giovanni Jacopo, Adamastor's description does not fit the persona who emerges from the earlier poems. It is, instead, a caricature of Livingstone himself, and suggests that he is hopelessly ineffectual in his attempts to combine his avocation as a poet with his workaday occupation as a marine biologist. There is no trace of Giovanni Jacopo's strength and simplicity, and his versatility becomes, in this distorted picture, a dissipation of energy that is part of his slide towards disintegration:

> Unravelled Fool, as soiled as any Navvy,
> The Vessels of Research have you decked out.
> The Ocean yields its Wares unyieldingly,
> & then: burnt Shoulders in the Shower; your Hands
> Sliced to the Quick by Wire, yearn after Ink.
>
> In earning daily Crusts, there is not Time
> — You bleat — to write, to read, to sleep, to eat.
> Each Night's a geodesic Frustulum
> Too shrunk for getting drunk, or happy Love;
> & you've eschewed a Patron, slewed your Pen.

The emphasis in Section VI is on what Livingstone has spoken of as "the hesitations and self-doubts and failures that have dogged my heels for more years than I care to remember".[15] It is this section that finally and firmly places Adamastor's charges: they are distortions and generalizations and half-truths, with doubts masquerading as incontrovertible facts, imperfectly realized intentions represented as abysmal failures, and the human struggles of the poetic process depicted as final defeats. Adamastor's intention is that the poet — indeed all poets — should give up trying. Giovanni Jacopo's, and Livingstone's, is that they should go on.

240

In combining the two voices of Adamastor and Giovanni Jacopo in this way, Livingstone has found a means of clarifying, without cynicism, his complex sense of the perpetual presence of the temptations that attack the poet as Word, and a means of asserting, without heroics, his belief in the persistence and courage that are needed to overcome those temptations. The mode is characteristically comic, the matter characteristically serious. And the serious view of the poet's vocation that emerges is not very far from the view of an earlier poet who was also concerned with "the intolerable wrestle/With words and meanings"[16] and who, like Livingstone, saw the integrity of the poet as so essentially related to the integrity of the person that both could be described in the same language:

> And right action is freedom
> From past and future also.
> For most of us, this is the aim
> Never here to be realised;
> Who are only undefeated
> Because we have gone on trying;
> We, content at the last
> If our temporal reversion nourish
> (Not too far from the yew-tree)
> The life of significant soil.[17]

NOTES

1   Livingstone, Douglas *The Anvil's Undertone* (Johannesburg: Ad Donker 1978).

2   Chapman, Michael *Douglas Livingstone: A Critical Study of his Poetry* (Johannesburg: Ad Donker 1981) p164.

3   Livingstone, Douglas *A Rosary of Bone* (Cape Town: David Philip 1975) p3.

4   "And I wanted to try to describe to you the shimmering experience, the moments of true cohesion a person experiences when he is struggling to turn a mass of ordinary words and thoughts into a poem; and how the poetic is not at all a separate stratum in the business of living." Livingstone, Douglas "Graduation Address" in *University of Natal Graduation Citations and Addresses 1982* (Durban: University of Natal 1982).

5   Livingstone *A Rosary of Bone* p12.

6   Ullyatt, A G "An Interview with Livingstone" *UNISA English Studies* 24 (1) (April 1976) 45—49. Here Livingstone is quoting from his own radio play *The Sea My Winding Sheet.*

7   Camoens, L *The Lusiads* translated by W C Atkinson (Harmondsworth: Penguin 1952).

8   Livingstone, Douglas "The Sea My Winding Sheet" in *Theatre One* edited by Stephen Gray (Johannesburg: Ad Donker 1978) 95—122; p116. This play was first published in an abridged form in *The Sea My Winding Sheet and Other Poems* (Durban: Theatre Workshop 1971).

9   Livingstone, Douglas *Sjambok, and Other Poems from Africa* (London: OUP 1964).

10 *Theatre One* pp121—122.

11 See also Roy Campbell's poem "Rounding the Cape" in *Adamastor* (Cape Town: Paul Koston 1930) and Stephen Gray's fuller treatment of the myth in his *Southern African Literature: An Introduction* (Cape Town: David Philip 1979).

12 Livingstone, Douglas "Ten Comments on a Questionnaire" *London Magazine* 4 (8) (Nov 1964) 33—34; p34.

13 Ullyatt "An Interview with Livingstone" p46.

14 Ullyatt "An Interview with Livingstone" p47.

15 Livingstone "Graduation Address" p28.

16 Eliot, T S *Four Quartets* (London: Faber 1944); from "East Coker II" p17.

17 Eliot *Four Quartets*; from "The Dry Salvages V" p33.

In a Free State:
The Exile in South African Poetry

Any contemporary account of South African cultural history must recognize the co-existence of two nationalisms, the one defined within the borders of the country and the other banished to host countries beyond those borders, but each having its own clearly defined ideological function and with its own tradition of popular heroes and observed anniversaries built into its mythology. Similarly, any attempt to chart the course of present-day South African literature must recognize that together with the establishment of an indigenous literature claiming the title South African, there has emerged a literature in exile. The chief contributors to that body of writing must be identified as belonging to a tradition with equal claim to the name South African.

Thomas Mann's statement from the United States in 1939, "Where I am is Germany"[1] indicates the analogy with German literature between 1933 and 1945. It was neither arrogant nor intended as a taunt to the National Socialist regime in his country of birth; it was simply the expression of a cultural reality and has, in effect, been reiterated by every exiled South African writer. The authors who were exiled from Germany constituted what has become loosely known as the 'other Germany'; similarly, South Africa exists in a state of particular self-awareness wherever South Africans produce its literature. The comparison prompts a further consideration: the history of modern German literature could only be written after the two streams had been rejoined in 1945; the proper history of South African literature must await some similar date in the future. In the interim it is important that special attention should be paid to those South African writers in exile whose works reveal, in addition to a strong sense of their personal plight, an awareness of the general category of exile. Bertolt Brecht considered it in 1937:

243

I could never agree with the name that was given to us. Émigrés are people who emigrate, but we did not leave the country of our own free will to go to the country of our choice. Nor did we emigrate to stay in that country, perhaps forever. We had to flee. We were driven out and banished. And the country that received us is no home but a place of exile.[2]

As in the case of Germany, the other South Africa is not comprised only of those writers who have embraced the extreme course of exile: the loss of citizenship, being declared an enemy of the state, or the confiscation and banning of their books. The other South Africa exists equally, although not with the same freedom of utterance, within the borders of the country itself. Like the expatriates, the internal exiles who have transgressed the rigid social and political frontiers by which South Africa has so obsessively defined itself and who have consequently been exiled from the larger community by way of detention, imprisonment and banning, are both the products and important determinants of South African history.

Although there is a general (and somewhat vague) sense in which every sensitive imagination which separates itself from a society can be regarded as in exile, and an equally loose sense in which all writers can be called imaginative exiles or even internal émigrés, it is worth bearing in mind that true exile — as opposed to voluntary emigration — is compelled.[3]

The experience of exile can be psychologically damaging, even morally corrupting, and for the poet imaginatively debilitating. He shares the general difficulties common to all exiles (obtaining financial support, involvement in tedious bureaucratic procedures in the host country, and adjustment to an alien environment); he also has, because of his special and intimate relation to his native language, the additional problem of an audience. His words can become incomprehensible or even irrelevant in his new surroundings. This verbal impotence can result in creative impotence, especially when the poet's feeling of obligation towards the political struggle causes his art to deteriorate into propaganda, when the fine and over-determined language of his poetry degenerates into bald sloganeering. Or alternatively, over-whelming nostalgia for the country he has left can result in his closing himself off to the outside world and expressing himself in a language rooted in his past. In his study of ex-colonial English writers, *Writers in Exile*,[4] Andrew Gurr argues that exiled writers spend much of their creative lives constructing a vision of their lost home by way of therapy

244

for the disease of alienation.

Although exile can and often does inhibit the poetic faculty, it may also serve to release the imagination. When he translates his own experience into the mythical world of his poetry, the exiled South African poet is able to respond positively and creatively to the fact of his personal exile. In a particular kind of mythopoetic activity, he imaginatively assimilates his own condition of exile and is then able to extend his imaginative sympathy to the figures of the political prisoner and the popular leader.

* * * * *

The actual experience of exile is well documented in contemporary South African poetry. In *Autopsy*[5] Arthur Nortje evokes the community of exiles: men with the shared knowledge of flight or expulsion, their vital connections with their native country severed and the old security replaced by temporary existence in a host country:

> In the towns I've acquired
> arrive the broken guerrillas, gaunt and cautious,
> exit visas in their rifled pockets
> and no more making like Marx
> for the British Museum in the nineteenth century,
> damned: the dark princes, burnt and offered
> to the four winds, to the salt-eyed seas. To their earth
> unreturnable.
> The world receives
> them, Canada, England now that the laager
> masters recline in a gold inertia
> behind the arsenal of Sten guns. I
> remember many, but especially one
> almost poetic, so undeterrable.

In *Immigrant* Nortje achieves a wry detachment from his own involvement in the process of expatriation thus reinforcing the vision of himself as translated from individual to international type:

> X-rayed, doctored at Immigration
> weighed in at the Embassy
> measured as to passport, smallpox, visa
> at last the efficient official informs me
> I'm an acceptable soldier of fortune . . . . (92)

He confronts the knowledge that his has become the emotional and intellectual baggage of the transient, and this serves as therapy for the soul-sickness of total anonymity:

> I walk with an address book
> full of crossed-out numbers, party contacts,
> once-met twice-kissed women who have moved
> to somewhere I will never be . . . .
>
> (*Return to the city of the heart*, 102)

Other poets find that their poetic sensibility only intensifies the malady. The condition of deracination becomes insupportable, the rootless movement it imposes is too depersonalizing, the psychological damage too great. Perpetual anonymity leads to anxiety, human resources are worn thin, become brittle and must eventually break down. Dennis Brutus finds that this predicament is mirrored in the lives of fellow exiles and the collective experience magnifies rather than eases pain. Acknowledgement of the community of exiles who share an anguish does little to console, for it is the type that he finds untenable. *For James Cooke arrived from South Africa on an exit permit*[6] succeeds in depicting the process of emigration from the vantage point of the already established exile. The vision in the poem is both prospective and retrospective, a complex overlay in which the description of Cooke's physical translation from South Africa to England is both a rehearsal of personal experience and analysis of Cooke's arrival in exile. The sad wisdom of hindsight has produced an ironic foresight. It is the element of paradox in the condition of exile that addresses itself to the imagination of the already exiled poet. He sees the flight into exile as a rite of passage from life to a living death; the forceful thrust of the aircraft and the confinement of its passenger become images of the interplay of restriction and freedom in exile. All the momentum of physical emigration is ironically dissipated into the scattered and precarious life awaiting Cooke as his certain sense of himself and his energies are absorbed into the ragged and stretched fabric of a torn, anxious mind. In the transition from South Africa to Europe, vital

246

emotion is translated into brooding consciousness as anger congeals partly into rational awareness of the motives for flight and partly into deliberate identification with the lot of the displaced person in history. A degree of artifice has necessarily to intervene to hold off the raw agony of exile. Only in equipoise of heart and mind can the poet function at all: the recognition of self as abnormal in a world that is disconcertingly normal, and the internalization of all former energies into a preoccupation with the role of the exile.

The geographical locations liberally furnished by Brutus after many of his poems are more than simply informative appendices; they are arguably an integral part of these poems dealing with the spiritual geography of exile. They first occur, tellingly, at the end of poems written by Brutus while still living in South Africa. These indications of exploratory journeys within South Africa prefigure the litany of information which traces the journey into exile. Thus places of poetic inspiration or composition demarcate specific stages in his state of exile; his is an unenviable internationalism and each new frontier crossed heightens his awareness of severed roots. The journey of exile is in many ways a cyclical one. Each new arrival signals an already known situation; each novelty experienced summons up memories of a familiar world lost; intellectual and cultural enrichment also means spiritual impoverishment; and free movement across borders only serves to emphasise the confinements imposed by such a life.

*　*　*　*　*

One of the most entertaining paradigms of the state of exile in modern literature is given by Italo Calvino in his tale *Baron in the Trees*.[7] The eighteenth-century Baron Cosimo Piovasco di Rondò's flight up an oak tree and subsequent life in the treetops begins as an adolescent act of rebellion. His story is a parable of flight from intolerable social pressures, and his life of exile in the trees offers valuable insights into the ambivalent awareness of the social outcast.

Cosimo's first lesson is that from the treetops everything looks different, and this altered perception is of course metaphorical. His kingdom in the trees has no borders; he is able to cross from estate to estate and even venture across national frontiers. What might initially have seemed to be a self-imposed restriction on his movements becomes unprecedented freedom. An instinct for survival teaches him that he is bound to continue on the road he has chosen, and he finally compels his father's admission that "Rebellion cannot be measured by yards. . . . Even when a journey seems no distance at all, it can have no return." (131)

His borderless state leads to new avenues of inquiry, to new habits of intellectual curiosity and introspection. He becomes confirmed in his need to make himself useful to others and in his commitment to the commonwealth. "This he understood, that association renders men stronger and brings out each person's best gifts, and gives a joy which is rarely to be had by keeping to oneself." (176) The notion of distance with all its philosophical implications begins to preoccupy him. He begins to compose utopian tracts, and comes to be regarded in turn as eccentric, mad, revolutionary, a Freemason, political reformer, and finally as a universal genius respected all over Europe. At the end of a life spent in perpetual flight from society, Cosimo is a celebrated and legendary figure, a living demonstration of the truth that "anyone who wants to see the earth properly must keep himself at a necessary distance from it." (213)

Engaging as the details of Cosimo's history are, what remains is the impression of the *figure* of the exile and not the particularities of an individual life. A kind of mythopoesis has occurred: the characteristic experiences of all exiles have merged into one representative life. This mythopoetic syncretism also occurs in the lyrical poetry of exile. When the exiled writer is least successful, he manages only to give his own experience a forced archetypal inflation; but in the best works the writer succeeds in holding the immediate reality of exile constantly before one while keeping the universal figure of the exile equally present to bestow lasting symbolic meaning on the specific instance. When Brutus concludes a short poem dealing with his estrangement from both African and European culture (*I am an alien in Africa and everywhere*, 121) with the statement that only in himself, occasionally, is he familiar, his claim points beyond mere solipsism; understanding and self-acceptance of a sort can come only from identifying his lot with that of the figure of the exile through history. He also declares as much in the opening line of one of his most successful poems of exile, *"I am the exile."* (137)

Two other poems stand out as combining the authenticity of lived experience with a comprehensive definition of the figure of the exile: Breyten Breytenbach's *Luistervink*[8] (Eavesdropper) and Arthur Nortje's *Native's Letter*. The poems should be considered in conjunction with each other for the composite image they provide of exile as an existential state. Breytenbach's poem begins rhetorically: "jy vra my hoe dit is om in ballingskap te leef, vriend —" ("you ask me what it's like to live in exile, friend —") and proceeds with a lyrical exposition of the compounded ironies of exile, of the paradoxical state and ambivalent attitudes of the exile as divided man. His response to the opening question is an image of himself without the solace of angry resentment or resignation, but constantly reminded in his own personal crises of his membership of the community of the maladjusted, the rejected and the impotent — an impasse, in effect, of individual distress and group malaise as he is accommodated by the unaccommodated. He is the victim of withering loneliness and nostalgia, reduced to begging for news from home and dredging up images from the remotest recesses of memory to alleviate the longing. He is caught with others in a private limbo between "do you remember?" and "one day". Ultimately however, as even memory is numbed and faces are dimmed, the imaginative capacity to project visions of future return becomes deadened as the individual is absorbed into the "shuffling mass of anonymity/ of prematurely aged revolutionaries/ mute poets and sightless painters" — the living death that is barely more than a temporary exile from death itself. It would be tempting to read the poem as ending on a note of insight and benediction; it remains, however, a vision of paralysing ambivalence. Only by becoming emotionally and creatively crippled has he arrived at an understanding of those who preceded him in exile and he can do no more on their behalf than ask for compassion for those who must inevitably follow.

Arthur Nortje's poem complements Breytenbach's in that he also explores the mental terrain of exile, the "bitter clay" inhabited between the homeland and the "northern waters". Like Breytenbach he acknowledges its ambivalences, but he suggests that this ambivalence should be exploited to generate a creative energy to counteract its otherwise enervating effect. The exile should convert the imaginative reserves released by incessant melancholy and the "keening on the blue strings of the blood" into supportive myths. Rather than resort to memory as a palliative, it should be employed to identify and recreate the heroic elements in the history and folklore of the resistance struggle. Then the exile can become an exploring instead of a despairing consciousness, turning physical and cultural distance to his advantage and relying on the dual perspective of estrangement to compensate present loss with future gain. Borderlessness need not be only debilitating; it also frees the exile into new imaginative structures and possibilities. In the often quoted last two lines of the poem Nortje fixes the relationship between freedom fighter and poet in exile.

Hospitable planets are unknown or too
far away from us to be
of consequence. To be of
value to his homeland must the wanderer
not weep by northern waters, but love
his own bitter clay
roaming through the hard cities, tough
himself as coffin nails.

Harping on the nettles of his melancholy,
keening on the blue strings of the blood,
he will delve into mythologies perhaps
call up spirits through the night.
Or carry memories apocryphal
of Tshaka, Hendrik, Witbooi, Adam Kok,
of the Xhosa nation's dream
as he moonlights in another country:

but he shall also have
cycles of history
outnumbering the guns of supremacy.

Now and wherever he arrives
extending feelers into foreign scenes
exploring times and lives,
equally may he stand and laugh,
explode with a paper bag of poems,
burst upon a million televisions
with a face as in a Karsh photograph,
slave voluntarily in some siberia
to earn the salt of victory.

Darksome, whoever dies
in the malaise of my dear land
remember me at swim,
the moving waters spilling through my eyes:
and let no amnesia
attack at fire hour:
for some of us must storm the castles
some define the happening.
Toronto, May 1970 (117)

250

In *Embracing Exile*[9] Lindiwe Mabuza also sees herself as caught up in a much larger historical current, her life in exile controlled by its forces and the end of her exile determined by the power of its thrust. Exile is not an inhibiting but a shaping factor in her life. And in *Faces of Commitment*[10] she spells out the ironic truth that participation in the liberation struggle grants an exit to life, that flight from South Africa both disperses the exiles and binds them together. These exits to life extend the landscape of South African poetry into the most unexpected areas. Barry Feinberg's poem *We Found Common Song* on the occasion of the Afro-Asian Young Writers' Conference, September 1976 in Tashkent brings Africa into conjunction with Soviet Asia. The mythical worlds of Samarkand, Tamerlane, Ghenghis Khan and Marco Polo are used to reinforce the informing myths of present-day South African life: the reactions demanded by the events of Soweto and the need for future Shakas. The landscape is of course ideological, its purpose solidarity, but Feinberg does achieve an almost surreal fusion of Africa and Asia in this otherwise didactic poem about forced exile:

> And Uzbek sands
> grow green
> and Uzbek skies
> glow red
> and Africa
> echoes home
> in this brother
> continent.[11]

Keorapetse Kgotsitsile's response to the same conference is much more explicitly revolutionary. His poem *South Africa Salutes Uzbekistan*[12] is stridently militant and as a 'freedom poem' demands to be justified in terms of its own radical aesthetic. Important for the purpose of this article is the evidence of a positive interpretation of exile — here a deliberate delving into an exotic Asian past in order to fashion the political myths that must sustain a South African future. The unity evoked by Kgotsitsile in *Song for Ilva Mackay and Mongane*[13] is the bond between international revolutionaries and with his characteristically curious blend of steely — almost menacing — elegance and crude political bludgeoning he endorses the brotherhood of freedom fighters. Exile has made him international in a very particular sense.

Total wholeness of the alienated spirit must, of course, await the

251

crossing of the final frontier — the exile's homecoming. In the early stages of exile this is still a matter of urgency. The longing remains at the surface of consciousness, the pain of separation is acute and the anger of displacement at white heat is part of a 'necessary wounding'. The myth of future return develops into the ultimate artifice employed by the exile to mediate his anguish: as the life-giving certainty of that return slowly evaporates, it sustains the exile as a vision forged precisely out of his awareness of its loss. "Mayibuye"[14] is the creed of the exile. It underlies the theme of Duncan Matlho's poems *Biding Time* and *Building a Future*,[15] and in Lindiwe Mabuza's poem *Forward Ever!*[16] it is the "brave dream" that leads to utopian "new horizons". Nevertheless, Klaus Maphepha acknowledges in *Our Home-Coming*[17] that this article of faith is not unequivocal. Victory will be attained, he is sure, but the celebration he envisages is sobered by the knowledge of the "blood that we shall have shed." This dual recognition is echoed in Mazisi Kunene's poem *Unfinished Adventure*. The final return home is vindicated, however, by the certain belief that

> There we shall meet with our broken selves
> Giving them the fulfilling word of life.[18]

The myth of homecoming expresses on a personal level the exile's search for psychic unity and on a national level his faith in the possibility of the restoration of a fragmented culture.

Exile and home are, in a very real sense, mirrored worlds in the literature of exile. For instance, in *Cosmos in London* the insular security of England paradoxically reflects the island imprisonment of Dennis Brutus and Nelson Mandela, so that Arthur Nortje can say with perfect ambiguity:

> It seems at times as if I am
> this island's lover, and can sing her soul. (39)

In *London Impressions* an ironically observed courtship in Hyde Park recalls his own youth "in the Union of South Africa", (57) and in *Dogsbody half-breed*, *Poem*, and *Poem: South Africa*, all three written in Toronto, it is the image of "my now distant land" that finally superimposes itself on his impressions of Canadian life. There is of course the danger that this imaginative reconstruction of home can degenerate into sentimentality, but Arthur Nortje avoids this by postulating a rational basis for the analogy between home and exile. It has needed the perspective of exile to perceive the fact that South Africa has always stood in the sign of exile and that there is in effect no break between his former and his present states:

Exile from the first

Exile was implanted
in the first pangs of paradise. This land became
a refuge for adventurers.
And who remembers history
need not trouble my
head with tales. I underwent the fire
baptism, reared in rags, schooled
in the violence of the mud. (140)

* * * * *

Mythmaking is a dynamic activity of the imagination and it would misrepresent its true achievement to see the exiled poet as merely creating nostalgic reproductions of his condition in static images of home. In *Exiles and Émigrés*,[19] a study of the modern English writer's relation to his work and culture, Terry Eagleton considers the general paradox that the literary artist has to maintain an operative distance from his object, society, while simultaneously needing to be intricately involved in it. Great art, he argues, has been produced "from the subtle and involuted tensions between the remembered and the real, the potential and the actual, integration and dispossession, exile and involvement." (18) This double-vision of the exile — his capacity for close scrutiny as well as the overall view — is fundamental to his mythopoetic faculty.

To sum up the mythopoetic capacity of the exiled imagination and the way it operates at this stage, it might be useful to consider some of the recent work of Mongane Serote from Gaborone, Botswana, and so define more closely what appears to be its most characteristic activity: an obsessive return to a vision of home born out of and reflecting the alienated state of that imagination. In *The night keeps winking*, the titles given to the last two poems, *once more: The Distances* and *The Long Road*, are by now recognizable signifiers of the dislocations of space, time, thought and feeling that complicate the condition of the expatriate, but it is the poem *Exile* that presents the most graphic illustration of the way the imagination of the poet in exile works:

Exile

it is quiet here
the silence is blue, large and far from the tree tops
it hangs above, this silence, concave and massive
always threatening to cling to one's shoulders
the silence here is as hard as the mountain and so unmovable.
Like a tick
it hangs like ivy does on walls, its thin feet stuck to the sun's
                                                        eyeball
ah,
when the eyes move
to look, they make a noise like iron scraping the earth —
so I would like to say, when people ask, how is exile;
it is quiet here.
here, the bad things I once said about memory
come back.
memory is a thin red-hot membrane on the brain
it vibrates all the time
makes sounds
rings and chimes
and once
when over-used, can shrivel like burning plastic —
do not ask me what life is
for
like memory it is thin it vibrates and can shrivel
and, once, long ago
I believed some people who talked about life being birds
                                                flying freely:
you see what memory can do?
but listen
now, when people say "interesting", "nice" and smile
I think of June 16th, I think of Solomon
I say yes,
it will be nice and interesting.[20]

The world of exile is one of simultaneously expanding and contracting horizons as the spirit is drawn out into the enormous landscape, freeing it from the mundane concerns of self; it also shrinks from this foreignness into the security of consciousness, only to become imprisoned by minute perception and cogitation. The liberating space of this world with its balm of silence paradoxically confines the poet in a close verbal reality, the absence of sound heightening his sensory perception of the otherwise inaudible. Because his situation is essentially inexpressible, he is forced to withdraw beyond articulation into the realm of ambiguity and memory. Alienation compels introspection, and introspection results in microscopic absorption. The inner eye produces images of burning intensity and the inner ear resonates thoughts uttered but no longer heard. This introspection constitutes life for the exile and is, of course, also a metaphor for the way the creative imagination functions. It is a tenuous kind of life and ironically recalls the more ample former life, but out of this precarious hold on reality a different kind of reality is created. Out of memory (here of the anniversary of the Soweto uprising and of an executed guerilla) the creative imagination makes myths, and myths salvage life out of death and sustain that life for future action. And out of the confidence of this knowledge of life Serote is able finally to formulate a response in words invested with meaning well beyond the ordinarily referential. The silence of exile has become totally internalized only to emerge again in a statement that is both ironic and threatening in its tone.

The state is more cryptically expressed by Arthur Nortje in his poem *Cosmos in London*:

We are here, nameless, staring at ourselves. (39)

Self-reflection arising out of anonymity and alienation. It is an act, Nortje says in *Waiting*, of mutilating solitude and aesthetic necessity:

The isolation of exile is a gutted
warehouse at the back of pleasure streets:
the waterfront of limbo stretches panoramically —
night the beautifier lets the lights
dance across the wharf.
I peer through the skull's black windows
wondering what can credibly save me.
The poem trails across the ruined wall
a solitary snail, or phosphorescently
swims into vision like a fish
through a hole in the mind's foundation, acute
as a glittering nerve. (90)

The translation of exile into art may have its beginnings in a necessary response to circumstance, but it quickly becomes, as Keorapetse Kgositsile suggests in the poem *Mayibuye iAfrica*, deliberate and purposive, "translated memory rides/past and future alike."[21]

The truly creative myth-making function of the exiled poetic imagination is two-fold. First, the expatriate poet is peculiarly equipped by virtue of his own excommunication to understand and demand our sympathy for those exiled within the South African community through imprisonment, detention and house-arrest. And secondly, through his exaggerated sense of his own individuality, he appreciates the distinctive heroism and also the vulnerability of popular leaders. Imprisonment, like exile, Dennis Brutus knows from his own experience of both, demands a new definition of self. Isolation and deprivation give events a fresh dimension; the prisoner learns the value of endurance and extrapolation. The response to imprisonment virtually parallels the response to exile as a comparably barred existence. Conditioned by the experience of house-arrest, Brutus in his poems from actual exile returns almost obsessively to the earlier equivalent experience. Every aspect of exile occasions some reflection on the plight of those still incarcerated on the Island: the English quicksilver dusk and soft spring rain perversely recall the Island's desolate dusks and haunting rain; South African Freedom Day conjures up a vision of how it will be observed in prison; the distress and anxiety of exile requires comparison with the suffering of confinement in jail; and even on another island (New Zealand) during the long endless night of his exile he feels obliged to find a parallel with the endless night of the men on the Island.

Other poets also project their exiled state onto the internal exiles in South Africa. Some do it in more general terms like Mazisi Kunene in the poem *The Political Prisoner*.[22] Others do it more specifically like C J Driver in *To the Dark, Singing* where his variations on the refrain "Though we sing when we die" extend an analogy between poetry in the living death of the exile and John Harris who allegedly went to his execution singing *We Shall Overcome*:

> Each of us makes a separate peace
> With the dark . . . .[23]

Or Hugh Lewin in *The Wedding*[24] where he dramatizes the isolation of Solly Nathee "banned from social gatherings" and having to stand on the koppie overlooking his home to watch his daughter's wedding alone. The distanced poet is watching Solly Nathee who is in turn being closely observed by the Special Branch with him on this koppie that overlooks his house and from which he is virtually having to spy on the guests who have come to see the bride and groom. One is inevitably reminded here of Calvino's moral, "anyone who wants to see the earth properly must keep himself at a necessary distance from it."

Sceptics might well dismiss the celebration of popular heroes as propagandist adulation or even a kind of self-aggrandisement, but this would be a failure to recognize a fundamental empathy between exile and popular leader that is a second important aspect of the myth-making function of the poet in exile. Dennis Brutus's poem *For a Dead African* (John Nangoza Jebe: shot by the police in a Good Friday procession in Port Elizabeth 1956),[25] for instance, reveals an understanding of social pathology in South Africa that is far more penetrating than mindless hero-worship. And in his poem *The Guerillas*,[26] dedicated to "the fighting men in Southern Africa", Brutus contemplates their larger social and political context from a perspective framed by the experience of exile.

Although Rebecca Matlou's poem *A Soldier at War* (*To the Year of the Spear*) is such patent propaganda, she introduces her celebration of the spirit of Zulu resistance with a line that practically sums up the experience of exile: "a soldier alone in reality I live."[27] Similarly, what strikes one most forcibly as the dominant feeling in Cosmo Pieterse's poem *Guerilla* is the anguish of exile rather than irrational hatred:

> I sometimes feel a cold love burning
> Along the shuddering length of all my spine;
> It's when I think of you with some kind of yearning,
> Mother, stepmotherland, who drop your litter with a bitter
> spurning.[28]

The suffering of rejection remains with the reader as a troublingly real emotion long after the forced ineptitude of the poem has been forgotten.

It goes without saying that the exiled poet turns to the figure of the popular leader as an inspirational force, figures such as Albert Luthuli, Nelson Mandela, J B Marks, Jack Hodgson, Solomon Mahlangu, Joseph Mdluli, Abraham Tiro, and Steve Biko. It is the experience of exile that determines the translation of these political figures into mythical heroes. David Evans's reinterpretation of Bram Fischer, Nelson Mandela and "other South African fighters against apartheid" in *African Prometheus*[29] ends with the image of rebellious consciousness in exile, and in *Before Interrogation (An Epitaph to Ahmed Timol and*

257

others)[30] A N C Kumalo recreates the dread and dependence of the political detainee driven to suicide, with the exile's understanding of the ambivalent emotions of the solitary individual towards a controlling authority. Finally, perhaps the most ambitious mythopoetic undertaking in South African poetry of exile is A N C Kumalo's poem *Child of Isandhlwana (For Solomon Mahlangu, executed on the anniversary of Van Riebeeck's landing at the Cape of Khoisan)*[31] in which he interprets Mahlangu's death against a history of black resistance. It is a poem in memory of an internal exile in a country that, in the words of Arthur Nortje, has known "exile from the beginning."

* * * * *

A body of mythological thinking has come to be identified as underpinning literary expression within South Africa: the notion of a paradisal world forever lost and a yearning to recover it; rebellious flight from authority; journeying in an unmapped interior; the effect of the immensity and sheer monotony of the South African landscape on the mind; a definition of self deriving from conflict with other indigenous cultures and the often violent resolution of such conflicts; and an increasing inhabiting of an interior realm. South African historiography has produced the figures of the frontiersman and the transfrontiersman, the latter as a type of the person who has crossed frontiers of race, religion and language. Only by recognizing that these South African myths and mythical figures apply equally to the South Africa that is in exile can the full operation of the South African literary imagination be appreciated and a more complete sense of the vitality of South African literature be gained.

NOTES

1   Quoted by Hans Meyer in "The Suffering and the Greatness of Thomas Mann" *Exile Literature 1933—1945* (Bad Godesberg: Inter Nationes 1968) p47.
2   Quoted in *Exile Literature 1933—1945*, p1.
3   See also Wegner, Matthias *Exil und Literatur: Deutsche Schriftsteller im Ausland 1933—1945* (Frankfurt am Main: Athenäum Verlag 1968) 11—31.

4   Gurr, Andrew *Writers in Exile: The Creative Use of Home in Modern Literature* (Sussex: The Harvester Press 1981).

5   Nortje, Arthur in *Dead Roots: Poems* (London: Heinemann 1973) p52. Page references to Nortje's poems given in brackets in the text, are to this volume unless otherwise specified.

6   Brutus, Dennis *A Simple Lust* (London: Heinemann 1973) 112—3. Page references to Brutus's poems given in brackets in the text, are to this volume unless otherwise specified.

7   Calvino, Italo *Baron in the Trees* in *Our Ancestors* translated by Archibald Colquhoun (London: Picador 1980). Page references given in the text refer to this edition.

8   Breytenbach, Breyten *Kouevuur* (Cape Town: Buren 1968) p63.

9   Mabuza, Lindiwe in *Poets to the People: South African Freedom Poems* edited by Barry Feinberg (London: Heinemann 1980) p89.

10 *Poets to the People* p96.

11 *Poets to the People* p37.

12 *Poets to the People* p47.

13 *Poets to the People* p44.

14 'Come back', in the expression 'Mayibuye iAfrika' — 'Let Africa come back'.

15 *Poets to the People* pp113—5.

16 *Poets to the People* p90.

17 *Poets to the People* p107.

18 *Poets to the People* p80.

19 Eagleton, Terry *Exiles and Émigrés: Studies in Modern Literature* (London: Chatto and Windus 1970).

20 Serote, Mongane *The night keeps winking* (Gaborone: Medu Art Ensemble 1982) p17.

21 *Poets to the People* p46.

22 *Poets to the People* p77.

23 In *Seven South African Poets: Poems of Exile* edited by Cosmo Pieterse (London: Heinemann 1971) p64.

24 *Poets to the People* p81.

25 *Poets to the People* p1.

26 *Poets to the People* p7.

27 *Poets to the People* p126.

28 *Poets to the People* p159.

29 *Poets to the People* p12.

30 *Poets to the People* p55.

31 *Poets to the People* p69.

SOUTH AFRICAN VOICES
FROM ABROAD

Perseus Adams

The Owl of Minerva, Hegel once said, flies only at dusk. If this is so, perhaps it is not too surprising then that in that land of scorching sunshine, big Broeders and assisted or induced suicides, you would have to use a radio telescope to find even a feather of one of its chicks.

Before I left South Africa at the end of March 1977, I was forced out of the teaching profession (which is primarily how I earn my living) by a directive from the Department of Coloured Affairs in Cape Town to the principal of the coloured secondary school where I was employed as an English teacher. It said, and I quote: "Mr P R C Adams's services will terminate with you as at the end of term on the 27th March." No explanation for this decision was given and I was asked by the principal to contact the Department and try and find out why I was being dismissed. "We need you here — you're a life-line to us," he said. "If you like, you can tell them you're asking on my behalf, that I have a report recently issued by the inspector praising your work."

I did as he asked and after the familiar experience of being fobbed off from one official to another (all of them white Afrikaners), I was eventually informed: "It's not our policy to give reasons for the dismissal of a teacher."

"Is there any point in my applying for a post at some future date?" I asked.

"No, quite frankly there isn't," I was told.

The principal of the school seemed genuinely sad when I relayed this information to him. Almost every window in the school was broken, there were not enough text-books or reading books for the students and of those in use, many had pages missing.

At that time I had had twelve years' teaching experience in five countries. (Now it is sixteen years in seven countries.) Respecting the law (though, along with many of my colleagues, I considered it a

263

bad one) I had never discussed local politics in the classroom. If any of my students asked me a question relating to this subject, I would say, "Ask me that question outside the school gates and I'll be pleased to answer you." Some did and I tried to deal with it as honestly, as forthrightly and as objectively as it lay within my powers to do.

Going by my previous experience, it would have been pointless trying to obtain a teaching post in a white school. My curriculum vitae recorded an international background and to most members of school committees and to senior officials in the Cape and other Provincial Education Departments, internationalism = communism. At least, if they did not form an exact equation to them, they comprised an approximate one, which was almost as bad. (What was he looking for in Hong Kong, Greece, England and Iceland that he couldn't find in Blikkiesdorp or Stellenbosch? Something funny there . . . Also, word has it that he's a poet, and we all know what *they're* like. No, far better play it safe and give him a thumbs down.) My application to teach had been rejected by them many times (or the Department concerned was withholding confirmation of my appointment). Whichever it was, the effect was the same.

To be quite fair, I never felt comfortable teaching or living in South Africa. The magnificent untamed landscapes, the majesty and variety of its physical setting always inspired me, but one can't always withdraw to a mountainside or a solitary beach, even if one wanted to, and one can't talk to trees. You have to relate to the society of which you are a part, and I saw this society (and still do) not only as a citadel of puritan authoritarianism, but also with its evil, officially endorsed racialism, as a blot upon the face of the earth, an obscenity, a boil over-ripe for lancing. Nevertheless, for me the central South African tragedy is not the white-black mélange, the first choice of the politicians, the media and writers with limited imaginations and bandwagon needs, but that a land built for gods and giants is inhabited by so many 'pygmies'.

I have had to endure a good deal of discrimination because of my links with South Africa and because of the widespread human tendency to form stereotyped judgements. A few years ago I was (much to my surprise) selected out of 340 candidates to take charge of the English teaching programme at one of the biggest oil companies in Libya. I was told that I could save at least £500 a month. Fantastic, I thought. In ten months I can save £5 000 and then I shall be able to buy myself a cottage on one of the Greek islands and spend the rest of my life writing. A week later I heard from my interviewer, the British Personnel

264

Manager, in Libya: the Government there had refused to grant me a work permit. They gave no official reason, but he was informed privately it was because "Mr Adams has been educated in South Africa, he has worked there, and Colonel Gaddafi wouldn't like that."

Most of the time I have lived in London I have been employed as a teacher of English as a foreign language. The pay is poor and with high unemployment (about 30 000 teachers are jobless in London alone) there is stiff competition. On several occasions my South African accent has been mimicked and parodied by other teachers in front of the foreign students, presumably in the hope that they would either reject me, or feel hostile towards me. The only effective answer I had to this was to work harder and for longer hours; to raise the standard of my teaching until any prejudice the students might feel towards me was cancelled out. In the main I succeeded, but at some cost: it reduced my slim social life to practically zero.

For some time I resented my circumstances, the poverty, the insecurity, the prejudices, and gave way to bitterness and self-pity. Since then, however, I have learnt to regard it as a spiritual boon. I realised that the experience was giving me a deeper insight into the suffering of black and brown people in South Africa, besides which my own trials and tribulations as a misfit, an outsider, were small indeed. It also added to my understanding, my appreciation of what other exiles (and there are a good many of them) are going through. Besides, loneliness and isolation were not new to me. In South Africa — where your skin is your uniform — I often felt more of an exile, more of an outsider than I do here.

Where or what is exile? Is it to live in a country far from where you were born, where your accent and your ways mark you out as a foreigner? Or is it to be estranged from values that are not only dear to you, but that the mainstream of civilization respects and clings to as being the right ones? To the extent that the first holds true, I am an exile. To the extent that the second is valid (and it is for me), I am not.

I would go further. I believe that the position of the resident white South African artists (including writers) is morally indefensible. They live in a concentration camp — not with the victims, but with the guards. They share the guards' food, their privileges, their comfortable life-style. "But we bear witness," they respond. "We offer words of hope, of comfort, to those going to the gas chambers tomorrow." Tell that to Nelson Mandela and to the ghost of Steve Biko. Even if you protest that your main reason for remaining there is to resist oppression and injustice, all the signs are that you have failed. And remember —

the government there, *your* government — can call upon you to fight under its flag, to spill blood in its name (and we all know whose blood that will be) right up until the time you are sixty years old.

I am glad that I am not you.

Jack Cope

How do you set about becoming a writer? The question in one form or another has been put to me many times by young hopefuls. Depending on the seriousness of the questioner, I usually answer somewhat to the effect that the only way is to sit down and start writing. There is a rider I have up my sleeve if the would-be scribe has already produced some writing that contains more than a spark of promise, and it is this: Get out of the country — go as soon as you can, preferably before you are twenty, and stay away for as long as possible.

There may be a good many objections to sentiments such as these. Do I imply a basic criticism of South Africa as a social background for the production of genuine or serious literature? Would I give a similar answer to a young person of any racial, language or economic group regardless of whether she/he is a privileged white or a black student from Soweto or the Transkei? Am I not generalising from my own narrow experience and therefore handing out misleading and possibly irresponsible advice? Is my advice not unpatriotic and provocative, if not a downright corruption of youth, for which the only just requital should be the hemlock cup?

I guess the answer to all these questions is — Yes! I am quite willing to face the music on every point. But since the target in this brief commentary is the South African writer and his/her work in relation to the country or sub-continent, perhaps I should start with a rundown of my own case.

I had the good fortune at the age of twenty-two to be literally removed from Durban and dumped in London as a newsman in the offices of the South African Morning Newspapers. For four years and more I was based in Britain though work and travel took me far and wide over Europe. From being a country bumpkin in the most provincial corner of an isolated and blinkered colony on the borders of nowhere,

267

I rapidly became something of a world citizen footloose in an ugly Europe boiling up towards World War II.

Journalism is no apprenticeship for genuine writing. I watched the towering hypocrisy naked under my eyes, the cynicism and treachery on both sides as the leaders scuttled about like rats under a haystack — until the stack caught fire and the flames spread. Early in 1940 while the 'phoney war' period was still on, I pulled out and returned to the family farm in Natal — bitterly anti-war and full of a realisation that journalism tends to serve the evil of whatever system it is attached to. However idealistic (as I think I was), the individual becomes part of the evil he tries to combat. His work is a futility. His writing is warped, and in any case what is printed today is forgotten tomorrow.

I decided by my green candle, as Ubu Roi would say, to become so far as possible independent, a freebooter in a world I totally mistrusted and despised, a law unto myself and at the same time a kind of Robin Goodfellow tripping up the smug, and dedicating my work to my friends, those heroes and heroines of real existence, "the injured and insulted". I had been attracted at the age of seventeen to Bernard Shaw's brand of witty and ironical socialism, but had evolved towards what now looks more like a kind of intellectual anarchism. *L'homme revolté.*

On the farm in an atmosphere of unreal isolation and tranquillity, considering the raging turmoil around the globe (Let them get on with it, the bastards!) I tried to write my first novel, going back two generations to the Zulu Rebellion of 1906. Sadly, I discovered that I had to start all over again as if I'd never written a word in my life. In the exact meaning of the words, I had to learn how to write. My teacher was myself, propped up by the shining models of writers like Joyce, Hemingway, Conrad, Eliot, Gorki, Sartre, Camus, Babel, Mansfield — oddly enough, most of them 'exiles' who had fled from the horror or boredom of their own countries while I had, for the time, fled back to mine. Of course I had long since absorbed the South Africans from Schreiner and Pauline Smith to Campbell, Plomer and Millin, and these were useful to me as examples of how under any circumstances I did *not* want to write.

Well, it was fourteen years later, with long breaks and three rewrites, that my first novel, *The Fair House,* was published in London. At the same time my short stories began to appear in New York and London. The rest, I guess, can be taken as a kind of intermittent quest for some goal beyond the known horizon, like Henry the Navigator's captains and pilots creeping ever further in their efforts to discover the road to the golden East. On its modest scale mine was also a venture of discovery

268

not only in the objective field of literary expression but in a more urgent and painful sense, a discovery of the self. Each novel, story, poem started and ended somewhere along that sea-road. It will not stop until the day I go to join my ancestors and am "hidden in the hills", as the old Zulus say.

Trying to look back, I think I can say candidly that I never questioned or became over-concerned about my relationship to my native country, South Africa. I do not picture myself as a patriotic this or a loyal that. I belong to no literary category, grouping or tendency. I feel no need to beat my breast for having been born into a privileged section of society or lived under a regime of repression, injustice and wrong. Nor do I begrudge the inordinate share of my life's capacity and energy spent in the hurly-burly of struggle against social evils and suffering wherever I happen to have been: not for personal emotional reasons but out of a belief that those who enjoy the gift of life have a sacred obligation to extend its opportunities in whatever way they can.

Getting out of South Africa must be seen as a process of education especially for students in the arts and literature. The scene there is becoming every year noticeably more isolated, stifling and hermetic. Lacking mental stimulation, even among intellectual circles, there is, I think, a narrowness of horizon or a complacency that is anything but healthy. Where minds are at work, their lucubrations seem from the outside to be amazingly unrealistic. Standards are falling just at a time when, I believe, the stage is set for a burgeoning of good writing in English, Afrikaans and, hopefully, those marvellous and as yet hardly ploughed up languages of the Nguni, Sotho, Venda and other indigenous groups.

Relationships? In my view it can be misleading to categorize writing in terms of national, geographical, racial or other non-literary parameters. Central in all instances is language — language in all its connotations and history. Take for instance Modern English going back age by age into the dim past, Middle and Old, Latin, Greek, Sanskrit, like a family tree with all its intermarriages, miscegenations, seductions, rapes etc. All enriching, mind-expanding.

On this scale there can be no place for 'South African' literature in English. By the nature of its difference, experiential influences and its flirtation if not closer bond with other languages, writing by those immersed in our scene can be regarded as a regional branch of Modern English. Paton may be loosely branded as a South African writer. But it is far more meaningful to place him as a Natalian regional writer in the mainstream of Modern English. Gordimer spreads her wings over the continent and in terms of time into the past, present and future, yet her regional basis remains Johannesburg, just as Dickens is essentially a London writer (Johnson too, although he was a Staffordshire man) and Hardy a Dorset regional writer. The exiles and immigrants who adopt a new home country or who enter the mainstream of English from another language (Bosman or Van der Post or Serote) bring with them their own historic nuances. Then there are the 'internal emigrants' — those who withdraw into themselves and distil out of their own joy and suffering and empathy, wherever they happen to live, writing that for its crystalline quality becomes universal. Among these I would place Clouts, a Capetonian transplanted to London.

Regional writing (literature) leaps all frontiers by reason of its quality. And here I think a very important distinction should be made between regionalism and provincialism in writing — provincial in the dictionary meaning of "thought peculiar to a province or country district . . . ignorance and narrownesss of interest . . . peculiar or uncultured in thought and manner; not urban; countrified . . . ." Matthew Arnold castigated the *provincial* spirit that "exaggerates the value of its ideas, for want of a high standard at hand by which to try them". Unhappily an excess of writing by our wielders of the typewriter falls into this category, particularly in the area of criticism.

I do not think emigration and exile should be overestimated as crucial factors. Writers, like anyone else, take with them, wherever they go or stay put, their own impedimenta of talents, gifts, faults and defects. At the same time I realise only too keenly from observation that the creative faculty can be an exceedingly delicate plant, easily snuffed out by the trauma of an enforced or unhappy change of social environment or linguistic surroundings, as it can be also by censorship and repression at home. But these are different factors from voluntary travel abroad as early and frequent as possible for aspirant writers.

Modern Afrikaans literature is inconceivable without the background of those magnetic points of attraction overseas — Paris, Amsterdam, Berlin, Rome. Writing in English focuses on London, New York and, to a lesser extent, the wider continent of Europe. Black writers using English train their antennae, consciously or not, on New York and further South as well as on the global centres of culture — all following the trail in one way or another of that "high standard" Arnold spoke of a century ago. Eventually the traveller may hope to acquire and establish standards that raise his/her literary output above the level of provincialism.

Hemingway said "every writer has got to have a built-in automatic shit-detector". Notwithstanding our era of high technology, such devices are not easily obtainable. In the "beloved country" of South Africa they seem to be unusually scarce.

C J Driver

Letter To Breyten Breytenbach From Hong Kong

Another holiday.
          The kids away,
My wife, the dogs; I here, alone at home,
Working, as always, with words, while they play
Sporadic games on a beach, and miss me
To catch the high ones, or fetch the picnic
From the car-park.
          Musing on you, I write
With my head still buried in Africa,
Which I abandoned, when I was younger,
Before it abandoned me, or stranded
Somebody a little bit like me then,
For the years I did not care to barter
For my own or someone else's freedom.

Now in front of my window a blank wall
And coils of wire — conditional enterprise
To keep the felons out, to keep me in,
In a great city on the edge of China;
And I remember you in gaol, whom no one
Trusts any more, not entirely.
          Van Wyk,
Named 'Spyker', has obviously learned by now
How to fish for poets, both thin and tall —
You catch them with words, a little bit bent
And baited with action.   They are too trusting
For words.   You pull the buggers in like eels.
They pant under the lights.

                              In Pollsmoor Gaol
You joke with the warders — a traitor, true,
But still their kind, the volk. The prison governor,
Whose mind is almost his own, commissions
(Not too abstract!) paintings. Poems are harder;
You can't be always sure that what they say
They really mean: they might be in a code
Or tell your readers what is best concealed.
It must be hard to try to represent
A Revolution when you want to be
A revelation. Out of words we make
Sporadic fictions, now and sometimes then.

Since I am hardly what I seem to be
What seems to me may not be you at all —
For self-concealing me, read you, romantic:
Your France, my England; your Pollsmoor Gaol,
My Asian exile. Yet we must be shared . . .
The world feasts on writers, especially
When they're wrong. You cannot mean those lies.
And yet you meant them, just as I meant mine.

Oh Breyten Breytenbach, we take our gaols
On our backs like pilgrims, and Giant Despair
Inhabits cities anywhere airlines
Care to dump us and our lame histories.
The choices that we make are not so sure
As policemen think, and what we make ourselves
Flickers like gunfire over the borders.
Traitors are traitors, even our own kind;
We gave away our futures long ago.

QUINTET

About Time Too

At four in the morning, I wake
To look at the strange lights
In the foreign harbour.
Across the dark and silver water
Go home the exiled ghosts
To their distorted distance.
Tensions of light
String from anchored boats
To anchored buildings,
And something like contentment here I note
To see so little so late.
I have no past, no people;
I belong nowhere now —
Here in the water-margins
Of China
And history.

Not Quite

Home at nine, after a long day
At desk, interviews, and meetings
With that ache more of eyes than head
Like a slow progress up stairways
With small prospect of arrival,
        Not quite, I said, not quite.

Meaning not very much, I guess,
Being polite, or meaning more
But not the end, not absolute
As if by saying that I tried
To turn aside what might be worse,
        Not quite, I said, not quite.

Being busy and middle-aged,
I have the usual fantasies
Of return and recognition:
There are times when I even seem
Something like my own father was,
          Not quite, I said, not quite.

Walking in town with my tall son
We were stopped by a red-faced tourist:
How very much alike you seem,
Your father's son, your son like you.
I stammered back embarrassedly:
          Not quite, I said, not quite.

How little now I have to say
About the things concerned me once.
Sons matter more than politics;
It is the milkman knocks at dawn;
My country recedes to headlines —
          Not quite, I said, not quite.

Somewhere Else

One grows used to it in the end, I guess,
The condition of exile. One talks of one as one
And writes one's love-songs to the Emperor
Who sent one packing to a far-off town
In a province of harsh barbarians.
We know all about exiles in China,
Says my scholarly friend in the grey silk:
A poet's home is always somewhere else —
No one ever sees again the cloud-cloth
Draping the mountain, the white waters foam
Among the pine-trees, the bright-speared aloes;
These are images of childhood, not place —
We see ourselves in time.

                                    Shall I never,
Never again see the lowveld?   Never.
Shall I never hear the hah-di-da birds
In the dusk across Grahamstown, nor smell
The pepper-corns in the rectory sandpit?
One grows used to it in the end, I guess —
And one does one's best not to remember;
One does one's best to think.   One learns to smile
At strangers who stare at one in the street,
At the clack-clack-clack of their dialect.
It is the dust which makes my face look grey,
And the north monsoon which reddens my eyes.
The Emperor was, as I said, quite crazy,
And the fire leaping across the tree-tops
Explodes like gunfire in the black townships.

Now And Then

The face on the torn page
Under the headline,
The torn face on the page —

That it should come to this
At midnight, on a Sunday,
On the edge of China

More than half a life-time
Swept out like dust
From a corner of my mind

And what seems tragic is not
Heroes in a death-cell
But a child on a road-side

An angry farmer in a big car
And a photographer pausing
For a newsprint epitaph.

And So On

It's a habit one grows into
Unwittingly at first, then wittily

To hide behind, to cover up,
A nicely English etcetera

To survive a revolution
By painting orchids prettily

A brush-stroke here, downwards,
Dividing subtly into segments

One hesitates to be definite
And then one weeps, and so on.

Bessie Head

A SEARCH FOR HISTORICAL CONTINUITY AND ROOTS

In March 1964, barely a day's journey separated me from one way of life and another. Until that day in March I had been a South African citizen. A very peripheral involvement in politics resulted in a refusal of a passport and I left South Africa on an exit permit. Great events were taking place then. Most of Africa was gaining independence and I was a part of the stirring of the times. It was consciously in my mind that African independence had to be defined in the broadest possible terms. I was twenty-seven years old and had lived those years like most black South Africans, an urban slum dweller who survived precariously, without a sense of roots, without a sense of history. A short train journey and a day later I awoke to a completely new world, Botswana, (then the British Bechuanaland Protectorate) and a way of life unknown and unfamiliar to me. South Africa, with its sense of ravages and horror, has lost that image of an Africa, ancient and existing since time immemorial, but in Botswana the presence of the timeless and immemorial is everywhere — in people, in animals, in everyday life and in custom and tradition.

I hope two disparate worlds could be considered to have combined harmoniously in me. I have never been able in my writing to represent South African society but the situation of black people in South Africa, their anguish and their struggles, made its deep impress on me. From an earlier background, I know of a deep commitment to people, an involvement in questions of poverty and exploitation and a commitment to illuminating the future for younger generations. I needed an eternal and continuous world against which to work out these pre-occupations. One of my preoccupations was a search as an African for a sense of historical continuity, a sense of roots, but I remember how tentative and sketchy were my first efforts, not finding roots as such but rather putting on layer after layer of patchy clothing. This

278

patchy clothing formed the background to most of my work.

It was my habit to walk slowly through the village and observe the flow of everyday life — newly-cut thatch glowing like a golden hay-stack on a round mud hut, children racing around, absorbed in their eternal games or a woman busy pounding corn for the evening meal. I would pause a while near a yard where a tall, slender woman pounded corn in a stamping block with a long wooden pestle, her bare feet partly buried in a growth of summer grass. It was a scene that had been a part of village life since time immemorial but to me it was as fresh and new as creation itself. The woman's form would sway to and fro with the rhythm of her work, her face closed and withdrawn in concentration. The warm slanting rays of the late afternoon sunlight seemed to transfix that timeless moment in my memory. I would turn and look at the distant horizon. Beyond the last hut, beyond the perimeter of Serowe, the land lay in an eternal, peaceful sleep, the distant horizon hazy and shrouded in the mists of the earth. I would reflect that the dwelling places of all the tribes had been, for ages and ages, just such small, self-contained worlds, busy with the everyday round of living.

Such peaceful rural scenes would be hastily snatched to form the backdrop to tortuous novels. Perceptive fans sensed the disparity, the disparity between the peaceful simplicity of village life and a personality more complex than village life could ever be. They would say: "I like the bits about Botswana life but I found your second/third novel difficult to read. . . ."

But it still goes back to a question of roots rather than the small, stolen patchy scenes which would seem implicit in my early work. Later, much later, I became acquainted with the history of Botswana and it was like becoming acquainted with a way of life that was applicable to all the tribes of Africa. The high clamour and violence of South African history dominates all the southern lands so that they are written of in the history books as mere appendages of South African history. Botswana is no mere extension of South African history and the great arid wasteland the history books would have us believe. It was a British Protectorate and as such has a distinct and individual history of its own, a history whereby a colonial power was sensitive to human grandeur, even if it turned up in a black skin, and it was a country that provided one such leader at a crucial moment, Khama the Great, who made known the people's preferences as regards their independence and the ownership of the land. We have a situation where the people never lost the land to a foreign invader and in the rural areas the ancient

279

African land tenure system of communal ownership of the land still operates. It is on this peaceful base of security of tenure that one begins to assemble the history of the land.

One has so many options and choices of study that are sure, steady and sane and simply another addition to mankind's history. One can concentrate on the impact of Christianity on the tribes, the power and influence of the missionaries and the London Missionary Society and changing patterns of culture and learning. Thus, the refrain of recorded history begins very much the way it began in Europe: "When the Romans first took learning to Europe, the tribes there were just like the tribes of Africa, not knowing anything about learning and progress. . . ."

We can look back at the old men, who until the missionaries introduced a new form of learning, were the only libraries the people had and the repositories of all tribal learning and knowledge. We can look back at the earlier religions of the tribes and the persuasive voice of Christianity in modifying and transforming custom and tradition. We can look back on a history that is not sick with the need to exploit and abuse people.

I have found the tensions and balances of the rural parts of Botswana, of a fine order. Enough of the ancient way of African life has survived to enable the younger generations to maintain their balance with comfort and ease, while almost daily with independence, new innovations, new concepts of government and critical, complex situations invade the life of the country. It is in such a world that one puts down some roots in the African soil and one finds a sense of peace about the future.

Carol Hermer

The quality of the light here is different. Two halves of an exposed spool; first the northern sun struggling through a film of grey, then the brilliant colours of a Cape summer. Now, between phrases, I stare out at forests about to change shade after only two months of summer. I remember the brightness of the sand and water that I saw from my other window, from that other life.

As a child I was fascinated by a story of a little boy who dug a hole in his garden right through the world and climbed out into China. If my little boy were to dig that hole he would emerge in the ocean, quite close to the beach where he once lived. What can I know about South Africa from this great distance? My current information comes through the static of news stories, picked up today but with no sequel tomorrow when space or time doesn't permit. The papers that arrive through the mail have the facts but lack the emotion of immediacy. So if I write about South Africa now I am no longer describing a reality but a memory, planned around carefully chosen words and therefore still further distorted. And even that memory changes from day to day depending on my mood.

I remember sitting around a clear pool cut into the cliffs of a Koue Bokkeveld farm. How often did I do that? Twice, three times. Walking along Clifton Beach on a cold, wild-water day, climbing over rocks that the winter seas had exposed. A hundred times, maybe? The fawn that stepped out of the mist onto the winding Kloofnek road. Just once. Yet all memories and all with equal weight in my mind. Some must be more accurate than others but which ones? Do I still remember each turn in the road to Hermanus? I think I do. Did I really laugh more often? Was Cape Town only a sort of childhood candyland of endless summers and cold wine and mountain paths? Of course not.

I think I remember the people more accurately. I still ache from the inability to maintain the continuous tie that comes from utterly aimless conversation touching on nothing. But whereas you can slot back into a true friendship instantly, a move away from your homeland changes your relationship to it for ever. You pass through many stages when you voluntarily move away. The initial pain of leaving is acute. The first year is miserable with self-pity at this self-imposed loss of background, familiarity and privilege. But gradually you adapt, start to feel in the skin of the new environment. Home? No, it's not home. You no longer have a home. You just live somewhere. Somewhere else. Not South Africa.

Being part of a country, being 'home' in a country is a feeling that overwhelms you. Your actions take place with reference to an inner core of knowledge, a collective conscience. An expatriate has no collective conscience. The old one doesn't fit and the new one will take decades to develop.

Going back after three years I attempt to integrate my mental thesis with reality. But the reality of a holiday in South Africa is not the reality of living there. The return is a nightmare of carefully allotted time, of scheduling people into compartments as if gracing them with the gift of your presence, maybe for a whole evening, maybe only a phone-call. It is a feeling of being eaten alive by relationships with little or nothing left over for the hikes in the country that I need to renew my attachment to the land. The reality of South Africa has become a succession of people: to welcome, avoid, embrace, repel. I leave exhausted, and only when I'm back in that new place can I analyse the experience, which is, once again, a memory but being more recent becomes more 'real' than my whole previous life. My existence in that previous life has lost its substance. I have moved from landmark to landmark trying to recapture what they once meant for me but discover that the true meaning is bound up in day-to-day living.

It is easier to 'see' in Johannesburg which is not as familiar. I am surprised by the redness of the earth and its creep up the endless white, pink, brown walls, hiding the houses from the street-life outside. I am aware of the parties in the hot nights, the conformity of the clothes on the guests, the weird coupling of events that is taken for granted in a class-bound society, one party on the patio and its impromptu mate in the kitchen and backyard. But these are the musings of a tourist.

Part of the problem is inevitably, political. I get angry with white ex-South Africans who say they left for political reasons meaning that they could not bear the inequities of the system. The majority of us carefully chose our times of departure to coincide with the least loss of comfort. We are not exiles. We do not plot and plan from afar and pray to return to our beloved country. We go back regularly to visit. We have, in essence, removed a tight pair of shoes, and we return only if the new shoes prove to be even tighter.

I have started to wear glasses to shield my eyes from the weak northern sun and my children cry out at the glare they encounter when they step off the plane in South Africa. I am becoming acclimatized. I still care about South Africa but it no longer hurts. It is only an active exile group that maintains a true contact with a country. You have to have daily involvement with a land to know it. I am not an exile. I chose to leave — for reasons that appear more complex the more that time has distanced me from the emotions that went into the decision.

True exiles have always feared that leaving would dry up the flow of words, that the separation from the homeland would remove the force that nourishes the muse. Up to a point that is true for us expatriates too. South Africa is a place that nurtured me and shaped my thinking and my values but I can no longer write of it in the present tense. I can read news cuttings and analyse political developments but I cannot feel the omnipresence of a society any longer. I can write as a tourist or I can write within my memories. For me South Africa has become fixed in time. I can imagine what someone could have said in 1978. But not 1979. I do not know what he could have said then. I cannot feel it. I wasn't there.

Christopher Hope

Living abroad I find myself constantly turning and returning in spirit to the place I left behind, blinking in disbelief, then wheeling back on my tracks for a more distant yet sharper view of South Africa; this activity being a predictable form of homesickness and yet something considerably more than that since, as others have experienced before me, I felt distinctly homesick even when I lived at home. And I can recall reading somewhere years and years ago that there were no South Africans and I remember how logical and unsurprising that seemed, a positive relief in fact to one who had begun to suspect that there was no such place, and the country so confidently named amounted to no more than a geographical convenience, a rallying point for political opinion, somewhere you assumed for the purposes of argument but which was, to anyone with half an eye, very little more than a nest of shadows. It was as if we had been raised with the kinds of expectations we associate with the great Russian landowners of the last century, taught to take for granted our absolute right to ownership of great estates while all the time knowing in our hearts that really we had only taken possession of the maps. Because the real world, where events occurred and people acted, lay elsewhere, we had no history, only excuses.

For this reason I read Herman Charles Bosman with such pleasure abroad. I read him for reassurance. I read him as my ticket home and because he shows in stories such as his wonderful little parable, *The Music-Maker*, how well he understood the characteristic desire "to get into history". As the schoolboy Stoffel Lemmer discovers, Vasco da Gama visited the Cape and got "into history". But as the inhabitants of the Marico know, things are not as simple as that. After all, Dirk Snyman once visited the Cape and never got into history, instead he got onto a tram and "a kafir came and sat down right next to him. . . ."

284

Worse still, nobody seemed to think anything of it. Then there is Manie Kruger, the concertina virtuoso, who knows that the Marico district is so inimical to art that he will never make a concert career and its climate so dismayingly healthy that it is difficult to catch a cold, never mind dying dramatically of consumption in the arms of a beautiful princess like another musician he has read about. No, the answer must be to get out; reality lies elsewhere.

And so, like Manie Kruger, one sets off and travels hopefully — indeed, like Bosman himself. For although it is perhaps not widely known, Bosman spent many years abroad and he wrote *The Music-Maker* about midway through his sojourn in Europe which lasted from 1930 to 1939 (and might even, when one considers the significance of that date, have lasted longer had the War not intervened).

Of course questions arise when you come to settle in that 'elsewhere' and yet continue to look homeward in your writing as I have done: questions of identity, of motive. Am I an immigrant? To the extent that the word refers to one seeking a new home in a new country, the answer is negative. I confess that the term 'expatriate' holds a certain appeal, conjuring up images of seedy agents in Graham Greene novels or elderly colonels in sweat-stained alpaca sipping beer on Egyptian verandahs, and for those very reasons will not fit. And then 'exile' is a status so brutally forced upon many who do not want it that it seems wrong to use it, and 'voluntary exile' is surely a contradiction in terms. Well then, retaining as I do that early, inbred passion for classification of my native land, I search until I find a name that fits: I am an escapee. I have gone over the wall and mine is a view from the hills.

But that is only half an answer; there remains the question of why I should continue to write about the place I have left. White South African writers frequently display a preference for living among the high moral peaks and hurling the boulders of their opprobrium upon their lowly readers for their lack of racial charity, with a fervour in which there is to be glimpsed an inverted sense of the old, ingrained superiority; it is not enough that we are bad, we must be worse than anyone else. Self-examination shows me that my reasons for writing are rather more basic and far less commendable; quite simply I am out to get the fellows who ruined my Sundays, who put an end to history as we might have known it from 1948, when the shades came down and whenceforth we were expected to defend the laager against the forces massing to attack what was called, in that cudgelling phrase, 'our traditional way of life' — a triple lie since it was neither 'ours', nor 'traditional', nor in the least like 'life', but a siege existence which had in it about as much joy as you will find in Potchefstroom on a wet religious holiday. Very early on there was born in me the realisation that future events were not going to be as advertised and I began most fervently to wish to have a few words with the organisers.

This deliberately backward view from my distant hideout inevitably means a certain amount of dwelling in the past and this sometimes stirs up a mixture of reproof and disbelief as if 'the past' were an unsalubrious suburb discerning people should avoid. And of course there are some who feel those too far away from 'home' can no longer write about things as they 'really are'. This is something I admit with alacrity. I go further and say that when I recall in a poem or a story the old Marine Hotel on Durban Bay, or the colourful crush of humanity on Diagonal Street in Johannesburg, or the eternal sales in the Indian shops at the lower end of Church Street, Pretoria, or the painted houses of District Six in Cape Town, I am not only recalling things as they no longer are, I am writing about places which have been literally wiped out. The result of course is fiction but the strange thing is that the lovely, fugitive gleam which lures me on is the desire, somehow, to put these experiences, these places, "into history".

In *The Music-Maker* Bosman throws light on this problem. Manie Kruger's bid for history ends dismally in a Pretoria bar. The warning to the would-be escapee is unmistakable. Yet there is something enormously encouraging about the story all the same. We fully, and embarrassingly, grasp the reasons for Manie's failure to escape, nonetheless we sympathise with the attempt, doomed as it may have been. When one remembers that the little tale is now almost half a century old, something of the nature of Bosman's achievement becomes clear. For what has happened to challenge his distant vision of events? Who would seriously deny that the bar in which poor Manie Kruger so sadly fetched up is still to be seen? Or that Dirk Snyman would be any less puzzled by the public transport system in Cape Town? Or that the climate of the Marico is one whit altered in its depressing healthiness? Though all this might once have purported to be fiction, it has been Bosman's achievement quite magically to resolve it into fact, to get it "into history". When this is grasped I think it becomes plain why Bosman is the best of all tickets home for someone on the run, and why I will persist in believing, *pace* poor Manie, that escape, though impossible, remains desirable and one can only register the deeply fictional nature of South African life with little fictions of one's own in the hope that one day they may turn out to have been, well almost, true.

286

Dan Jacobson

A WAY OF SEEING

Not long ago I was watching a BBC television documentary about a person who had undergone a sex-change operation. The presenter repeatedly pressed the subject of the programme to tell him why anyone who had been born as a male should have felt compelled to have such drastic surgery performed on himself. In reply, the victim or victor of the operation said that she had always known "in herself" that she was actually not a man but a woman. "I felt like a woman," she said over and over again. "I knew I'd always really been a woman, as far back as I could remember." Whereupon the interviewer suddenly turned on a young, female member of the camera crew and asked her, "Do you feel like a woman?" The startled girl answered, "I don't know what that means. I feel like *me*!"

When I am asked to comment on how I believe my "connection with South Africa" is reflected in my work, I find myself in a position rather like that of the second of the two interlocutors quoted above. Anyone who voluntarily expatriates himself is no doubt performing an act of radical psychic surgery on himself; it may be thought, therefore, that it is the first speaker whose experience is in some way analogous to my own. However, when I came away from South Africa I did not do so because I had always known "in myself" that I was something else, in terms of national identity, to which I could have given a name before-hand. Far from it. It is true that I wanted to become a writer; true also that that ambition seemed easier to fulfil outside South Africa than inside it, for reasons which had more to do with 'culture' than with 'politics', and had as much to do with my personal situation as either. But the point I have to make is not merely that all I had to write about, when I left South Africa, and for many years after that, was what I had seen and learned there during my childhood, boyhood, and early man-hood; much more significant is the fact that the very modes of seeing and learning which made me the person I was had been determined (forever) in South Africa, and I could no more deny or repudiate them than I could deny or repudiate my eyes or my hands or my brain.

That is the essential point. It is also, by definition, one which it is difficult if not impossible to write about discursively. Obviously such connections as I have with people and places in South Africa — the external connections, that is — are very different now from those I had twenty-five years ago. The attrition of time, with all its deaths and separations, has done its work; places which are no longer lived in by the people with whom we associate them are themselves no longer the same places for us, as Proust observed. ("The reality which I had known no longer existed . . . . Places we have known do not really belong to the world of space in which, for our convenience, we situate them . . . . Houses, paths, avenues are themselves as fugitive, alas, as the years.") The internal connections, however, remain: memories, in the first place; and beneath even the deepest of memories, those modes of apprehension through which the world makes itself known to each of us, and which thus create our individual past, present, and future, and our sense of the relationship between them.

None of this has much to do directly with the "broadly political matters" and the "current developments" to which, in the letter of invitation I received from the editors of the present volume, I was asked to relate my work. Of course, like most other expatriates, I continue to follow social and political developments in South Africa with a special degree of interest; of course I have opinions (which I sometimes express, and which I sometimes revise) on those developments. But however important my opinions may be to me, I do not believe that any special value is conferred on them by the fact that I write novels and stories. Nor, per contra, do I believe that my opinions on any subject whatever can add one cubit to the stature of my novels and stories. Less and less, as I grow older, do I find that that which really matters in imaginative literature emerges from the level of consciously held opinion or belief in the author, or speaks to that level in the reader (whether to confirm or change the opinions he holds, or, for that matter, to incite him to act on them). Rather, poems and stories have value because they reveal to us and illustrate for us, as nothing else can, the quasi-instinctual, self-creating modes of apprehension I referred to earlier, and the worlds which have been made available through them to the writer.

I do not know whether or not I shall again write fiction which is explicitly and unequivocally set in South Africa. It is a long time since I last did so. On the other hand, I do know that everything I write has something more than its origins there.

Daniel P. Kunene

My very first piece of writing that survived its first draft and eventually got into print was a poem entitled *Walking Walls*, which I wrote while living in Los Angeles. It was occasioned by the death of my father in 1965, two years after I left South Africa. The loneliness of my grief, among strangers in a foreign land, pointed with poignancy to the political significance of my trauma. The poem therefore made both a personal statement and a political comment.

From that time on, all my writing, which has included poetry and short stories, has been dedicated with a passion to the struggle for liberation, with particular reference to South Africa. My first volume of poetry, *Pirates Have Become Our Kings*, derives many of its themes from my South African experience: the demolition of Sophiatown, a pass office scene, Sharpeville, daily experiences of a slum existence, and so on.

I saw 'Sharpeville' with my own eyes as it manifested itself in Cape Town with the massive march down De Waal Drive to the city, led by Philip Kgosana. I heard a first-hand account of the siege of Nyanga from a white student of mine at the University of Cape Town, who was 'called up' and helped to man the siege while the police charged with fury into the location assaulting man, woman, child and aged indiscriminately after the marchers had been tricked into going back to their ghetto on the basis of empty promises. The student was in a state of shock and didn't say much. My short story *The Pit of Hell* focuses on the emotional turmoil of a character who participates in the march and then, when a general strike is called, has to resolve a dilemma resulting from the contradiction between an immediate family crisis facing him, and supporting the strike.

Works such as those cited above have resulted from a vivid recall of some of these events and situations. The pass laws, specifically the face of a black brother peering through the little window, handing papers hesitantly to the stern white face inside, while I, no less black, am being bribed with a seat and a cigarette inside the office, talking to a higher-up official, about . . . *getting a pass.* The face, with pain wrinkling its brow, vanished. *Where did that face go?*, a poem in *Pirates*, was the result. And so too was the short story *The Spring Of Life* whose hero tries hard to live within the system, but is eventually left with no option but to escape and join the liberation army.

But nothing quite like 'Soweto' happened while I was still living in South Africa. Soweto, which exploded on June 16, 1976, brought children, teenagers and sometimes even younger, into direct confrontation with the monster of racism which, without any hesitation whatsoever, turned into an insatiable Moloch demanding more and more children to be sacrificed. For me, one of the most tragic consequences of this is that black children are denied the carefree years of childhood.

My second book of poems, *A Seed Must Seem To Die*, is dedicated to the courage of the children of Soweto. I experienced 'Soweto' vicariously. It was the most serious outburst of police violence against the oppressed since I left in 1963. The theme poem of this collection is entitled *Soweto* and is written for a twelve-year-old school girl who was shot dead by the police in Alexandra Township during the Soweto rebellion because, they alleged, she was looting. In this poem the child, as she lies dying in the dusty street, is heard holding a dialogue with the voice of death. Death maintains his distance as long as possible. He is sympathetic to the child and the struggle for which she is dying. He tells her: "You, child, are like a seed that must seem to die in order to produce a young shoot se'en days hence." He knows he must eventually embrace the child, but it will be in order to make her sprout anew. It is the same death that asserts

> I walk freely in the streets of Soweto
> raising my mutilated children
> out of these blood-washed particles of sand

in the poem *To Kill Death*. The struggle cannot fail for, in the same poem, death proclaims:

> My loins are quick with life
> I am the Hydra
> I am he who lives twice when you kill him once.

My nineteen-and-half years in exile have sharpened my awareness of the tragic events in the land of my birth for which my love has not diminished. The racist regime continues to regard ideas as its worst enemy. The voice of truth is silenced with censorship, with restrictions of movement and association. The writer is hampered and harried and hemmed in, and generally treated like a criminal. How many writers in South Africa have fallen victim to the censor's guillotine? My own book, *Pirates Have Become Our Kings*, became a casualty in 1981. I salute my fellow writers who continue to operate from South Africa and to face these challenges with courage.

The message of our plight is needed as much here in America as it is in South Africa. Or maybe more. America's participation in the economic exploitation that has reduced blacks to no more than beasts of burden, buttressed by racist laws, extends the battle area, and you soon realize that the blacks in South Africa are facing a much more formidable enemy than is at first apparent. When I read my poetry here, I aim to raise the consciousness of the American people of their government's complicity in apartheid which results from the greed that has victimised many Americans themselves. The poem *The Dreamers*, in *Pirates*, in fact came to me as I pondered 'The American Dream' and realized that it remained just that, a dream, for the majority of the population.

I also see South Africa engaging in acts of terrorism and sabotage against its black neighbours, which further widen the field of operation. These are situations which no writer can ignore without becoming a pitiful escapist who is not relevant or useful to his/her society.

Through its characters, fiction creates for us neighbours of flesh and blood and places them in situations not unlike our own. We empathize with our neighbour, the character, even though we have not met him personally. Herein lies the power of literature as an instrument of persuasion. And the poetry, if it is to fulfil its function of rousing those overcome by inertia and inspiring those already in the fray to even more daring feats of self-sacrifice, must be clear and unambiguous. As long as the writer writing about South Africa is part of the war of liberation, I would not mind his sacrificing some obscure though beautiful metaphor in the interests of clarity.

In sum, then, I see my task as that of a writer actively contributing to the overall movement of liberation through the awakening of political consciousness.

Roy Macnab

I have never thought of myself as a South African poet in exile and even find it difficult to accept that I am an expatriate. In 1966 when I was living in Paris, Anthony Delius, in an article about South African writers abroad, said: "Roy Macnab writes from a different kind of exile, one in the South African diplomatic service . . . although this distant regard is not an entirely warm one, it remains troubled and cannot be detached." Jack Cope wrote later, "he is restless and driven always by a ferment of doubt, of rootlessness, searching for a purpose and meaning." If this is true, and I fear it may be, it could be one of the hazards of the diplomatic life, of working abroad in some sort of representational capacity. I find, therefore, that although I have spent most of my adult life abroad, it has always been within a South African context, working in someone else's country, while concerned with the external affairs of my own. This is a position — the French call it *à cheval*, on horseback literally — which cannot but have its effect on one's literary alter ego. It's a double dose of everything. During the past decade which I have spent in London, I have often found myself shaking my head over Britain while wringing my hands over South Africa. It is not so much a double loyalty as a dual involvement. However, it is not always all tears; it is a way of life that confers great benefits on a writer, and I have found it illuminating to see how some really distinguished writers were affected by this combination of literature and diplomacy. Among Anglo-Saxons there are not many. Lawrence Durrell and Robert Conquest are exceptions. The French are the most impressive, the Quai d'Orsay having produced two career ambassadors who are among the great names of twentieth-century literature, St John Perse whose poetry won him a Nobel Prize, and the poet and playwright, Paul Claudel. Claudel's most famous play, *Partage du Midi*, was written while he was serving in the East where he became Ambassador in Japan. St John Perse wrote his remarkable poem *Anabase*, translated by Eliot in 1931, in a disused temple near Peking, where he was *en poste*. One still writes from one's own culture, from one's own particular national background, but the framework is broader, influenced by the other environments, the other cultures in which one is working. You stand at the window of your embassy, and your feet are legally on your own home ground, but your eyes look out on to another country. One has only to study Durrell to see what an impact the Mediterranean world had on him while working there. *Esprit de Corps* and *Stiff Upper Lip* might indicate a not very serious attitude towards diplomacy, but he took it seriously enough to resign during the Cyprus troubles about which he wrote his *Bitter Lemons*. This raises an important issue for a writer who lives within the discipline of a service, diplomatic, military, religious. Do you not put constraints upon your literary freedom, even get yourself wrong-footed? Denis Saurat wrote: "Claudel is essentially a reactionary Catholic in the service of the diplomacy of an anti-clerical regime." He also inferred that Claudel's rather bombastic way of writing might have been a way of letting off steam. A realistic South African Foreign Minister, now dead, once told us the country expected its diplomats to serve all governments with equal loyalty and equal contempt. That gives one scope.

To be a South African writer abroad is almost as difficult as being one at home. Some give up the struggle and try to be something else but seldom succeed in writing about anything other than South Africa. One can reject the kind of society we have and most of us do. When calamity and tragedy arise, as they do from time to time, I think of another ambassador-poet who won a Nobel Prize for literature, the Greek George Seferis. In 1941 he was serving at the Greek Legation in Pretoria, the Greek government was in exile, the Germans were occupying his country. He kept a diary in Pretoria and he wrote of the misery in his country: "All sorts of faces jump up in front of me. The begging soldiers in the streets of Athens. The Cretan women who were taken via Kavaala to Germany because they fought alongside their husbands on the island. My people, my relatives." In another context, at different times, the news from home has created for me the same kind of helpless misery and "All sorts of faces jump up in front of me." Seferis passed his time in Pretoria on his study of Cavafy, who, according to Auden, was one of the few poets who could write a patriotic poem that was not embarrassing. I find Seferis equally unembarrassing, but then I am not embarrassed by patriotism, which unlike nationalism, has no poison. But what does one mean? In my series of poems *Winged Quagga*, all written abroad, I tried to define "the Africa in me", in evoking my own particular piece of the world where I was first conscious of the earth's light and sound and colour. This is the kind of attachment to a landscape, both physical and personal, that survives the strains produced by "news from home". As my academic training and part of my writing is as an historian, I have tried to take comfort in the long view, but there again doubts arrive. I found myself in Paris once with Dr Harriet Sibisi, the distinguished Zulu anthropologist, then an Oxford don. We were taking part in a French television programme about the Anglo-Zulu War. We had both been born and schooled in Natal, but our respective upbringings had given us a totally different concept of the same historical events. Ever since, I have felt that a true South African identity will not be possible until those two concepts of our story can be accepted by all of us as making a whole. And in the hope that we can somehow make it together in a still-to-be-recorded time,

> . . . keep clinging on
> without greed any longer but linger in pity
> on the raft of each other

There may be other ways of being a South African today, but I cannot think of them.

Zakes Mda

Theatre has always played a vital role in reform and reflection; and in South Africa, a society characterized by racial segregation, economic exploitation and political oppression, it continues to be a significant voice in the resistance of the repressed majority. This it does despite the censorious nature of the environment in which the artists work. In fact the harsher the hand of the censor, the more impressive our theatre.

When I started writing plays in the mid-sixties there existed in the various townships a form of theatre that seemed to be based on a set formula. The plays, and these always incorporated a lot of song and dance, were characterized by a policeman who was normally very slow-thinking and insensitive, a wily priest, a comical school teacher, the street-wise and fast-talking tsotsi, a diviner who was sometimes but not always a fake, a shebeen-queen, and a township gossip. The plot would involve a church service, usually of the 'Zionist' denomination, a jail scene, a wedding, and a funeral. There would be plenty of weeping, exaggerated gestures and forceful speech. The different storylines were almost always based on this formula.

The best of these works were often humorous social satires and were to a large extent relevant to the every day experiences of the people, but they did not carry any profound political message. A few did touch on political themes, but in most cases this would be incidental. The writers' intention was entertainment and the primary interest commercial. Of course the censor also played his part to make certain that whatever political matter was contained in the plays would be that which advocated political reactionism and the maintenance of the status quo. Playwrights were required to have their scripts read by government officials who knew nothing about theatre before they could get venues for the performance of their plays in the township halls.

New forms of stylistic expression emerged in the seventies. With the advent of plays like Maqina's *Give Us This Day*, although to a large extent set within the formula, we saw playwrights consciously and openly siding with the progressive tendencies of the political struggle. We heard theatre voicing the political aspirations of the South African majority. It is at this time that groups like Workshop 71, the Theatre Council of Natal, the People's Experimental Theatre and the Serpent Players emerged. Theatre became part of the whole liberation movement which culminated in the June '76 resistance, and continues today in the struggle that is going on within and outside the country.

As with most artists of my generation, the historical developments in South Africa, including the June '76 resistance, have had a great impact on my work. Although writing thousands of miles from the country, the characters and situations I depict in my drama continue to be motivated by social, political, economic and historical factors in South Africa. I have dismally failed to respond to the strange aesthetic concepts so cherished in the western world that profess that artistic creation is an end in itself, independent of politics and social requirements. I draw from the traditional African aesthetics where art could not be separated from life. In our various African societies the artist was a social commentator. *Imbongi*, the praise singer, also became a social critic. Among the Pende the *Mbuyo* masks were made to represent certain people in the society, and through choreography and music the performers would vent social criticism by miming certain behaviour patterns of the rulers with whom they were dissatisfied. In this way wrongs were righted. I do not believe in the universality of the human condition, for the human condition is always determined by social, political and economic factors. It therefore changes from time to time, and from place to place.

Fortunately for me, I have not felt the setbacks that are suffered by most South African writers living outside their country. Although I live in the United States now, I have spent most of my life in, and hold the citizenship of Lesotho, which is just a stone's throw away from South Africa. In this way I have been able to keep in touch with the country at close quarters.

My work has also played a role in informing the Americans of the situation in Southern Africa, of which the media has effectively kept them ignorant. Our writers such as Dennis Brutus and Keorapetse Kgositsile are among the most active in the campaign for disinvestment and cultural boycott of South Africa. The other day I was at Harvard

University where my play, *The Road*, was being performed at the Loeb Experimental Theater, when the young man who was directing it came to me with a message from Dennis Brutus who had been there a few days before for a lecture and poetry reading. "He asked me to tell you to boycott Athol Fugard's plays, because Athol is a cultural ambassador of South Africa." That week Athol was preparing to take his Broadway production of *'MASTER HAROLD' and the boys* to the Loeb, and apparently in his talk at Harvard and elsewhere he had spoken against the cultural boycott of South Africa, in favour of what the liberals of the western world call constructive engagement. As a result a boycott is being organized against him and his work. Such is the fate of the writers who have identified themselves with unpopular political issues.

Since the transition from the township theatre to the radical one of the late seventies and eighties we have seen greater commitment on the part of both the writers and the audiences in South Africa. It is not unusual for a play like Manaka's *Egoli* to be performed not only in theatres and halls (that is, before it gets banned), but at weddings and funerals. The people want to see this tragedy at a happy event like a wedding, for as an optimistic tragedy it embodies the will of the oppressed to continue the resistance and to overcome in the end.

Rose Moss

South Africa is the soil of my imagination. It appears in my work continually as the original world where things are as they must be. This world — sun, sky, stone, grass — has been, is, will be. If language allowed, I would not use a verb with a tense. The seeing of childhood does not know that anything changes or suffers history.

It feels comfortable and intimate to write to you in South Africa "sun, sky, stone, grass". I believe that the images you will bring to these words are the images I would invite. It feels comfortable to write without simultaneous translation, feeling that you hear the words I use without a foreign accent. Usually, even when my subject is the unitary vision of childhood, I must find my way through words I learned later than childhood. This morning as I walked in Cambridge, Massachusetts, among leaves falling and fallen at the early end of summer, a bitter smell in the transparent air between suburban gardens put me among Johannesburg plane trees at autumn and an afternoon after school. If I were telling an American about this instant of common sensation that fused my present and an afternoon when I was fifteen, I would identify the tree whose leaves smell bitter with the name I learned in this country, sycamore, translating.

When I grew up in South Africa I translated the other way, as children in a subordinate culture do. With language itself I lost connections with my own daily experience. I used words for what happens in England and Europe. I had learned them from books, and books rarely had South African words like khakibos, or blackjacks, or bluegums. The things I knew and did, so dense and rich, were things without their own names. When they were dressed in words from overseas, what I had known hid behind cardboard masks. Now that namelessness of South Africa feels stronger. When I came to the States, unexpectedly starved for the country I had left, I read voraciously about South

Africa, and felt again and again that foreigners get it wrong. I believe that by now I also get it wrong. My main connection with South Africa now is through books, rare articles in newspapers, a few visits. I do less inner translating, though Americans still hear me with an accent. My written voice too remains South African, in rhythm, in accent, and most of all, in irony.

By irony I mean seeing simultaneously from two or more points of view, an adult vision unlike the unitary vision of childhood. Irony is endemic to wanderers. They see unquestioned certainties in one city with eyes that saw them as exotic in another. The practice of colonial translation taught me one kind of irony. 'May' might be spring or fall in any sentence, 'June' roses or frost. The year began with Janus facing two directions.

My South African irony goes deeper than language, into gesture. When I try to see what I mean, I think of the way I walked down a street in Johannesburg and my eyes met the eyes of other people. Immediately there was that wealth of exchange and intimate knowledge we have when we look into the eyes of another person. The whole life is there, and floods out like light. People in cities learn not to look at each other that way. Everyone knows that when the subway stops or the light changes the person you are looking at will move on. You will never see each other again. You do not look into the eyes of strangers. But before I had learned urban reticence, I looked into people's eyes on the street. Sometimes the person I looked at, looking at me, was black, and part of the life streaming between us included knowing that we were set apart. The naked knowing of our seeing was forbidden. In South Africa blacks and whites learn to not look at each other, even when they are not strangers.

I suspect that when I first looked at black people as though they might be equals or friends, I looked as though I had learned to look when a black nanny held me or fed me. Somewhere I must have learned that the intimacy of unreserved knowing, of touch, or smell, has nothing to do with the way things are. The sensuous base of trust in another person who picks you up when you fall and feeds you when you are hungry can disappear because that person is a servant, a nothing. A servant is not a friend. A servant may be exchanged tomorrow for some advantage of price important to adults. A servant may go forever for the whim of a law that sends the intimate nanny away from the child's white world.

Perhaps I learned that sense of irony some other way, though I try to describe it as being at once close as a child to its mother and as distant as white from black. However I learned it, it structures the way I know everything. A field of namelessness separates what I know at skin level, at smell, at slouch and balance, from the official words I inherited. To fill that field I write, searching for words and shapes of story that fit and link. Other writers, not South African, have written to find out who they are and how they live. For me that field of namelessness close to myself, *terra incognita*, has a few landmarks I call South Africa.

I find another trait of my voice and imagery South African. I see the present itself from another point of view, as though over the present looms an apocalyptic sense that something must change, will change, in destruction and tears, but with some justice, some necessity. The apocalypse calls for biblical language to imply that it will be a judgement which will make clear the meaning of what is happening now. I used to think my apocalyptic imagery my private thing. Now I see it in many other South African writers. Some northern writers also have a sense of impending doom. They foresee universal destruction that will be simply absurd, as meaningless as it will be terrible. The underlying vision in South Africa is revolution, in the United States, nuclear extinction.

Sharpeville was, for me, a foretaste of revolution. I left South Africa soon after, despairing that the change Sharpeville had seemed about to initiate would not come after all. Soweto opened the issues of Sharpeville again, but I have changed. I see now what it would take to change apartheid with greater sadness and less anger. I am less impatient for revolution, and less able to believe that it can lead to a just society. I have lost or grown out of the unitary vision of justice or injustice in which apartheid felt almost uniquely dreadful. I have learned that it is not unique. Soon after I left South Africa, the United States plunged into Vietnam. Again I was living in a society that behaved with intolerable injustice. I write this in a week full of two new words, Shatila and Sabra.

Mbulelo Mzamane

For a long time after my apprenticeship as a writer in the late 1960s, my commitment remained quite ambiguous, often consisting of a few sneak lines against the authorities. That was the dominant style among us in the precautious 1960s, following the elimination of our predecessors through banning, imprisonment or exile. None of us really wanted to go down the same drain. My first collection of short stories, *Mzala* (1980), made up of selections from stories I had written since my undergraduate days in the late 1960s, was of the variety which aspires no higher than to provide pleasant reading material. From this apolitical stance, I was always trying to throw sneak punches at the Bantustan policy, migrant labour, job reservation, influx control, laws prohibiting sex across the colour line and at the apartheid machinery in general. That is not to say there are no valuable things for me in that book.

In many of the stories from *Mzala*, the narrator is the son of a minister, very much a centre of social life, who observes what is going on around him, recounts and comments, sometimes with irony and always with some measure of involvement. The stories portray low life in Soweto, the shebeens, the underworld etc, and the characters that live in it. The stories also recreate the bourgeois life of African ministers, doctors and the educated elite. In all the stories, I attempt to bring out the variety of life in Soweto and the way in which class differences are expressed socially. Some of the themes are familiar ones — eg the 'Jim-comes-to-Jo'burg' motif which is very familiar in South African literature, black and white. But I try to handle such themes in a fresh manner. Thus one of the characters is Mzal' uJola, the narrator's country cousin, who comes to Jo'burg and shows the greatest originality in surviving (and survival is the key theme running through most of the stories) and learning his way, indeed often showing the way, around the world of petty crime in Soweto; a remarkable character in what I conceive of as a rogue's gallery.

Despite what I now perceive as some positive elements in my early work, I was always painfully aware of a groping, of something lacking in my work, the absence of an ideological framework to elevate my work to the standard I so admired in the work of Alex la Guma, Keorapetse Kgositsile and a few more of my compatriots. I had been 'educated' to believe that literature and politics did not mix, that to mix them was a recipe for poor art: "the journalistic fact parading outrageously as imaginative literature" (which is how Lewis Nkosi who, like me, had internalised the bourgeois concept of art and beauty, categorised fiction by blacks in South Africa). However, I studied African oral traditions closely; read the great Russian novelists; the committed novelists, dramatists and poets of our time: Brecht, O'Casey, Hasek, Gide, Camus, Sartre and Steinbeck; the African novelists, Ngugi and Ousmane. They exploded the great liberal myth I had come to espouse. Politics, economics and social concerns of every description did, in fact, mix in literature of the highest order.

The advent of Black Consciousness was an important watershed for most of us. From the beginning I subscribed in broad terms to the concept of Black Consciousness. I became reconciled to the sad fact that, in the final analysis (when the chips were really down), the black person was, indeed, on his own. I came to disregard criticism of racial exclusiveness levelled against us in those days, even by liberal activists of Alan Paton's and journalists of Donald Woods's hue. These charges were mere red herrings, diversionary tactics. The fact of the matter, I came to realize, was that redemption would be meaningless, holding little scope for fulfilment, unless it came from within. No real salvation would come from the hills or from abroad.

For many of us, the events which broke out in Soweto in June 1976 caused a great deal of soul-searching. Two to three years previously I had decided to drop creative writing for a while to concentrate on literary criticism and teaching. Perhaps, in the process, I would discover the ideological framework I had missed: a clear literary theory that would embrace the totality of our experience as the disadvantaged and oppressed people of South Africa and reflect the reality of our situation, without idealization or romanticization. I wanted to create art and not just utter political statements, no matter how profound; or, perhaps, I wanted a fusion between the two. I was groping, painfully, painstakingly. Then Soweto exploded in our faces. How could I continue along the subtle path, when they were shooting my kid brothers and sisters

302

openly in the streets, in broad daylight? My quest was complete. Only the right serene setting "to recollect my emotions in tranquillity" was lacking. I found just such surroundings as I wished for along the Cambrian coast in the tiny university town of Aberystwyth, Wales, where my wife, Nthoana, was completing her doctoral studies in pasture agronomy. After a break of nearly six years — four years since the Soweto revolt — I resumed my interrupted creative writing career. The result was *The Children of Soweto* (1982), in which I wanted to convey, in a way that the several accounts of the students' and workers' revolt written by journalists and academics do not, what it *felt* like to be one of those involved and how life in the townships was transformed in response to the call of the students.

The Children of Soweto is a trilogy, an experiment with a kind of situational trilogy in which continuity occurs through the developing (or is it deteriorating?) political situation rather than through the same characters or their descendants in a linear time sequence.

The first story, *My School Days in Soweto*, is a very long story that reads like the first chapter of a novel, which is what the story is in relation to the complete work. It maps the gradual progress which led to the crisis and offers an inside view of the student grievances, motives and their organization. Through the memories of their teachers, reluctantly catapulted into the centre of the struggle, we are made aware, too, of earlier political campaigns of resistance — the anti-pass campaigns of the Sharpeville era, the ANC inspired Defiance Campaign, the 1940s 'Sofasonke' squatters' movement, going right back to the frontier wars of African resistance to European encroachment. In other words, the students' response is seen as part of a long tradition. This historical perspective was sadly lacking among the students at the time and its absence weakened their struggle considerably, as Njabulo Ndebele so graphically illustrates in his moving poem, *The Revolution of the Aged*. Mandlenkosi Langa, too, shows that the students were no more than "the children of the hour", leading as transient an uprising as Philip Kgosana and, before him, Bransby Ndobe had done.

The Day of the Riots is a more orthodox kind of short story. It describes the events of June 1976 and their devastating effect as seen through the eyes of a Soweto father of three, a commercial traveller, who returns to Soweto with his white senior colleague after a long trip to the north the day the revolt erupts and the police run riot. The drama involving the white man trapped in Soweto illustrates the complex network in which both blacks and whites are caught in South Africa. As Mongane Serote and Sipho Sepamla teach, the black is the soul of the white person and any white person who rejects the complementary nature of the relationship is condemning his own soul to perdition.

In the third and main part of the book, *The Children of Soweto*, I tried to limit the work to a strict time sequence by compressing all the action, which took place over the greater part of a year, within the first week of the uprising. It is a day-by-day account of student activities, as narrated by one of them (with the benefit of hindsight) from exile, and the reactions of the people of Soweto and the authorities to the events. In this work, my method of characterization tends towards the collective, to emphasize the collective effort our struggle calls for. In *The Children of Soweto*, the community as a whole is the hero. As a chronicler, I chose the role of the traditional *griot*, who is the custodian of his people's oral tradition, their verse and songs, their history and culture of resistance.

There are, of course, a number of us who have moved in this direction in our most recent work. So that just as our predecessors were preoccupied with Sharpeville and its aftermath, Soweto is our Sharpeville.

In South Africa, you are not just a writer, a critic or a teacher. You are either an enemy or a supporter of the regime, either part of the problem or the solution. Our tragic predicament in South Africa lies in the fact that whether you resort to action or inaction, protest or silence, you are either abetting the system or helping to advance the dawn of a new era. The situation allows for no prevarication, no literary quislings. Perhaps a time will come when we shall sit back and review one another's work primarily as literary creations. For now, we have very pressing problems to which we must harness all our resources, physical and spiritual.

Sheila Roberts

When I left South Africa in June 1977, to take up a job offer to teach creative writing at Michigan State University, I was sure of one thing only (apart from my desire to go) and that was that the visa I had been granted was valid for a year. This particular visa, the H1, was renewable at the discretion of the U S Department of Immigration if the applicant's services were still required in the job in question. I could not be sure that Michigan State University would want to keep me (I had never taught creative writing before) or, even if they did, that the U S Department of Immigration would see fit to renew the visa. I mean, which South African reaches adulthood without acquiring a profound distrust of bureaucracies — even if one is white?

But the English Department at MSU (Moo U, as it is popularly known, having been an agricultural college in those days when the Chippewa Indians still called Lake Michigan 'Gitchigoomie') did decide to keep me on. During my first year in Michigan several of the other universities there, hearing about a creative-writing denizen from some place called South Africa, a place they knew was south of Cairo and probably at walking distance from Nairobi, invited me to give readings of my work. I made an extra hundred bucks that year just on honorariums. These reading sessions were stimulating, sometimes stage-frightening, but certainly conducive to keeping South Africa not only in the forefront of my imagination (which it still is) but also constantly on my tongue.

Within a month of my arrival at Michigan State University, the *Washington Post* phoned to tell me that the *Pretoria News* had phoned them to ask me to comment on the news that my novel *He's My Brother* had been banned. I was stunned. I could not believe that a manuscript that had already been through a process of self-censoring, at the encouragement of the publisher, could possibly invite banning. For about half a day I mourned (and still miss the loss of meagre royalties)

305

but soon began to realize that the banning turned me into a curious kind of *persona grata*: black South African students on campus would now deign to talk to me; the anti-South African African Studies Center at the university invited me to give a reading; some people thought I was myself a banned person; and the Chairman of the English Department was able to make a case to the Provost about retaining me, not only for my hard work (I hope) but also because of my status as some kind of refugee. A couple of weeks ago, in fact, my very own niece, a South African who should know better, asked me whether the Secret Police had "thrown me out" of South Africa!

In any event, my employment at the university was extended and I was placed in the 'tenure stream' down which I have been swimming until this June when I was promoted to the steady ground of Associate Professor and given a permanent post.

In 1980 the banned *He's My Brother* was brought out in New York under a new title — *Johannesburg Requiem* — a much more ominous one really but a change that has not helped the book to sell. This year the censors decided *He's My Brother* was no longer offensive and so they unbanned it, something which also has not helped its sales in spite of a sharp attachment to the rather plain cover saying "Just unbanned!"

I cannot stop writing about South Africa. I have published only a few stories in the United States and about a dozen poems, but a recent novel, *The Weekenders*, was brought out by Bateleur Press in 1981, and Ad Donker has entered into a contract with me to bring out a further collection of short stories to be called *This Time of Year* in 1983. I am grateful to Ad Donker: it was he who first took the risk of publishing me when he brought out *Outside Life's Feast*, a collection of stories which won the Olive Schreiner Award in 1975. But in accepting the new collection, he threw out my *only* American story, one I am particularly fond of called *Iced Lake* — in Michigan I live on the shores of a lake which freezes over to a depth of five feet each winter. But, again, what was a disappointment seems to be turning into an advantage. I can see so clearly now how the short story can be extended into a novel, so in between teaching at the University of Natal this year [1982] I am trying to work on my first American novel. Maybe I'll be able to break through the geographical limitations to my creative impulse and write about my American experience. Maybe not.

I like living in America, but the first thing I look for each day in the daily papers is news of South Africa, and I hope to be back in the future frequently to 'check things out' and compare reality with what must become a stationary time-sense of the place in my mind.

Douglas Reid Skinner

FREE VERSE, OR, WHERE THE HEART IS FULL OF

At the age of nineteen, and with Russian tanks churning up the streets of Budapest, my friend Nick was slipped over the border into Austria. The cold war was strangling the world. He emigrated to America, went to college, was married, and began to earn a living teaching German to high school students. The paradoxes of exile! His poetry, couched in American phraseology and slang, is unmistakably European in style and sense. The paradoxes of exile — physical, cultural and spiritual; he dreams of return. Twice in recent years he has visited Hungary, full well knowing the political and social realities of life behind the Iron Curtain. Still the heart does not listen. . . .

In archaic societies, Geza Roheim tells us in his illuminating work, *The Origin and Function of Culture*, the medicine men act as ". . . the lightning conductors of common anxiety. They fight the demons so that others can hunt the prey and in general fight reality." This role points to an aspect of the poet's work. Measured and sung language is and has been a functional paradigm in human culture, entirely significant in the very complex of pattern and rhythm which defines our and all existence. The work of storage and transport of culture is the poet's primary domain; consciousness and communication, intensified in condensed and specialised language-use, are primary in the maintenance of and connection to the symbolic and mythic base of the culture.

There is a fundamental spiritual unity underlying human culture in all of its astonishing diversity of colour, form and content. Thus, as Ananda Coomaraswamy holds, mythopoesis is a common 'language', and mythological variation is dialect. South Africa, like many modern societies, is a polyglot culture, one of many streams and shards, a composite of the Tigris-Euphrates city-state model societies from Europe and the tribal societies of Africa, and it incorporates mytho-logical and social elements from both. The literary traditions reflect the varied language and cultural origins; but it is writing in English which has received the most exposure internationally. South Africa is notable for the number of its writers who have left its shores to live and work elsewhere; sometimes with success, sometimes with tragedy.

The political and social realities of South Africa, as with much of the world, are based too little upon compassion and rational understanding, too much upon prejudice, power, greed and superstition. It is a society organised by caste and privilege, dominance and subservience, leading inevitably to repression and guilt. For the conscious sensibility, that is enough reason to leave, for it is actually impossible to dismiss oneself from the common culpability engendered by a myriad of voluntary or legislated participatory factors. Taxation with representation and democracy are illusions in the context of a state which imprisons its citizens for what they write and say.

But there are other, more important reasons for journeying out from one's culture of origin. In the growth of the individual, the passage of birth from the physical womb must be reiterated in a subsequent birth from the mythic, social womb. As Campbell has extensively documented and argued, this is a central meaning of the hero's journey, marked by the formula of separation, intensification, initiation, transformation and return. Inasmuch as the spiritual growth of the artist requires the transcendence of individual history and limitation, so does the maturation of the society and culture. For the maintenance and extension of the mythical and symbolical base of the culture it is clearly vital that the artist knows what the 'local' *is* and what it *is not*.

The journey is both inner and outer, the former mapped by the texts of human culture, and the latter achieved through direct exposure to and experience of other cultures. Which raises some interesting paradoxes. To understand one's society one must leave it, an action simply denied a great many in South Africa. Access to texts is burdened by one of the most repressive censorship systems in the world, levied by those who arrogate to themselves the right to interfere with the affirmed possession of choice in knowledge — a patrician, intrusive and absurd process of denial. Such limitations are always evident in the form, if not the content, of South African writing; as elsewhere, it leads to codification and esoteric symbolism.

For poet and writer, censorship is a particular affront, a denial of fundamentals in that work. A culture's greatness seems tied to what it affirms, knows and transcends, rather than to what it represses, evades and debases. Education is the very essence of liberation, thus it is no surprise that denial of texts should appear overtly and, more often, covertly as a central theme in much writing. It is no surprise that Soweto should erupt in response to stupid and flagrant intrusions upon the rights of choice in knowledge.

There is a sense in which a writer never leaves the culture of his or her origin, no matter what alternative domicile is chosen. Both in memory and in essence one always lives close to the *genius loci* of one's birth and upbringing. But the longer one is removed from that locality of culture the less precise one's sense of the daily life, the quiddity. One relies upon memory which aggregates. One relies upon news media which are controlled, biased, selective, ethnocentric and compromised. One relies upon the snapshots afforded by personal correspondence. One relies upon the texts originating within the society. The human tragedy of the Cape Flats has not the same dimension *within* oneself when experienced from 14 000 miles away. And so it is with writing. Imposed exile is akin to death. The voluntary exile is drawn back again and again to the paradox of sameness and difference where nothing changes and everything has changed.

As George Steiner says, "A poetic form *acts out its meaning*, and is inseparable from the complete formal motions of that action as is, in Yeats's famous query, the dancer from the dance." The text approximates an analogue of *condition*. Thus it is that the writer in exile is compelled to write *in exile*, no matter the disguises employed. The prodigal dreams of his father's house, Odysseus of Ithaca and Penelope. This is a paradigm of the human spiritual condition, and the poet in the very nature of that work is compelled to write at some level of metaphor *in exile*. The society of South Africa is spiritually malformed, a society always in exile from unity. Legislation imposes fragmentation and the book burners condemn themselves to disintegration.

A text is measured against all that has been; thus it is not the responsibility of a poet to *report* the news, what is current, what is fashionable. The long list of human tragedies in the history of South Africa are projections of the human soul in all its darkness and light. It is with the soul that the poet must deal, not the quiddity. As Montale succinctly puts it: what is important is not the content, but the form. Shakespeare's greatness is in his portrayal of the soul, not in the historical accuracy of the represented Elizabethan life. Concrete detail, the basis of all texts, is not enough *in itself*.

Poetry in the context of South Africa is inevitably politicized by the very polemical nature of the society. As Camus said during his acceptance of the Nobel prize, "By definition (the writer) cannot serve those who make history; he must serve those who are subject to it." In a society which assaults the veracity of language and historical fact, the symbolic and mythic base of the culture is in jeopardy and a contest must arise between the keepers and the abusers. It is an old enantiodromia: repression begets dissension and dislocation; abuse of language begets a radicalized literature.

The reflection of social realities in the current writing in English by South Africans is inevitable and varied in form, from direct political statement in text to a communication of spiritual despair. But it is the *how* of this that is clearly of paramount importance, not the *what* of it, for that is surely the basis of critical review. Much of the overtly political work published succeeds as journalism or polemics but fails as art, for it so often lacks a broader understanding and synthesis and leads to a trivialising of the tradition.

I am, not only as a poet, but especially as a poet, tied to South Africa, to its history — past and in the making — to its mountains and jacaranda trees, by an invisible umbilical cord. A storm has been invited into the house of our culture and society and will cloud the pages of all writers at home and abroad as it gathers momentum with historical certainty. Writers risk redundancy by ringing the alarm bells, but ring them one must. It is a fundamental element of the work. It is equally important to reflect the forms of wholeness which the culture so desperately needs in the midst of fragmentation, a model available in the tradition of visionary poetics. To have history is to maintain texts; to understand history is to transcend it; to ignore it, to deny it, is to become its victim. Who listens? Who affirms freedom of information? Who listens to the wisdom of the heart?

David Wright

I left South Africa at the age of fourteen, not for political but personal reasons. In those days the only school for the deaf in the world that could educate its pupils to matriculation standards was the Northampton School for the Deaf in England. Personal reasons (the long life of my mother) brought me back to South Africa for six visits in the seventies; for the impressions these visits have afforded me I cannot be sufficiently grateful. They are recorded in *A South African Album*, *A Letter to Isabella Fey*, *Notes on a Visit*, *A Letter from Westmorland* and *Easter at Machadodorp* (the last, still uncollected, published in *The Bloody Horse*). However, it is for political as well as personal reasons that I probably would not return to live permanently in South Africa. Though I don't believe that an artist, *as artist*, should do or not do anything whatever for political reasons. His function is to see, and celebrate what he sees, even if he condemns; condemnation being a form of celebration.

On the dustcover of my collected poems I call myself "a South African poet who lives in England, and thinks of himself as an English poet who was born in South Africa". To that there is little to add except in the way of obfuscation — eg by going into too much detail.

I am South African in so far as I was born in that land and come from 1820 Settler stock; and because I spent the most impressionable years of life, from birth to the age of fourteen, in the sometime Union. Again, if I am a poet at all (a matter of opinion), I am an English poet in so far as English is my mother tongue and the language in which my verse addresses the Muse: as English a poet as, say, Roy Campbell or William Carlos Williams or W B Yeats or even, despite the dialect, Hugh MacDiarmid.

The artist can't get away from his earliest impressions because these are the most profound. They shape him. They are his material, because crucial to his life, and life is the material of art.

He cannot get away from his medium, whatever it may be: wood, stone, paint, or sound. These he must obey or they will not obey him. The medium of poetry is language, and the one in which I work was shaped by Chaucer and Wyatt and Shakespeare, Dryden and Milton and Pope and Wordsworth; but not by Thomas Pringle — or at any rate not much.

Index

Abrahams, Lionel, xii, 3—5, 15
  The Celibacy of Felix Greenspan,
    4—5
Abrahams, Peter, 41
Achebe, Chinua, 79
Adamastor *see* Livingstone, Douglas
Adey, David, 197n
Africa South, 78
African languages, 269
African Literature Association, 93—4,
  95
African Music and Drama Association,
  219
African National Congress, 35—6, 303
African Writers' Association, 93
Afrika Arts Week, Turfloop 1973, 46
Afrikaans as instruction medium, 171
Afrikaans language, 99, 148
Afrikaans literature, 8, 270
Afrikaner nationalism, 143
Afrikaners, 29, 47, 145, 150, 189, 201
Afro-Americans, 78, 80
Afro-Asian Young Writers' Conference
  1976, 251
Aidoo, Ama Ata, 79
Albee, Edward, *The Death of Bessie
  Smith*, 40
Algijew's Pina-Culo, 40
Alternative Theatre, 215—29, 230—2
American influence, 78—9
Anglo-Boer War, 35, 149, 153
Angola, 59—60
apartheid, 7, 14, 41, 47—8, 50, 52,
  59, 64, 82, 83, 84, 93—5, 172—3,
  203, 291, 300
Aristotle, 121, 123
Arnold, Matthew, 270
Art and Revolution in South Africa,
  203—5, 214n
Auden, W H, 70, 293
Awoonor, Kofi, 79

Badsha, Omar, 38, 50
Bahul, Julian, 40
banned literature, 17—8, 37, 81, 161,
  198—9, 244, 301, 305—6
bannings, 38
Banoobhai, Shabbir, 42
Bantu Dramatic Society, 215, 218
Bantustans, 52, 301 *see also*
  Homelands
Baraka, Imanu, 48
Barthes, Roland, 11—3
Beckett, Samuel, 24, 126—7, 226
  Watt, 125
Biko, Steve, 203, 257, 265
Black Alliance, 50
Black Consciousness, 38—52, 85, 151,
  161, 171—2, 175, 181n, 215,
  218—25, 302
black literature defined, 92
Black People's Convention (BPC), 40,
  181n, 215
Black Renaissance Convention,
  Hammanskraal 1974, 43—4
Black Review 1973, 42
black theatre, 215—32
Blake, William, 9, 71, 108, 118,
  120n, 201
The Bloody Horse, 311
Bolt, 41
Bosman, Herman Charles, 3, 35, 270,
  The Music Maker, 284—6
Botswana, 278—80
boycotts, 72, 171, 205, 296
Brecht, Bertolt, 37, 220, 223, 243—4,
  302
Breytenbach, Breyten, 272—3
  Kouevuur, 259n
  Luistervink, 248—9
Brink, André, 47, 90
Brutus, Dennis, xv, 246—7, 248, 252,
  256, 296—7

316

318

319

Uilyatt, A G, 49, 236, 242n
Union Artists, 215, 219
university courses in South African
    literature, 54
University of the North (Turfloop),
    41, 46
Urban Areas Act, 220
urban blacks, 44, 50, 78—9, 149—51

Vandenbroucke, Russell, 202, 214n
van der Post, Laurens, 55, 270
Vanguard Booksellers, 78
van Ijzeren, Barbara, 148
Van Vechten, Carl, *Nigger Heaven*, 78
van Wyk Louw, N P, *Raka*, 8
Variava, Sadecque, 223
Venda, 60
vernacular writing, 44
Vietnam, 21, 48, 107—8, 113, 300
Vilakazi, B W, 79
Vista, 6
Die Volksblad, 148
Voorslag, xi, 55

West Rand Administration Board, 220
Wilhelm, Peter, xiv, 101—4
    At the End of the War, 101, 120n
    LM, 101
Williams, Mance, 229n
Williams, Neil, 42
Williams, Raymond, 224, 229n
Workshop'71, 232, 296
The World, 171
World War I, 149, 153, 220
World War II, 21, 58, 149, 153
Wright, David, *Easter at Machadodorp*,
    311
    A Letter to Isabella Fey, 311
    A Letter from Westmorland, 311
    A South African Album, 311
Wright, Richard, *Uncle Tom's
    Children*, 78

Xhosa customs, 148, 150

Yeats, W B, 69, 71, 309, 311
Yevtushenko, Yevgeny, 84